It Never Rains in Rowayton

A Memoir and Narrative on Hope, Love and American Culture

Joyce Hizer Meurer

No part of this book may be reproduced, distributed or transmitted in any form or by any electronic or mechanical means, including information and retrieval systems, without permission from the author except for brief quotations in a book review.

Copyright ©2025 Bell Island Enterprises. First edition: 2025
Printed in the United States of America. All rights reserved.
Paperback ISBN: 978-0-9615148-0-8

Design and cover photos: Mark Smith
Select photography: Carola Precht

Front cover photo: View from Roton Point in Rowayton, Connecticut, looking toward the Rowayton Beach Association beach and entrance to Five Mile River

Back cover photo: Green's Ledge Lighthouse, one mile offshore, Rowayton, Connecticut

The material related in this book is a collection of stories compiled from various sources, including my own recollections. I have in my possession my diary from 1962 when I was a freshman in high school that was immeasurably valuable. Whenever possible, I consulted my pocket calendar from each of the last 45 years. I sorted through boxes of photographs and files that helped jog my memory. I drew from all available records and known information on the Hizer and Meurer family histories. And I asked a lot of people, including those from historical societies, questions in order to learn the details. I also researched dozens and dozens of sources to verify facts, statistics and background material. Every attempt has been made to tell the stories as they actually occurred.

It Never Rains in Rowayton

Joyce Hizer Meurer

Happy reading!
Joyce

"This wonderful book is so much more than a memoir. As well as a story of how both hard work and hope can make dreams come true, it's about life and culture in America. Every page is a delight, a feast for the heart."

The Reverend Cynthia Hizer, sister

"My friendship with Joyce is a precious gift from God. I wish everyone could have a best friend like her with whom to share the ups and downs of life. From small town girl growing up in Indiana to living and working on the East Coast, she has not forgotten her roots, morals and values. Her book is a page-turner – I couldn't put it down. With much love to my dear friend."

Loisann Crimmins, lifelong friend

"It was a pleasure and enriching experience sharing the leadership role of Wilson Cove Yacht Club with Joyce. And it's a joy to witness someone who so passionately loves boating. I wish I would have had the opportunity to get to know her and Ray much earlier in life. I will treasure this book as a wonderful memory of Joyce and our friendship."

Carola Precht, co-commodore and friend

"Joyce, thank you for your exceptional editing of another annual report letter. You are a fabulous partner. All our best."

        Jamie Dimon, chairman and CEO, JPMorgan Chase & Co.
               Judy Miller, chief of staff to Jamie Dimon

"Thanks, Joyce, for sharing this delightful memoir with me. You were a key player on the annual report team year after year, and our financial folks adored you. Your competence and confidence were great for everyone's morale, and to this day, each of us remains grateful for all we learned from you."

                      Rich Feldheim, former president
      John F. Murray Advertising Agency, Wyeth Pharmaceuticals

"I really did love the book. Your writing is engaging and warm and sensitive and honest. A welcomed style in today's literary world."

                          The Reverend John Livingston
                              The United Church of Rowayton

A Taste of What's to Come

Get ready to read stories that will make you laugh and cause you to cry. Triumphs and tears: It's all here for your reading pleasure. Following are excerpts from *It Never Rains in Rowayton*.

"John Hizer was able to outsmart his captors. With herculean effort akin to what we see in the movies, he devised a plan of escape that included dodging bullets and plunging into the river on horseback, ferociously swimming to safety."

"Year round, I would sing the words to 'Silver Bells' and fantasize about the hustle and bustle on the busy streets of the city – the people dressed in their finery, the traffic jams, the honking horns (all a far cry from life in Grass Creek and Hizer Hatchery)."

"I was confident and ready for the next chapter of my life. As I made my way around the stadium, I had a vision and told myself, 'Someday, I'll work in the heart of New York City in a floor-to-ceiling glassed-in office with a view of skyscrapers in every direction.' "

"I had achieved my goal – that vision I had had on the IU campus oh! so long ago."

"Yes, in America, you can do anything, and you can be anything. It is the Land of Opportunity. You can achieve and live the American Dream."

"I am proud to be an American and think the United States of America is the greatest country in the world. If you work hard and play by the rules, every person here has the opportunity to make their dreams come true."

"Infuriated that our lives and the boat had been needlessly endangered, Ray grabbed the mic to the VHF radio and shouted, 'Is there no law and order on the Cape Fear River?'"

"With a fistful of matchbooks (I thought) and a happy voice, I loudly called over to Ray, 'You just can't get enough of these!' 'These,' it turned out, were not matchbooks – they were condoms! The diners smiled from wall to wall."

"Oh, the price we pay for honesty, but that is a principle that has always been important to me."

"As with most families, the Meurer lineage is peppered with accounts of courage and fortitude along with tales of embarrassing moments and secrets in the closet."

"He slipped away on a Saturday night at 7:30. Ray died in my arms – his breathing just got shallower and shallower until it stopped. I couldn't speak much during those last few moments so I just whispered over and over, 'Everything's going to be *just* fine' as he had said to me so many times in his life. As sad as it was, it was beautiful."

"I filled the shot glass with the remaining liquid of the finest of scotches – and made a toast to the finest of men."

"I take in the salt air. I watch the gulls soaring through the sky. I marvel at the cloud formations above the water and the breathtaking sunsets. Life is good, and I am thankful every day for all the gifts that have been bestowed upon me."

Acknowledgments

Throughout the pages in this narrative, I have singled out certain people who played an important role in my life's story. I thank each of you for your contribution to the book and to my life in general.

Your encouragement and support are deeply appreciated. In particular, I thank my dear sister Cynthia Hizer, my close friend since high school Loisann Hartzler Crimmins and my good friend Carola Precht.

I also want to thank Carola for taking all those dozens of photographs from land and sea. They make the book come alive.

There are many of you who provided love, support and comfort from the day Ray was diagnosed to today and beyond, and I want to take this opportunity to thank you once again.

You are from far and near. You sent flowers. You brought food. You brought bedding. You lent equipment and medical supplies. You set up the hospital bed. You opened and closed the air-conditioning vents. You replaced the water filter in the fridge. You fixed the back door. You helped with the canvas on the boat. You ran Blue Heron to winter storage.

The same is true when COVID-19 changed all of our lives. You sent emails and texts. You called on the phone. You were always there. I thank you.

Joyce

Dedicated to the memory of my beloved husband
Raymond F. Meurer

My dear friends,

Not that long ago, life was happy, carefree and full of promise. Ray and I cherished every day we had together and looked forward to enjoying many more years side by side. But the seas keep changing, and we have to cope with the unforeseen storms.

Thank you for your support, love and the myriad of ways you have shown your heartfelt concern during these difficult times. May our beloved Ray rest in peace knowing he lived his passion and was loved and respected by so many wonderful people.

With love,
Joyce

Ray on his boat, Blue Heron.

Contents

Prologue   1

The Early Years   5

The Move to Greenwich   75

Boating   106

Work Highlights   152

Sports Fan   193

Life in Rowayton   217

The Meurer Heritage   285

Saying Goodbye to Ray   320

Prologue

Summer 2020, Rowayton, Connecticut

It's 2020, and people around the globe are experiencing a pandemic. The coronavirus has changed our life as we are urged to stay inside.

On March 13, President Trump declared a national emergency so all businesses and schools and other organizations have been closed. Only essential workers are allowed in the workplace. When we do venture outside, we are to wear a mask and gloves and stay six feet apart from the next person.

We are to wash our hands often, wipe down countertops, disinfect all boxes and containers when we bring them inside, and rinse fruit and vegetables. We are not to be around people other than those with whom we live, even on a boat.

COVID-19 affects people of all ages, but those over the age of 60 are particularly at risk. Since I'm in that group and could easily fall victim to this deadly virus, I decided it would be a good idea to get the most important events of my life down on paper. Pandemic or not, I urge every person who reads this story to do the same (and we all have so many stories). Otherwise, those memories will be lost forever.

This project is giving my days structure and purpose. And it's a tribute to Ray, my beloved husband who died of cancer in July of 2019, as many of the events chronicled involved both of us. I'm finding writing about those memories therapeutic. It has also been fun to write these stories. It's made me think about my life and has put everything in perspective.

I am glad this pandemic didn't happen a year ago. It would have been even harder to deal with impending death and anticipatory grief in an environment where social distancing is mandatory.

My heart goes out to those who are sick and those who are caring for someone who is sick with such restrictions in place.

I'm missing Ray so very much these days. Since his death, I have been dealing with my grief by being extra social. I tried to plan an activity every day that included others, and I attempted to broaden my circle of friends. I also continued to work, particularly during the annual report and proxy season.

Overall, I was feeling as if I was getting stronger and would be okay. And then the pandemic hit. I still feel that I will be okay, but the lockdown has thrown all of us into isolation. So I'm spending nearly all the days and evenings alone.

That's the hard part.

I've been blessed to have had a very full and rich life. From rural Indiana to a successful career in the New York City metro area and 40+ years with the love of my life, I've had a happy and meaningful journey. So this is my story. It's a story about having goals and dreams and following your star. It will take you back in time as the description of the early years depicts life in the '60s, '70s and '80s. There's quite a bit of detail, and that's intentional.

I've included a lot of facts. Maybe the accounts will be somewhat educational and you'll learn something new. I know I did from doing all the research. I hope the historical information and happenings will provide a sense of perspective of the culture of America at that time.

It's also the story of a powerful love. I end this memoir with my farewell letter to Ray. My dear friend Loisann Hartzler Crimmins read the letter at Ray's memorial service, and it is a testament of the deep love and wonderful life we had together, thus the title *It Never Rains in Rowayton*.

When my time comes, I truly believe I will be reunited with my beloved Ray in heaven.

Summer fun on Five Mile River at the Boathouse beach
across the street from our home.

"It never rains in Rowayton." – Raymond F. Meurer

Ray coined this term. He would call me at home in Rowayton every afternoon from his office at IBM in White Plains, New York, just to touch base.

Many times he would comment, "It's raining buckets outside," and I would respond, "It's not raining here."

Ray would answer with, "It never rains in Rowayton."

And that became a motto because our life in Rowayton was happy and carefree, and the sun shone on us.

The Early Years

Grass Creek

From an early age, I was interested in business. I spent many hours with my dad, Fred Hizer, in his office running the chicken hatchery and feed business in the small rural town of Grass Creek in north central Indiana, one of 12 states that comprise the Midwest.

Dad taught me how to keep track of the accounts, order inventory, pay bills and manage relationships with customers.

Grass Creek stretches about a half mile east to west on State Road 17 and is bordered by two 90-degree turns on each end. It is an unincorporated community located in Wayne Township in Fulton County.

In the 1950s and '60s, the only street in town boasted a small dry goods/grocery store, a gas station/garage by the railroad tracks, a grain elevator with a luncheonette on one side, a hardware store that carried everything from nuts and bolts to John Deere tractors and other farm equipment, a post office on the first floor of a residence, the school (grades 1 to 12 – there was no kindergarten in those days) and a church.

There wasn't one stoplight or stop sign.

Grass Creek is still about the same today – no stoplight or stop sign. What is different is that most of those establishments are gone.

Generally, people drive 15 miles south on State Road 17 to do their shopping for food and essentials in Logansport, a former railroad hub that in the 1920s maintained nine lines radiating in all directions. Because of the rail activity, it was a booming town then with lots of opportunities.

When I was growing up, the Hizers owned a 20-acre farm right at the bend of the most westerly corner of "town." The property housed the farmhouse and a large barnlike building where incubators ran 24 hours a day and thousands of baby chicks were hatched each spring.

In the back of the hatchery, there were brooders where the chicks were kept for about six weeks until they were ready to be sold. Heat lamps kept the air temperature at 90-95 degrees the first seven days, decreasing the heat by five degrees each week until the chicks' juvenile feathers were developed. In another part of the building, there was a haymow and storage area and, of course, Dad's office.

The words Hizer Hatchery were painted in large red letters for all to see on the front of the two-story white clapboard building.

Adjacent to the hatchery, an outbuilding and a number of small wooden structures were situated around the property housing bags of chicken feed that farmers from the area came to purchase (many a meal was interrupted by a customer). Dad or the buyer would heft the bag up onto their shoulder and carry it to their truck. Upon request, Dad would make deliveries to the customer. The cloth bags holding the feed became sought-after fabric for the farm wives to use for sewing their daughters' dresses.

Four one-story henhouses stretched down a long lane to the east where 10,000 laying hens (primarily leghorns) were raised. We referred to

A photo published in the January 12, 1995, issue of *The OBSERVER*, a weekly newspaper based in Kewanna, Indiana, five miles north of Grass Creek, shows an aerial view of Grass Creek (circa early 1960s). It identifies six business establishments as follows: Young's General Store, Cunningham's Garage, Hoover Welding & Repairs, Sommer's Elevator, Thomas Hardware, Hizer Hatchery.

The OBSERVER was read from cover to cover by eager eyes as it carried news about who had visited with whom, upcoming and past events of interest, school menu for the week and a column titled "Looking Back" that noted news items from decades past. The newspaper no longer is being published.

Excerpt from *The OBSERVER*, May 30, 1996, "Looking Back, Forty Years Ago": *Several friends of Sharon Slater, daughter of Mr. and Mrs. Gale Slater, helped her celebrate her ninth birthday Sunday afternoon in her home. Guests included Shirley Fultz, Yvonne Thomas, Charlene Thomas, Joyce Hizer, Shirley Scott, Jean and Judy Dague, and Kenneth Slater.*

the henhouses as #1, #2, #3 and #4. Henhouse #3 was 100 feet long, and #4 was 200 feet long. Eggs were used for breeding stock in the hatchery. The remaining eggs were sold to a distributor for commercial use.

Young chickens (from 15-20 weeks up to about one year of age) are called pullets. Once pullets start laying eggs, it takes about a month before the eggs are of normal size. These pullet eggs are smaller (three pullet eggs to two large eggs) and are creamier than regular eggs.

Most hens lay, on average, one egg a day for the first three years, and then their production ceases. From time to time, Dad would raise capons for special occasions. A capon is a male chicken that has been neutered at a young age and fed a rich diet. The result is fattened meat that is especially tender, juicy and flavorful, well-suited for roasting.

The rest of the 20 acres was used for farming, generally corn.

In the succeeding years, in addition to the hatchery business, Dad bought tracts of farmland around the township and entered into cash rental agreements with the locals, particularly the Herrolds. He deeded farmland to each of us three kids (my brother Alan, five years older than me, and sister Cynthia, three years my junior).

The home property has been owned by the Hizer family since 1832, when John Hizer ventured north from Rising Sun, Indiana, and started accumulating land in Fulton County.

His father Jacob Heiser was born around 1740 in Germany. Many of his ancestors came from Wittenberg, about 70 miles southwest of Berlin (about halfway to Leipzig) so it is assumed Jacob's roots stem from there as well.

In an attempt to verify Jacob's origin, my dad contacted city hall and some of the churches in the Wittenberg area in the 1960s. But after the bombings in two world wars earlier in the century, the buildings housing those records had been demolished.

Jacob emigrated to Shenandoah County in Virginia, changed the spelling of his surname, and became a farmer and landowner. He and his wife Susanna had five children.

In 1796 after Jacob's death, Susanna and their three sons, John, Daniel and Jacob, who were 20ish, left Virginia. They moved to Kentucky and lived in a settlement along the Ohio River about 40 miles west of Cincinnati. Nothing is mentioned about the two sisters. It is assumed they married and stayed in Virginia.

The community in Kentucky was just across the river from Rising Sun, Indiana. North and west of there in Indiana, bands of Indians ferociously protected their territory. It was extremely dangerous.

There are Hizers in Rising Sun today according to the record books. About 20 years ago, my brother Alan visited Rising Sun. He was sitting on a park bench when a stranger sat down beside him. They started chatting and soon introduced themselves and discovered they both had the same last name: Hizer.

Nothing further is known about Daniel or Jacob. John is my ancestor. So the Hizers who have resided in Rising Sun through the years may be descendants of Daniel or Jacob. We don't know for sure.

John Hizer spent much of his adulthood living by the Ohio River hunting, riding and becoming adept at all those skills necessary to survive in the wild.

More than once he had been kidnapped and taken deep into Indian territory. One time he was held captive for six weeks. Because of his expert marksmanship and horse-handling, the Indians allowed him to go hunting with them, and that opened up a way to escape. At an opportune time, he sneaked away on a horse. The Indians came after him with a vengeance, but he was able to maintain distance in a race for his life – beating them to the river and finding refuge.

On another occasion, John and two neighbor children were taken hostage for a year by the Indians. Hidden 40 miles into Indian territory, he taught the girls to hunt and ride and navigate the trails that would lead them to freedom. Again, he was able to outsmart his captors. With herculean effort akin to what we see in the movies, he devised a plan of escape that included dodging bullets and plunging into the river on horseback, ferociously swimming to safety.

John had other close calls, always managing to get away because he could shoot, ride and swim better than those who were in pursuit of him.

There are other legends about bears that range from funny to scary.

These stories are part of the Hizer family history as researched by my dad, Fred Hizer, in the 1960s. He spent a decade delving into the records and interviewing elders, who related facts and stories from earlier generations. Dad also visited Rising Sun, Indiana, to add to what was known about the early days.

My brother Alan compiled this information and wrote a narrative in the 1970s. What follows is a summary of John Hizer's move north to Fulton County and some of the adventures of succeeding generations.

In 1815, John Hizer, still single at age 40, married a young lady named Nancy Burns, who had been born in Edinburgh, Scotland. They stayed there on the river in Kentucky and had 10 children (three of whom died in the same year, possibly from scarlet fever).

Not too many years later, John and Nancy moved to the other side of the river to Rising Sun, Indiana. John's mother Susanna, the Hizer matriarch, lived with them until her death at the age of 80.

In about 1830 at age 55, John decided to move. Roughly 200 miles to the north, he eventually settled in Wayne Township in Fulton County, Indiana. He bought 80 acres of land from the government for $1.25 an acre. During the next few years, he continued to accumulate farmland and by 1839 owned a total of 440 acres.

Fulton County was Indian country, too, and nearly all of John's neighbors were Native Americans. But they were different from those he had known from his time in Kentucky and Rising Sun. These natives were honest and friendly as long as they were treated with fairness and courtesy. There were few skirmishes.

So life went on, and John tended to his land and watched his family expand. He lived to be 83 years old. He is buried in the Hizer family cemetery on what later became the Carl Dean Sommers farm about a mile southwest of Grass Creek. Approximately 25 Hizers from that era are buried there.

Being of German descent, my ancestors felt at home in Indiana right from the beginning. Germans became the state's largest immigrant population by 1850.

John Hizer's grandson Aaron David was father to my Granddad Hizer (Daniel). Dan was one of five boys, and they all stayed close to home and all but one raised a family. So there are lots of Hizers in the area, mostly second, third and fourth cousins.

Dan was the local mail carrier for Wayne Township. He was appointed to this position in 1900 at the age of 20 and worked in that capacity for 32 years.

In the early days, horses were used as the means of transportation by postal workers. Dan would start out early in the morning and deliver mail. He would return home for his noon meal and then hitch up a fresh team of horses for the afternoon run.

Note that mail was delivered twice a day until 1950. The afternoon route was a duplicate of the morning run.

In the later days, mechanical transportation became available, and Dan acquired a motorcycle for warmer-weather delivery, reverting to horses in the wintertime.

When automobiles became available, he was one of the early owners of the horseless carriage, making mail delivery easier.

Anna Olive Herrold's parents' house was on Dan's route. Time and again, she tried to get his attention and start a conversation, but he had a job to do and didn't take notice.

So she tried something else. She had a green thumb when it came to flowers and conveniently arranged to be tending to her colorful and blossoming garden when it was time for Dan to come by with the mail. And that did it – the blooms caught his attention, and she offered a tour of the garden. They started dating (double dating, in fact, with Annie's sister Pearl and her future husband Art Williams). Both boys were tall and thin, and the girls were petite.

Dan and Annie were married two years later in 1904 and had two children, Icel Caroline and Frederick Daniel (my dad). At some point, Annie studied to be a schoolteacher but never taught.

All told, Dan and Annie were married 56 years, and I remember them well. Oh, how she loved Dan to her dying day.

It was Annie who started the hatchery business when she ordered an incubator from the Sears, Roebuck catalogue in 1927 and had it installed in the basement of the house. The incubator was about the size of a grand piano, and she experimented and learned how to hatch chicks.

The operation was an immediate success. There was great demand for baby chickens.

Without a hatchery, farmers would have to hatch eggs naturally. This entails the mother hen sitting on her eggs for approximately 21 days, turning the eggs about 50 times during every 24-hour period and maintaining an internal egg temperature of 99.5 degrees. It's not an easy task.

Grandma Hizer ran the hatchery for five years, and then Granddad Hizer (Dan) retired from the U.S. Postal Service and joined her in the business. The year was 1932, the same year Franklin D. Roosevelt was first elected president. He would go on to be elected to a total of four terms. Congress later ratified the 22nd Amendment to the Constitution limiting the office to two terms.

And that was the same year that Dan and Annie's son Fred, my dad, graduated from Indiana University (IU) with a degree in economics. It also was during the worst of the Great Depression years. Jobs were nearly impossible to find. Dad was footloose and fancy free so he decided to try his luck at getting a job in Florida. He hitchhiked all the way to Miami. I remember him telling the story about seeing the Atlantic Ocean for the first time: "It didn't look as big as I thought it would."

For about a month, he worked odd jobs in exchange for room and board and then was offered a position as a bookkeeper at Miami Railway & Bus Company. He was fortunate to have a job – so many people didn't. He was employed there until about 1935.

One of the benefits of working for a transportation company was that he could take the train or bus for free and explore the state, which he did on weekends. And one time when the company was short on staff, he stepped in to serve as a guide and took a group of tourists to Cuba (there were no travel restrictions then).

Dad used to tell us a funny story about his good friend Barney Kent, a fellow bookkeeper at the company. One year, sometime after the holidays, a bus driver turned in a bundle of misplaced mail. The bag was tossed in a drawer and forgotten. In June, Barney came across the packet so he mailed the envelopes, mostly Christmas cards. He thought it extremely humorous because he said the recipients wouldn't know if the holiday greetings were late or early. Dad said people used humor whenever they could to make life during the Great Depression a little "less dreary and unpleasant."

After about three years in Miami, Dad took a job as an accountant for the Florida Power & Light Company in Jacksonville.

In 1938 in Indiana, Granddad Hizer had an appendicitis attack (perhaps rupture since he had a long rehabilitation). Fred was called home from Florida.

During his stay up north to help his parents during the recuperation, Dad saw that people from all over were seeking chicks. There was high demand and not nearly enough supply (remember he had majored in economics at IU). It wasn't long before Dad recognized the great opportunity the hatchery operation represented.

After six years in Florida, he moved back home to Indiana and jumped in with both feet to help grow the business. He and Granddad converted the barn into a hatchery and upgraded to bigger and more incubators, manufactured by the Cugley Incubator Company.

I remember the incubator room. It was filled with half a dozen or so dark wooden heated structures seven feet high with heavy floor-to-ceiling doors. Inside, there were racks that slid in and out containing first the eggs and then the chicks. A generator was installed so we wouldn't lose the whole clutch if the power went out before the eggs were hatched or the whole flock if they already were.

And I can still hear the sound of hundreds of baby chicks chirping away in their first days and weeks. It was a cacophony of sounds.

Customers came from far and near, and Hizer Hatchery became a thriving, lucrative operation.

The hatching season ran from late winter to June so Dad was able to go to Florida for the coldest months while his parents handled the chores and "held down the fort" in his absence. It was a good arrangement: He could be assured of employment at his former company and escape the snowy season. Then he spent the rest of the year up north.

Dad met my mother, Miriam Esther Hines, in the summer of 1939, when she moved to Grass Creek to teach business and music. He saw her in church that first Sunday. She was no ordinary girl. She had graduated as salutatorian of her class from Indiana State University and had an alto voice that resounded throughout the sanctuary. He asked a friend to introduce him to her that very day.

He wasted no time in courting that dark-eyed girl named Miriam, and it wasn't long before they were engaged. Then Dad went to Florida for the winter. He came back in the spring, and they were married on May 5, about three weeks after school let out for the summer.

The school year ran from after Labor Day in September to mid-April and was based around agrarian and climate considerations. This timing was scheduled to accommodate the farmers, who needed their sons available to help during the busy planting, growing and harvesting seasons. The other factor was the heat. There was no air conditioning back then, and it could get dangerously hot in those brick schoolhouses. It could get equally sweltering out in the fields, working the land under the blazing sun. Today, air-conditioned schools and tractor cabs make life more comfortable when it's hot.

In those days, female teachers had to resign if they married. So Mother left her job after the wedding. She and Dad went to Florida the next winter, and Mother worked as a secretary.

The newlyweds had a wonderful time and toured around the Sunshine State on the weekends. Then they returned to Grass Creek in the spring with the intention of starting a family.

Dad and Mother visited Barney Kent, the Christmas card jokester from Miami, a few times over the next 10 years. Then there was a 20-year hiatus before Dad and Barney saw each other one last time, in 1969. Barney died in 1971, and Dad died in 1972.

When World War II began, many of the men went off to fight, leaving a scarcity of teachers. Because of that, the rules changed, and married women were allowed in the classroom. The school administrators in Grass Creek begged Mother to return and even found a babysitter (Olive Herrold) for her six-month-old son. So Mother went back to teaching and continued on until she retired in the mid-1970s.

Dad and Granddad Hizer worked as partners at the hatchery through the 1940s. Granddad stepped out of the picture in 1950 after working 18 years in the business that Annie had started all those years ago and, prior to that, working for the postal service for 32 years. He was ready for retirement.

For the next seven years, he and Grandma Hizer enjoyed their life in Grass Creek eight months of the year and wintered in Palmetto, Florida, on the Gulf Coast.

A number of their contemporaries went to the Sunshine State, too, each towing a sizable house trailer, and it was like Fulton County South at the trailer park. The Hizers won several shuffleboard tournaments and went to the ocean beaches often. Grandma collected shells and used them to decorate lamps made of cypress wood.

I remember visiting them at Christmastime. We would drive down and back in our Oldsmobile, stopping at a motel at night. Note: The word "motel" is a blend of "motorist" and "hotel." These one- or two-story buildings offering a room and parking peaked in popularity in the '50s and '60s when Americans took road trips and didn't care about room service and frills.

On one trip, we couldn't find a room for the night. We finally saw a billboard for a veterinary office that offered overnight rooms to pet owners. We drove 20 miles out of our way and did find lodging but had to listen to sick dogs barking and howling all night.

Then there was one trip where we had to drive through a long tunnel in the mountains. It was raining, and we were tired. The traffic was heavy, and the glare from the headlights of the oncoming traffic was blinding. It was tense, and Mother was sweating bullets. Dad was driving and asked if she had the toll money ready, and she answered, "Right here in my hot little [sweaty] hand."

After Granddad retired, Dad handled the hatchery business alone along with an occasional hired hand. Early on, he had widened the offerings with some ancillary products. For example, when people bought chicks, they then needed chicken feed so that became an important business in and of itself. He built the new henhouses, and we produced a large quantity of eggs – more than what was needed for the hatchery business – that Dad sold to a distributor for commercial purposes.

My mother got involved, too, and helped out with the hatchery when she could. In fact, Dad and Mother drove to Iowa and took a course in incubation and hatching.

Mother led a busy life. Along with cooking and sewing and being a wife and mother, she taught school full time, directed the church choir and played the organ for worship service, sang in a county choral group, gave piano lessons to kids all over the area, played the piano for the high school musicals and plays and the Shrine Club minstrels, provided the music for countless weddings and funerals, and participated in a host of other activities. She made the Hizers proud.

Starting with Jacob and counting the birth of the newest members of the family, we are nine generations of Hizers.

My childhood was good. Our community was small so everyone knew everyone else. We kids went through the days living a happy life, riding our bicycles and frolicking in the yard, swinging and singing and laughing.

Pony "Bud" taking Joyce, Alan (center) and friend
John Costello for a buggy ride.

Florence Cunningham was the first-grade teacher for decades. She was loved by all and helped shape the character of the children in the community. She was well-known for telling a child who was pouting that she was going to place a rooster on his or her lower lip if they didn't turn their frown into a smile. I could relate with that, having grown up around chickens, and I tried hard to keep a smile on my face at all costs.

Janece Herrold is a former home economics and physical education teacher and a pillar of the community. She was the one who headed up the committee and made sure things got done – every time. In doing so all those years, she became the unofficial town matriarch. Janece is just a year shy of being 90 years old now and is the go-to person for any information about Grass Creek.

Like in many families, I shared a bedroom with my little sister (until our brother left for college when I started eighth grade and she took his room). I can remember drawing a line down the center of the double bed with my hand and demanding that she not cross over it – not even a toe or finger was allowed. I also forbade any squirming, and she says that mandate set in motion her habit that continues to this day of not moving while sleeping. Sorry, Cyn, for being so unrelenting.

Cynthia (left) and Joyce one Christmas morning.

Black and white television sets were prominent in most homes during the '50s, and color TV became popular in the early '60s. We grew up watching shows such as "The Adventures of Ozzie and Harriet," "The Dick Van Dyke Show," "Dragnet," "Father Knows Best," "The Honeymooners," "I Love Lucy," "Lassie," "My Three Sons" and "Perry Mason."

Dad especially liked the westerns and watched "Bonanza" and "Gunsmoke." Mother enjoyed the music on "The Lawrence Welk Show" on Saturday nights and especially appreciated the harmony of the Lennon sisters. And we all watched "The Ed Sullivan Show" on Sunday nights and were introduced to some of the day's brightest upcoming stars. Often, it was a family affair, and the parents and kids alike sat around the room together and enjoyed the program of the moment. And remember eating dinner on those individual TV trays?

Granddad and Grandma Hizer built a house next door when Mother and Dad got married so there was constant back and forth between houses. In fact, when the chickenpox virus was spreading throughout the community, I stayed with my grandparents and escaped contracting the disease (and, as an adult, I've still never had it).

On some Sunday evenings, I would walk with Grandma Hizer to the church service right down the road and around the bend. I also recall being with her when there was a church revival. It could get rowdy at times.

I remember Granddad Hizer, tall and thin, looming high above me and saying "Bah! Humbug!" He said it a lot. The expression was originally spoken by the curmudgeon Ebenezer Scrooge in *A Christmas Carol* by Charles Dickens.

Grandma Hizer had a strawberry patch behind her house, and I would help her pick the berries. One time I interrupted a nest of bees, and they swarmed around my head. I've had a phobia about bees ever since (the buzzing sound specifically). Grandma's early passion for growing flowers stayed with her all her life, and she always had a greenhouse or garden full of colorful blossoms.

Just beyond the strawberry patch, Dad installed a small wooden structure for me to use as a playhouse. I spent a lot of time in that make-believe environment. As I grew older, Dad upgraded my domain and let me use a bigger building where I would occasionally prepare real food and serve dinner to Mother and Dad, practicing my hostessing skills. Later on, Dad bought a ping-pong table and put it in Grandma and Granddad Hizer's basement. We kids spent endless hours playing the sport (I was pretty good at it and often beat the boys). Life was so carefree. Remember all those silly knock-knock jokes?

Joyce (right) celebrating Cynthia's birthday.

Mother and Dad kept busy socially and were part of a group from Logansport that got together regularly: the Reids, the Evermans, the Grafs. And we went to the Shrine Club in Logansport for dinner on most Friday nights except when there was a basketball game. Often, my friend Loisann Hartzler and I would go shopping beforehand, particularly for lingerie.

Bill Diveley, a distant cousin who grew up in Grass Creek, earned a doctorate in chemistry at Purdue and took a job in Wilmington, Delaware. He would stop at our house to visit whenever he was back in the area to see his mother Mildred, who was a friend of Mother's and a fellow teacher.

He would come to the house on a Sunday in the late afternoon and join us for a popcorn dinner (yes, that was the main course following a hearty meal after church, and, yes, popcorn dunked in soda (Coke) is quite tasty). Bill would talk about his work as a research chemist at

Hercules and life in the East, and it all sounded so exciting. The seed for my desire to live on the East Coast was planted during those visits.

During the 1950s, Americans became enamored with cars. A decade earlier during World War II, young soldiers and sailors had plenty of time between battles to reminisce and brag about the souped-up cars that sat on blocks awaiting the return of their owners.

Once back home, the hot rod craze began anew. These were cars that had been stripped down and the engine rebuilt or modified to make them go much faster. They were followed by the muscle car of the '60s that had a powerful and larger-than-usual engine and a broad, boxy shape and long hood. A few of the most popular were the Chevrolet Camaro, Chevrolet Chevelle, Dodge Challenger, Dodge Charger, Plymouth Roadrunner Superbird, Pontiac Firebird Trans Am, Pontiac GTO.

On another front, cars became a necessity for those living in the suburbs. After the war was over, millions of veterans went to college and then took a job in the city. They chose to reside in the suburbs and commute to work, thus spiraling the demand for automobiles.

With a booming economy, Americans had money in their pockets and were enthralled with style. "Flashy" anything was in vogue, and cars were at the top of the list.

My parents bought a new General Motors automobile every other year, usually an Oldsmobile. The cars of the '50s and '60s had a style all their own – long and sleek with fins and whitewalls and fancy taillights – and window vents and fender skirts and lots of chrome. They were beauties. Everyone loved those cars, especially the convertibles.

They were gas-guzzlers, too, but that wasn't a problem. We were still enjoying the golden years of cheap gasoline – in the '60s, a gallon of gas sold for an average of 31-35 cents. Miles per gallon (mpg) averaged an abysmal 8.0 to 14.0 (a few cars were rated as low as 5.5; my GTO, which you'll read about later, clocked in at 10.3 mpg).

On the opposite end of the spectrum, popularity of the Volkswagen

The Early Years 21

Beetle (known as "the Bug") surged in the '60s and '70s. This unique car was small, fun, affordable and economical, averaging 19+ miles per gallon. After over 80 years, production ceased in 2019. A total of more than 23 million VW Beetles had been manufactured.

Your car was your pride and joy. The boys would drive around showing off and then park in the school lot or the local drive-in and rev the engine (remember that guttural sound of the V-8s?). The girls would giggle and flirt. The scene was a national pastime for high schoolers.

Some of the conversations would go like this: "Man, oh man! He has a really sharp car" or "That's really neat" or "We drove like mad" or "We had a blast at the drive-in" (typical Midwestern speak).

The hit movie "Grease" starring John Travolta and Olivia Newton-John is always fun to watch. Its portrayal of teenagers in the '50s and their friendships, romances and adventures makes you smile. It brings back happy memories of high school – the music, the dancing, the clothes, the hairstyles, the cars and maybe even a few tears.

Drive-in restaurants – remember hanging out at the drive-in? It's where everyone went to see and be seen and to find out who had a date with whom. Round and round you'd drive and eventually park and turn your lights on as a signal that you needed service. A carhop dressed in a cute little uniform would come to your car (sometimes on roller skates!) and take your order and then deliver your burgers and fries. The food was placed on a window tray that was attached to the car door. You'd turn the radio up and sing along and watch to see who came by.

To see and be seen – the age-old pastime. It reminds me of Ego Alley (appropriately named) in Annapolis, Maryland. An endless parade of boats and yachts traverse this narrow waterway, the proud captains making their appearance and loving every minute in the limelight.

The drive-in in Logansport where we always went was named Harvey's. And farther to the west, Keitzer's was almost as popular. And in Culver, Indiana, where I spent my summers, it was the Original Root Beer Stand on the curve across the street from the beach lodge.

Of note, A&W Root Beer drive-ins captured a leading share of the market for many years. A&W's signature root beer float served in a frosty glass mug straight from the freezer kept customers coming back again and again.

So close your eyes and pretend you're sitting in your car at the famous orange and brown drive-in. It's a hot summer day, and the carhop has just delivered your root beer float. Draw in on your straw and take your first sip of the foamy brown liquid. Mmm mmm good!

Back to the cars: They were big vehicles. They swayed on the road and were almost like big old boats as they floated along (I think it had something to do with the suspension). A friend once said it was like riding on a flying carpet.

There were no bucket seats or seat belts in that era, just the bench-seats (that the teenagers loved for necking). The movie "My Cousin Vinny" is all about those unforgettable cars.

It wasn't until 1968 that the auto manufacturers were required to put seat belts in new cars, but even then usage was voluntary. In 1984, New York became the first state to pass a law requiring that a seat belt be engaged when operating a vehicle. The law mandated that all front-seat occupants wear a seat belt and, in the back, passengers under the age of 10.

Most farmers get gasoline and diesel fuel for their farm equipment delivered in bulk because it is impractical, for example, to get a tractor to a gas station (often called a filling station in the Midwest). Note that fuel consumed by vehicles not driven on public roads is eligible for an off-highway fuel tax refund. This applies to farm equipment, lawn equipment, boats, trains and planes. The refund can be sizable as some farmers can consume thousands of gallons of fuel a month during the busy seasons. Hizer Hatchery had its own barrels of gasoline for the vehicles. And every farm had a pickup truck. So I grew up driving a stick shift.

After Ray and I were married, he always preferred that one of our cars be a standard shift (usually the puddle jumper). Luckily, I had no problem with that since I had learned to drive a pickup back in the day.

From time to time in this book, I describe traditions and provide background information on certain topics. Let's take a minute to talk about funeral protocol in Indiana.

I grew up with the Protestant tradition of going to the funeral home the afternoon or evening before the funeral. It was a big event. Everyone in the community, it seemed, went to the visitation – it was almost a social affair.

People came from long distances as well. (For example, my friend Yvonne Thomas came from Indianapolis (90+ miles) to my father's funeral and to my mother's viewing.) The funeral parlor can get crowded. The line can wrap around the room and even stretch to the outside and down the street.

The visitation is the opportunity in which to extend your condolences to the bereaved family members – and perhaps reminisce a little and remember some funny incidents.

An open casket displays the deceased wearing his or her finest attire. Floral arrangements, each on a stand, adorn both ends of the coffin and spill out into the room. Sometimes a special ceremony is conducted if the person was a member of, say, the military or, as were my parents, the Masons or the Order of the Eastern Star.

I came upon a notation in my diary about a visit to a funeral home when I was 15 years old, and it reads like this: "Mrs. H died. Dad, Cindy and I went to the funeral home to see her."

This followed by, "She looked terrible" (oh, those innocent words that come out of the mouths of babes!).

The funeral is held the next day either at a church or at the funeral home, preceded by a short open-casket visitation. Not nearly as many people attend. Afterward, the casket is transported in a hearse to the cemetery for burial.

Then the entire crowd is invited to the funeral meal hosted by the Ladies' Aid Society. The meal is served either at the church or at a nearby community center.

Of late, small towns across America have been awarded grant

money from the federal government to build a community center. The public building is used for a variety of events, from civic meetings to class reunions to funeral meals.

All the food is homemade and delicious. The menu served at my mother's funeral meal is typical: chicken and noodles over mashed potatoes, a corn casserole, several other sides and a variety of freshly baked pies.

In the East, the protocol is a little different. More often than not, the body is cremated. This preference is becoming more and more the norm across America due to lower cost and added convenience.

So, generally, the ceremony, by definition, is a memorial service. There usually is no event for the public the night before. If there are calling hours, people often refer to the visitation as a wake (even if there is no body present).

After the service, a reception normally is held at the church or at a yacht club or country club or even at a local pub.

Our Jewish friends sit shiva when they lose a first-degree relative (parent, spouse, sibling or child). It starts after the burial and ends seven days later. Its purpose is to provide loved ones a time for spiritual and emotional healing. During that period, the family may hold an open house so friends and relatives can come and show their support.

Birth of an Entrepreneur
In 1960, my parents bought a second home on Lake Maxinkuckee in Culver, Indiana, 20 miles or 30 minutes north of Grass Creek. It is the second largest natural lake in the state.

Maxinkuckee is an Indian word. Its translation varies, but all versions pertain to water: sparkling water, clear water, diamond lake. It's pronounced just as you would expect: "Max-in-kuck-key."

The modest house is situated at the top of a hill on the west side of the lake, with a neighboring house within a few feet on each side (in the back, the House of Treasures gift and antique shop was located across the street for many years).

In the front, a 32-step cement stairway descends to the lake. About halfway down, an open-air deck was built atop a cinder block boathouse that was used for storing swimming and water ski gear and fishing equipment. At the bottom of the steps, a seawall extends from property to property, and you can walk along the lake at water's edge for stretches at a time.

Most lake residents own a boat, generally a speedboat, and keep it at a pier under a cover of some sort. In the '60s, it was popular to purchase a canvas-covered shed. The pier would be installed in the early summer and removed in the fall because the ice in the wintertime would destroy the structure if left in place.

Although a year-round dwelling, our family primarily used the lake house in the summertime with an occasional afternoon visit throughout the rest of the year. It was always referred to as the "cottage" (but it was a far cry from the "cottages" of Newport, Rhode Island, in its glory days as I would learn later in life). Mother named the cottage Kinjockity, an Indian word meaning away from the crowds, although it was anything but that.

Prior to the second summer there at the age of 15, I approached Dad with the idea of selling eggs to the neighbors at the lake. He thought that was a good idea and offered to provide the eggs free of charge if I handled all the details. So on Friday afternoons, Dad and I would transport a supply of fresh farm eggs to Culver. On June 16, Dad took me to the State Exchange Bank, and I opened my first checking account.

I didn't have a regular driver's license yet but was granted special permission to operate a car for business purposes both on the farm and around the lake (called a farmer's driving permit). I had taken the driver's education course, which was free, in high school the preceding semester.

Dad and Mother had bought a new turquoise Chevrolet Corvair, which I claimed as my own. (Remember the Corvair? The engine was in the back, and the trunk was in the front.) So on Saturday mornings, I would drive from house to house, knocking on doors and offering my wares to the neighbors.

People loved it! Who doesn't savor one-day-old eggs? Before long, I had a loyal following. If customers had to be out at delivery time, they just left the money by their back door along with a generous tip. I enjoyed talking with the people, and managing the egg route was a good learning experience.

Joyce playing the piano.

My egg business was a win-win from the beginning since I didn't have to buy product or pay expenses (such as egg cartons, gas or car purchase/repair). I soon became known as "the egg lady" and carried on with the venture for a few summers, saving every penny and building my bank account, a habit that has stayed with me all my life. Even in semi-retirement, I maintain the mindset that I have to make enough money each year to cover the expenses and not dip into my savings.

In research for this book, I came upon the fact that the late, great George Steinbrenner, former owner of the New York Yankees who had roots at Culver, also sold eggs (and chickens) when he was a boy.

In addition to helping Dad in the office, I had chores to perform, and I took them seriously. They included gathering eggs by hand (and keeping count and recording the numbers) in each henhouse.

Chicken nests had been installed along the walls of the henhouses. It was easy to merely pick up the eggs from an empty nest and place them in the basket. If, however, a hen was in the nest, the gatherer would have to gently reach under the hen and collect the eggs, which would still be warm to the touch. If an egg had been laid recently, it might have a few feathers stuck to it.

After the rounds were made and the baskets placed in the Corvair, the eggs were driven to the farmhouse and transported to the basement where the egg operation was set up. On these jaunts, I would dream of life in the city and say to myself, "Someday!"

Year round, I would sing the words to "Silver Bells" and fantasize about the hustle and bustle on the busy streets of the city – the people dressed in their finery, the traffic jams, the honking horns (all a far cry from life in Grass Creek and Hizer Hatchery).

Another popular song during those years was "Moon River." I would stand outside in the large parking area between the house and the hatchery (called the barnyard on a normal farm) and bellow the words "there's such a lot of world to see" with stars in my eyes.

Back to the chores: The next step after hauling the eggs was to wash the baskets of eggs in a washer and stack the yellow plastic baskets on shelving to dry. The basement was always damp and served as a natural refrigerator.

The egg sorting, or grading, machine was simple to use. Each egg was placed on a conveyor belt by hand and culled out if a blood spot was detected as the egg passed over a light (occasionally an egg would show a double yolk – a surprise bonus for some unsuspecting soul).

Once the egg reached the bottom of the sloping belt, it would roll down the tray to the weighing stations and, according to weight, spill into pens signifying the classification of small, medium, large or extra-large categories. Then, again by hand, each egg was placed in a cardboard filler flat containing 30 eggs. These crates were then placed in a cardboard case by size.

We called the whole process "casing eggs."

Special care had to be taken to prevent eggs from being broken or cracked, and, from time to time, there would be an accident (messy!). Eggs were collected twice a day seven days a week from the henhouses, and the cases were picked up by a distributor two times a week.

Through my adulthood, I have sought sources for fresh eggs. After Ray and I were married, we would visit his father Syl in Lakewood, New Jersey, and bring home farm fresh eggs and veggies. Jersey is well-known for its choice produce in the summer, as is upstate New York. Even Connecticut is beginning to be recognized for quality dairy products and fresh produce grown on inland farms.

Mother and Dad taught us kids to be responsible and to fulfill our obligations. Earlier, I had had a calf that I had to feed every morning before school. And, for a while, Cynthia and I had two baby lambs, named Lucy and Ricky, as pets. And, of course, there were dogs: A standard Manchester named Tinkerbell and a toy Manchester named Sparky were our favorites. The Manchester pedigree gets its name from the city in England where much of the breed's early development took place.

My parents were good friends with Bob and Lois Cherdron, who lived in Indianapolis. Dad and Bob had been in the same fraternity in college, Sigma Pi at Indiana University, and they remained friends for life.

Bob was an executive for a tool and die company, and Lois was a highly trained medical professional involved in the promising field of radiation treatment. They would visit us at the lake a couple of weekends every summer, and Bob was renowned for changing his fashionable wardrobe three or four times a day.

The rest of the year, our family would go to Indy every month or so for the weekend. Bob and Lois had a lovely home with a beautifully finished basement that displayed keepsakes from a lifetime of traveling.

I would spend hours in that spacious room playing records and looking through their treasures, dreaming about traveling to far-away places with strange-sounding names.

When Ray first met Lois, he asked her, politely, what it was like to grow older. She responded by saying that whatever traits you exhibit in your younger years merely become accentuated as you age.

Soon after I was legally old enough to work, I took a full-time summer job at the State Exchange Bank in Culver. Alan advised that I wait a year or two – he said that once I started working, I'd never stop. But I couldn't wait to get started. It was the same when I graduated from high school. I just couldn't wait until fall to start college so I went to summer school. I always was excited about the next step in life.

So at the bank, I served as a teller one summer and, since I had learned typing and shorthand in high school, as an assistant secretary to the vice president, Fred Adams, the next year.

The bank was progressive in its thinking. For example, lunch was served to all its employees free of charge. Any customer who happened to be in the building at lunchtime was invited to partake. Word got around quickly, and the bank entertained a few customers about every day. The cafeteria service was discontinued in the mid-1980s after carrying on the tradition for 40 years.

Dad was one of those people who, every couple of weeks, just happened to be doing his banking around noontime. The bank president, W.O. Osborn, felt offering a free lunch was a small price to pay for the goodwill it brought. He also used that opportunity to get to know his customers better. He said that if a person salted his or her food before tasting it, that person would not be a good candidate for a loan.

Mr. Osborn was the heart and soul of one of the most successful banks in Indiana at that time. I listened to his words of wisdom for the two summers I had worked at the bank and tried to assimilate his advice. His assistant was Charlotte Jung (whose title was senior vice president), and I admired her for climbing so far up the ladder in her career, which was not common for a woman in those days.

Then an opportunity arose that I couldn't resist. Mr. Osborn was interested in getting feedback about the bank's services from customers, as well as non-customers.

He presented the idea to me and asked if I would be interested in calling on people in their home to gather this information. So all summer long, I drove my little Corvair around the county, greeting people, offering all kinds of tchotchkes such as calendars and condiment containers, spreading goodwill for the bank and ferreting out any problems or unhappy customers. And in some cases, the sincerity demonstrated by the bank brought in a new customer.

It was a dream job.

The only downside was occasionally making a stop where there was a sign posted that read "Beware of Dog." I remember a couple of times where the person had to keep a snarling animal tight on its leash (or the owner wasn't even home, and the dog was protecting its turf). That was a little scary.

Speaking of the Corvair, as described above, it had multiple uses. When I was an upperclassman at Caston High School, I drove the compact back and forth to Fulton, eight miles due east. It was *my* car.

Most of the students old enough to have a license had access to a vehicle so their parents wouldn't have to take time to drop off and pick up the kids all year long or they wouldn't have to be restricted to the school bus schedule. Schools from four neighboring communities consolidated, and the trek to the high school could be as far as 15 miles each way (it was even farther once the new school building was built) so each trip took a chunk of time.

In addition to being a form of transportation, the Corvair served as a recreational vehicle. In the wintertime when the lake at Culver was frozen, I would host snow skiing outings. We would retrieve the summer water skis and tow line out of storage in the boathouse, and Dad would drive the Corvair across the ice and snow, pulling one skier at a time. The ice was that solid. All these years later when I see classmate Johnny Herd, he frequently mentions how much fun that was. And, occasionally, some of the kids would build a bonfire on the ice and sing songs until it became unsafe to stay any longer (of note, the lake was 90 feet deep in some places).

The usefulness of a good education came from both sets of grandparents. And Mother and Dad, each a college graduate, considered education to be extremely important (Mother went on to earn a master's degree and had her sights on getting a doctorate, but that wasn't to be – life happened. And it was rare for a male in rural America to have earned an undergraduate degree during the late 1920s and '30s).

My parents ingrained in us kids the value of learning and doing well in school. In fact, we were given a quarter for each A on our report card (B's didn't count toward anything). And Granddad and Grandma Hizer gave us a dime for each A.

Going to college was a topic of discussion starting at an early age. I remember a story that brings home this point. I was in second grade, and we were having a spelling bee. I drew the word "divided" and started spelling it: d i v i d e d *e d*. The teacher, Mrs. Miller, shook her head and said, "No, I'm sorry. That's wrong. You added an extra 'ed' at the end." I was horrified! I was crushed! I had misspelled the word!

Tears started streaming down my face. Mrs. Miller came to my side, put her arm around me and said, "Honey, it's not the end of the world. You'll get it right next time." I looked at her and sobbed, "But now I won't be able to get into college!"

In the end, all three of us kids completed undergraduate and postgraduate degrees: Alan earned a B.S. degree and a law degree, I completed a B.S. and two master's degrees, and Cynthia earned a B.S. degree, a master's degree and a divinity degree.

Mother and Dad kept their eyes open as to what was happening in the world. They took trips and tried to bring us kids up with solid values and ethics and to have an interest in and knowledge about more than just the small farm town called Grass Creek where we lived. They attempted to expose us to situations that would enable us to reach beyond our own views and experiences.

I thirsted to learn about other places and corresponded with pen pals all over the United States and even abroad until I graduated from high school. One gal was from Detroit, and we traveled to each other's home to meet in person.

In going through my diary from 1962 when I was a freshman in high school, I mentioned writing a letter to at least two people about every night – some were local, most were not – just before turning out the lights. I was religious about this and sometimes didn't finish until well past midnight – the beginnings of being a night owl (my brother is even more so). And, as noted in the diary, I received just as many letters in return, addressed to Post Office Box 353, Grass Creek, Indiana (notice there was no ZIP Code).

Recently, I came across a greeting card from my maternal grandmother, Edna Olive Hines, wishing me a happy birthday. It is dated 1963 and prominently displays a canceled 5-cent stamp on the envelope. (Note: "Olive," a common name in that era, was the middle name of my two grandmothers. I understand consideration was given to naming me Olive in honor of both of them.)

Grandma Hines wrote a postcard to Mother once a week throughout my growing-up years. It would always be a white index card, the address on one side leaving the back side open for five and a half inches of script. Grandma Hines had the most perfect, tiny penmanship and could write a full letter in that space. Back then, people regularly wrote letters to each other (long distance phone calls were expensive).

I enjoyed keeping a diary, and it has been revealing, as a senior citizen, to reread the thought patterns and processes of a 15-year-old. Many of my lifelong habits and pleasures took root back then, from an interest in words and business to list making. (At my wedding reception, for instance, someone took a photo of me at the head table where half a dozen sheets of notepaper were spread out detailing the order of events and other details.)

On May 9, 1962, Dad said he would give me 50 cents if I wrote down 1,000 different words – and I did. "It's fun to work with words," the diary reads. Dad enjoyed writing, and he encouraged me to write: letters, articles, a book, anything – "just get the words on paper," he said. My diary says, "I simply can't wait to get started writing a book."

After we kids were grown and out on our own, Dad would write on his manual typewriter one letter to my brother, sister and me using carbon paper, placing a check mark by our respective name. That was long before computers and printers made making multiple copies easy. I also read a lot of books and remember staying up way later than I should have, "reading under the covers" or writing letters. Mother would usually notice the light on from the stairway and call up to me to go to sleep.

A lot of time was spent in my (bed)room. It was a rather large area that I had painted aqua. Featured front and center was a huge desk (I think it was a former dining room table) where I organized my books and papers. There was a sizable walk-in closet and a newly added bathroom just beyond the door.

I studied there in my room. I wrote all my letters there. I entertained my friends there. It was my space. It was my domain.

Cynthia told me recently that, as the little sister, she used to envy those visits with my girlfriends, most often Yvonne Thomas and Shirley Scott and, later, Loisann Hartzler. We'd spend hours practicing applying makeup and talking about boys and playing the latest hit songs on the stereo and dancing. Cynthia couldn't wait until she was old enough to partake in these same adventures.

During my freshman year in high school, we added a family room on the first floor of the house with a storage area above. Access to that storage space was through an opening in my room, and in the winter, you could hear Old Man Winter howling. Wind in the

Midwest can get ferocious because the terrain is so flat – there aren't hills and mountains to block the wind from building.

The 1960s was a busy and successful era for NASA, and I recorded the historic events of 1962 in my diary. On Tuesday, February 20, I wrote: "John Glenn orbited the earth, and he went around the world three times in just under five hours. That's history! We had the TV and radio on all day." Glenn was the first American to orbit the earth. (Due to a mechanical failure, the planned seven-orbit flight was cut short.) The mission re-established America's position as a strong contender in the space race against the Soviet Union. On May 24, I wrote, "They shot M. Scott Carpenter into space today, and he orbited the earth three times. It was just like Glenn's flight." And on October 3, Walter Schirra orbited six times.

Keeping a diary was good training in many ways. On the blank pages after December 31, I summarized the highlights of the year and chronicled the most important events. Making lists and categorizing/summarizing data are tasks I've continued all my life.

No matter the season, we kids went to the movies and saw about every new release as soon as it came to a nearby indoor or outdoor theater. In 1962, just a few of the titles from my diary include seeing "Breakfast at Tiffany's," "State Fair," "Mr. Hobbs Takes a Vacation," "A Raisin in the Sun," "Birdman of Alcatraz," "Splendor in the Grass," "Psycho," "Pocketful of Miracles" (which I saw on two consecutive nights, each time with a different date), "G.I. Blues." Many of the movies from that era are classics today.

We especially delighted in going to the drive-in theater on the outskirts of Logansport on State Road 17. This is where each car is parked in a designated area beside a speaker, and you watch the movie on a large outdoor screen from inside the car.

Later in life, one time when Ray and I were anchored for the night in Coecles (that's pronounced "Cock-els") Harbor in Shelter Island, New York, there was a raft-up of about 25 boats. At dusk, some skippers hoisted a sail, stretched it across a couple of boats, secured it at the bow and used it as a screen for projecting a movie. The sound was magnified so all could hear. It was almost a replica of the old outdoor theaters popular when I was a teenager. Coecles was even better, though, because we were sitting in the cockpit under the stars and taking in the salt air and evening breeze.

Back to 1962 and high school: Everyone followed the movie stars, of course. I noted in my diary that Marilyn Monroe committed suicide on August 4. All the girls read *Seventeen* magazine and tried to emulate the models and their clothing styles. I made mention of buying a girdle that year: "It was aqua colored!" Most people today have forgotten that females ever wore such an undergarment. And remember sleeping in rollers every night? I'm glad that's gone by the wayside. Every September, the girls watched the Miss America contest on TV and dreamed of being glamorous. That year, Miss Ohio won.

Popular attire for the girls during their high school years consisted mainly of dresses and straight or A-line skirts and blouses with maybe a dainty ribbon under the collar. Note that in the early '70s, slacks and pants became fashionable, followed by designer jeans in the '80s, and have remained so to this day.

Footwear generally consisted of saddle shoes and bobby socks. Eventually, loafers made their way to the top of the list. On dress-up days, the high schoolers wore flats and hose. And for special and fancy occasions, every female learned how to walk in high heels.

The girls wore their hair teased in a bouffant or beehive using copious amounts of hairspray or in a flipped bob, trying to imitate the Jackie Kennedy look. Brigitte Bardot, Jane Fonda and Raquel Welch wore a sexy style called the bombshell.

The boys' hairstyles changed, too. The clean-cut side part and crew cut (or buzz cut) that had been popular for a long time fell out of favor. The neat, clean-shaven military look gave way to longer hair and sideburns.

Elvis Presley's first #1 bestseller, "Heartbreak Hotel," in 1956 ushered in a new era of music and culture. The girls swooned at the mere sight of the King of Rock 'n' Roll, and the boys mimicked his dance techniques and hairstyle. His pompadour (ducktail) came to be called "the Elvis cut," kept in place with lots of Brylcreem or other styling lotion. By the way, I was surprised to learn from my research that Elvis had been born a natural blond with blue eyes. By the time he was a teenager, his hair had turned medium brown. He had it dyed mink brown or black once he was in the limelight, thinking the darker color brought out his facial features better on film and had more sex appeal in general.

Elvis' first movie was "Love Me Tender." He went on to star in a total of 31 movies and two documentaries. For a few years, he was one of Hollywood's top box office draws and one of its highest paid actors.

The Beatles came along a few years later and made their first American appearance on "The Ed Sullivan Show" on February 9, 1964. A large percentage of the 73 million viewers were transfixed, and Beatlemania took over the country. Likewise, the mop top hairstyle the Beatles wore became all the rage.

Of note, the group selected "Beatles" as its name because the band members took to the idea of calling themselves some kind of insect. They had particularly liked the moniker "The Crickets," Buddy Holly's former band name. You may remember that the music world was saddened when Holly's chartered plane crashed in 1959, killing everyone on board, including fellow performers Ritchie Valens and the Big Bopper.

The Liverpool foursome selected "beetle" and changed the spelling to "beatle" as a pun on musical beats. John Lennon, Paul McCartney, George Harrison and Ringo Starr comprised the British rock group.

Once you became a senior in high school in Indiana, boys and girls alike took great pride in wearing their "senior cords" ("cords" is short for "corduroy"). Each student would have favorite items hand painted on a cream-colored corduroy pair of trousers or skirt that reflected his or her interests and captured their personality – activities, achievements, passions, aspirations.

Artwork could include images and cartoon characters of singing groups, nicknames, friends' names, boyfriend/girlfriend names, school mascot, clubs, catchphrases of the day, cars, hearts, hobbies, sports, special events, musical instruments – customized graffiti of sorts. Combined, they represented a walking yearbook.

The trend started in 1904 at Purdue University in Lafayette, Indiana. A group of senior boys noticed a bolt of yellow corduroy fabric in the display window of Taylor Steffen Co., a local tailor, and came up with the idea to have trousers made.

The flamboyant pants were a big hit, and the idea of decorating them grew to the point where they became a fashion statement. Classmates jumped on the bandwagon, and soon boys and girls alike were sporting their own set of senior cords.

Because it was a "Purdue thing," the students started using fabric with a tawny hue to reflect the Boilermakers' school colors of gold (and black). The fad spread to IU. Not wanting to use their archrival's school colors, an off-white, cream or beige shade became the norm (IU's school colors are cream and crimson). Soon kids from other colleges around the state picked up on the idea.

It wasn't long until the craze trickled down to the high schools. By the 1920s, senior cords had become a widespread tradition throughout the state. It was part of being a senior and represented a rite of passage. The students proudly wore their personalized trousers or skirts, and there were some kids who went all out and complemented the basics with shorts, vests, jumpers and/or jackets.

The custom remained popular until the 1970s and was unique to Indiana, primarily in the high schools (I don't recall any mention of it at IU when I was a student there in the '60s).

I personally remember there were times throughout the year at Caston that were designated as Senior Cord Day where the entire class was to wear their special attire. It was fun strutting up and down the hallways wearing the skirts and pants reserved for seniors and flaunting our superior upperclassman status.

Senior cords were so popular, in fact, that there were events planned around the theme. Bloomington High School, for example, held a Senior Cord Dance where everyone was to wear their creation. The dance was first held in 1952 and became an annual affair for several years. Prizes were awarded for different categories such as originality and neatness. School administrators and teachers served as judges. A disc jockey was hired for the evening and made the trip down from Indianapolis.

Today, senior cords are considered fashion artwork from a bygone era. The Elizabeth Sage Historic Costume Collection at Indiana University in Bloomington has been involved in bringing back an appreciation for these decorated clothes.

The staff of the Sage Collection is always looking to expand its inventory while these valuable items of social history still abound. So here's a call to action to my Caston classmates and anyone else you know who may have had the pleasure of wearing these fun clothes: If you still have your senior cords and can bear to part with them, contact the Sage Collection at IU. Your garment can be a part of history.

The tradition of senior cords has long since disappeared. The closest thing the kids do today is decorate the top of their cap at graduation.

The class ring was another ritual. Everybody ordered one from a wide choice of metals, cuts and stones. Mine was gold with mother of pearl. It sits in my jewelry box to this day and is still bright and shiny.

If a couple was "going steady," the boy often would give his girlfriend his class ring. The girl would wear it on a chain around her neck or wrap angora around the ring to make it fit better on her left ring finger. The task was time consuming, but it was a labor of love, and the fluffy wool looked beautiful. Or the boy might let his girlfriend wear his letter sweater or jacket.

These traditions, too, have been abandoned. If a token gift is made today, it might be a tee shirt or sweatshirt. And I understand it's common practice to exchange passwords to emails, texts and other digital platforms as a way of making a commitment.

By the way, the company that sold the class rings that year in 1965 was Jostens. If you still have your ring, you can see the company name inscribed on the inside.

Then there was the yearbook. Every high school put one out. Ours was called *Exodus*, and there were 26 seniors on staff in 1965. The publisher was the American Yearbook Co. Its name is embedded on the red back cover (Caston's school colors are red, white and blue).

One other company that specialized in the class ring and yearbook business was Herff Jones, based in Indianapolis. The company was founded in 1920 and is still in business today. You'll read later about the Meurer family history and Ray's father attending Carnegie Institute of Technology. Herff Jones ran an ad in his 1923 college yearbook – nearly 100 years ago.

Another rite of passage was the senior trip. All during high school, the class officers would organize projects and activities to raise funds to pay for a trip the students would take together in their senior year just before graduation. During our freshman year, I served as class president and enjoyed getting the kitty started. On April 14 of that year, our class held a scrap drive, and we made $125.

Let's talk about scrap drives for a moment. During the 1960s, they were a popular activity left over from World War II, when Americans wholeheartedly rallied to support war operations.

The federal government sponsored a Salvage for Victory campaign in 1942, and posters were displayed across the country. Americans jumped on board and scoured their homes, farms and businesses to help out, feeling a direct link to the husbands, fathers and sons (and a few women, too – more than 350,000 by the end of the war) who served their country. The crusade brought people and communities together in a united front.

Metal was used in the production of dozens and dozens of military vehicles and equipment. Everyone was encouraged to collect unused and unwanted metal that the government would melt down and reuse to build airplanes, armored tanks, battleships, weapons and all kinds of equipment with which to fight the enemy. Any type of metal was welcome: aluminum, bronze, copper, iron, nickel, silver, steel, tin.

On the farms, there was a plethora of barbed wire, broken-down vehicles, outdated equipment and rusty tools. Throughout the nation, people contributed everything from crumbling metal staircases and wrought iron furniture to expired license plates, old keys and common household items such as bobby pins, metal toys, pots and pans, tin cans, tin foil and used clothing with zippers.

Other everyday items included bed frames, bicycles, boilers, car batteries, cars, lawn mowers, old appliances, radiators, vacuum cleaners.

Metal wasn't the only category of materials that could be recycled to make war products – cooking fats, nylon, paper, rags, rubber and silk had important usages. Following are some examples.

Cooking fats were used in making ammunition and explosives, and women across America were encouraged to collect bacon grease and household fats for the war effort.

Nylon stockings were respun to make thread for the production and repair of parachutes.

Paper bags, books, boxes, candy wrappers, comic books, magazines, newspapers and wastepaper were used to make new paper and paper products for packaging explosives, food and materials.

Rags were used to make paper, of which there was a serious shortage, and for cleaning – from guns and machinery to barracks' floors and ships' decks.

Rubber boots, floor mats, garden hoses, hot water bottles, raincoats, rubber bands, swimming caps and worn-out tires were used to make gas masks, life rafts and tires for military vehicles.

Silk was reprocessed and made into bags housing gunpowder and other high explosives used in large-caliber guns. Silk was also a preferred raw material in the production of maps so they wouldn't fade and disintegrate in storm-tossed trenches and drenching rain.

The Early Years

Eleven months before the United States entered the war, President Franklin D. Roosevelt gave his famous Four Freedoms speech to Congress. The president reaffirmed America's dedication to protecting four essential freedoms that people everywhere in the world should enjoy:
- freedom of worship
- freedom of speech
- freedom from want
- freedom from fear

Just months later, America would once again embark on the fight to protect the fundamentals upon which our country was born: On Sunday, December 7, 1941, the Japanese attacked Pearl Harbor. The next day, December 8, at 4:10 p.m., President Roosevelt signed the U.S. Congress Joint Resolution declaring war on Japan.

It took a shocked America a few weeks to mobilize itself and prepare for combat, marshaling its troops and resources.

One of the first steps was to get U.S. industries into gear. Under the direction of the War Production Board, factories across the country immediately started retooling and converting their production of peacetime products into the manufacture of war munitions: airplanes, ammunition, battleships, boats, cannons, equipment, guns, helicopters, submarines, tanks, and components and parts for each.

Three months later, a number of programs were rolled out, and implementation commenced.

Examples of the magnitude of this effort are many. Contractors were engaged to build barracks. The auto manufacturers ceased making cars, trucks and auto parts for non-military use in February 1942.

Instead, they built military vehicles and munitions. That continued until October of 1945. And the garment factories took all the cotton, leather, nylon and wool they could muster to make uniforms and clothing, and sheets and blankets, etc., for the troops.

Everybody got on board. War plants were running three eight-hour shifts a day six days a week, hiring vast numbers of women because the men were off fighting.

The war meant that huge amounts of America's resources and supplies were needed for the war effort. In many cases, little was left over for civilians, but they were happy to make sacrifices to support the country's finest young men and women:

1) Enormous quantities of food and non-food products – from beef to butter and sugar to shoes to canned goods and processed food – were shipped overseas to our servicemen and women and our Allies.

2) The bulk of the country's supply of gasoline and, essentially, all rubber tires were dedicated to the military. Thus, transportation of foods and other commodities domestically was extremely limited.

3) Imported food (coffee/sugar) and other products were bound by wartime import/export trade restrictions set in place.

To meet the surging demand by the armed forces, the government instituted rationing protocol, an equitable way of distributing limited goods to the general public. Virtually every man, woman and child in America was affected and granted a monthly allotment.

The Office of Price Administration was established, and ration books with removable stamps were issued. The only way to purchase a rationed product was to present the cashier with the appropriate amount of cash and a stamp for that particular item. To prevent hoarding, the stamps carried an expiration date.

In the spirit of the war and patriotism, images of airplanes, corn, fruit, guns, tanks, wheat, etc., were printed on the stamps.

Items rationed included food; specifically, butter, canned goods, cheese, coffee, dried fruit, jams and jellies, meat, oils, shortening, sugar.

Non-food items included clothing, coal, firewood, gasoline, heating oil, metal, nylon, paper, rubber (especially tires), shoes, silk, toothpaste.

Ration Card #1 (called the "Sugar Book" because sugar was the first food item to be restricted) was issued in early 1942.

People living on a farm or in a small town were encouraged to grow their own vegetables. Approximately half of American families planted a Victory Garden.

The rationing of gasoline affected millions of Americans. Starting in May of 1942 on the East Coast, the program was rolled out across the entire country by December. Each motorist was assigned to a category, generally based on occupation, and was provided with a sticker to place on the car's windshield. Most people displayed the "A" sticker and were entitled to purchase (gas was 19 cents a gallon) three or four gallons a week (later reduced to two gallons). With such a minimal quota, those living in remote places were forced to stay home most of the time. Starting in January 1943, all pleasure driving was outlawed, causing public outrage. The restriction was revoked nine months later.

Certain groups were permitted an unlimited supply of gas: clergy, construction workers, embalmers, farmers, mail carriers, motorcycle delivery drivers (e.g., Western Union), physicians and healthcare personnel, truckers, VIPs. It's said that the paperwork required to be granted this status was so cumbersome that some who would have qualified didn't even apply.

People were urged to drive less and carpool whenever possible and to walk and bike more. Because bicycles were made of steel and rubber, they, too, were rationed. Bikes were used by the military and had been since the late 1800s. In World War II, for example, the Allied forces supplied paratroopers with folding bicycles for easy transport after landing (the lads actually jumped out of the planes clutching a bike!).

The national speed limit for cars was set at 35 miles per hour in order to reduce gas and rubber consumption. The thinking was that the slow speed would provide a longer life for the automobile in general and the tires in particular since new civilian cars were not being made and replacement tires, for all intents and purposes, were not available to the public. Like so many other restrictions, the speed limit was not lifted until 1945, three years later.

The real and underlying reason for gas rationing, however, was to minimize the consumption of rubber. Rubber conservation by the public became a top priority as it was critical in the production of wartime equipment. Early on, Japanese armies seized control of the rubber plantations in the Far East that provided 90% of the U.S. manufacturers' supply of rubber, the primary raw material for making tires.

On the domestic front, rubber or forms thereof, such as elastic, latex products and stretch fabrics, was being used in the production of many clothing items. Due to the scarcity of rubber, those items were hard to get or were not available at all; specifically, footwear, foundation garments, rainwear and waterproof gear.

As an aside, after Ray and I were married, we became friends with Alex Mackintosh and his mother Ann. In the early 1940s, Ann and her husband Don were living in Java (now Indonesia). He was working for General Motors and was manager of the rubber plantations there. They had a wonderful life – with servants to cater to every need. Once war was declared, the Japanese claimed the area and the highly prized and ample supply of rubber.

Don, Ann, Ann's mother and three-year-old Alex were taken prisoners of war. Don was sent to the men's camp and the others to the women's camp. They spent three long years under the most unpleasant of conditions and did their best to survive until being released. Ann used to tell the story of how she and Don saw each other one time during the years of capture. They secretly met in a park and sat on adjacent benches, pretending not to know each other. It was very risky, but they didn't get caught.

President Roosevelt generated enthusiasm and support for our troops through numerous campaigns. These are just a few:

- Curtail food waste. Eat leftovers and "lick your plate clean."
- Dress warm and keep the thermostat down to preserve heating oil.
- Take short showers to avoid straining fuel resources necessary to heat large quantities of water.
- Buy war bonds and fund the war. These were debt instruments issued by Uncle Sam to finance military operations in wartime. War bonds were popular, with 85 million Americans, or more than half of the population, purchasing these bonds during World War II.

Rationing ceased when the war ended in 1945 except for sugar, which was restricted until 1947. For much of my life, I heard my parents talk about the shortages and sacrifices – big and small – during the war (I was born one and one-half years after it ended). For example, my mother and her friends were happy to be able to buy nylon stockings again.

For years afterward, those of my parents' generation often asked, "Where were you on Pearl Harbor Day?" It's a question everyone had an answer for because it would forever be utmost in their mind (just like my generation asks, "Where were you when John F. Kennedy was shot?" I was a sophomore in high school. The teachers set up a TV in study hall so we could watch the coverage.).

On that December day in 1941, my own parents were returning to Grass Creek from Logansport after seeing a movie and heard the news on the car radio. Mother was about seven months pregnant with their first child (my brother Alan). She and Dad felt enormous uncertainty with the reality of war upon them.

From the very beginning, patriotism and personal sacrifice played a significant part in the Allied war effort. After four years of fighting, the war was won. The victory promised a bright future for our country and its citizenry and for our Allied partners and their peoples.

With peace restored, prosperity descended upon America. After "doing without" during the war and, before that, the Great Depression, Americans were ready to make up for lost time.

The 1950s ushered in a whole new level of consumerism and consumption – planned obsolescence and a throw-away culture. Called the Age of Affluence, the decade saw an unprecedented boom in the wealth of the country. As the economy grew, personal incomes rose. People had plenty of disposable income and were ready to go on a spending spree. And spend they did!

That attitude flowed into the 1960s, and life was good. As well, another type of patriotism was starting to evolve: taking care of the environment and recycling. The scrap drives of the '60s were a precursor to that mindset.

The idea of protecting the environment gained traction. The first Clean Air Act was passed by Congress in 1963. The first Earth Day was observed on April 22, 1970. And the Environmental Protection Agency was established the following December by President Richard Nixon. Its purpose was to protect human health and the environment. In 1972, the Clean Water Act was passed.

In the 50 years since, we've made great strides in many areas – from cleaner air to cleaner water and the adoption of renewable energy. It has become a worldwide effort.

Back to the scrap drives at Caston High School: Having organized scrap drives and other projects for four years, our class treasury was flush enough to subsidize some of the expenses for our class trip, which entailed a weekend in Chicago. We packed in as many sights and excursions as we could, including touring the Museum of Science and Industry and Shedd Aquarium, watching a major league baseball game, shopping at Marshall Field's and dining at restaurants.

Smoking cigarettes was all the rage so in preparation for the trip, I would sit on a chair in front of the full-length mirror in my bedroom and practice inhaling and exhaling. I wanted to look experienced and sophisticated. It's a habit I wish I had not taken up and one that is hard to break.

The senior trip in years prior to the Caston school consolidation featured a bus trip to Washington, D.C., and New York City. Mother, as faculty advisor, and Dad served as chaperones on a number of those trips, and I heard the exciting stories all my life (about the cherry blossoms in D.C. and the Broadway plays in New York, for starters). The Class of 1962 took the final senior trip out East. My parents went as chaperones, and I stayed at Loisann Hartzler's house while they were gone.

The Grass Creek High School typical class size of around 20 students was about one-quarter the size of our 1965 Caston class of 79 students. So the smaller group to more distant destinations (than

Chicago) was much more manageable and affordable than after the consolidation. The class trip was abandoned not too many years later.

A new facility was built a few years thereafter that housed all 12 grades under one roof. Until that structure was completed, the schools continued on in the existing buildings split into two campuses under the names North Caston (in Fulton) and South Caston (in Twelve Mile).

Fulton and Grass Creek comprised North Caston, and Metea and Twelve Mile comprised South Caston. (The name Caston is derived from a combination of the two counties in which the towns reside: Cass and Fulton.) Note: The blending of two words to create a new word is called a portmanteau.

I belonged to the North contingency. Our senior yearbook featured a full page of the Confederate flag and a full page of the Union flag at the beginning and ending of the book. So sometimes we were rivals, and sometimes we were cronies.

Teachers often were assigned classes in both locations and traveled back and forth. It was not uncommon for them to deliver "love notes" to a student's sweetheart at the other campus.

The makeup of a rural farming community is quite stable. Farmland customarily stays within the family generation after generation; thus people don't move away, and few move in. For the most part, your first-grade classmates will be the same kids with whom you will graduate 12 years later. In my case, there was an infusion of new blood my freshman year when Grass Creek joined the three other towns (Fulton, Metea and Twelve Mile) and consolidated into one school system in 1960.

But those early friendships during elementary school created a strong bond. I spent much time during those years with Yvonne Thomas and Shirley Scott, in particular, and sometimes Charlene Thomas. I have great memories of those days.

After the consolidation, we formed lasting friendships with our new classmates as well (for me, especially Loisann Hartzler). My new circle of friends also included Mary Ann Bailey, Gloria Birk, Sherry Brown, Jeanette Clemons, Judy Leavell, Jana Lowe, Julia Rose McCrosky, Marsha McDowell and Wanda Townsend.

Another feature of a small school is that any given student will join a number of clubs and organizations because "bodies" are needed to carry out the activities. So the high school experience is full and rich and well-rounded. For example, I was class president in my freshman year, class reporter of the school newspaper in my sophomore year and business manager in my junior and senior years, and activities editor of the yearbook staff in my senior year.

I served as backstage crew for the annual school play, was in the cast of the musical production *Caston Capers* all four years, belonged to the Pep Club, was a member of the Sunshine Society (doing good for others; our theme song was "My Sunshine Girl"), was captain of the Girls Athletic Association in my senior year, and qualified for and became a member of the National Honor Society in my junior and senior years.

Musically, I sang in the school chorus and performed in frequent programs. I sang in a duet, trio and sextet and was in the school band, the marching band and the stage band. I played the piano, organ, flute (first chair), piccolo and baritone saxophone and did well in state competitions in all four years of high school. And the marching band competed at the Indiana State Fair every August.

If you've never been to a state fair, it is a must-do. They are huge affairs, and there's something of interest for everyone. All but two states hold the event, and some patrons go from state fair to state fair to bid on choice livestock at the auctions for breeding purposes.

Indiana's venue is on the north side of Indianapolis, and the grounds encompass 250 acres. Nearly a million fairgoers typically attend either as a competitor or as a bystander.

It's a three-week event featuring all kinds of exhibitions, competitions, entertainment, and rides and attractions that will keep you busy from morning till night. Entrants from all over the state take great pride in being selected to participate in contests in dozens of categories

– from every kind of livestock to every kind of fresh produce along with baked goods, sewing, woodworking and flower competitions, to name but a few.

Earlier in the summer, every July brought the County Fair, a one-week event staggered throughout the month all around the state. Everyone went. The kids in 4-H entered into competitions of all kinds. Others went to see and to be seen. I usually went to several fairs: Fulton County, Cass County, Marshall County. Then there were festivals all over the state most anytime of the year. Of significance, the Johnny Appleseed Festival is held every September in Fort Wayne to honor the folk hero and real-life pioneer apple farmer who is buried there. John Chapman became known as Johnny Appleseed, having introduced apple trees to the heartland during the 1880s.

I also belonged to the International Order of the Rainbow for Girls, a Masonic youth service organization. It was good training as the members had to memorize rituals performed at the monthly meetings, and there was a lot of pomp and circumstance associated with the ceremonies. I was elected worthy advisor in my senior year, and Loisann Hartzler and I attended some state galas in Indianapolis, each wearing an evening gown and being escorted by a date.

In the '50s and early '60s, drive-thru and fast-food restaurants came upon the scene. McDonald's started opening sites around the state. I remember the first time I heard about the fast-food chain. My Uncle Warren Hines and Aunt Ann drove the 160 miles to Grass Creek from their home in Worthington, Indiana, and tried out the new phenomenon on their way north. They said it was wonderful that you didn't have to wait while your meal was being prepared. This was much faster.

Locally, the owner of Bob-O-Link Drive-In opened his doors in Royal Center in 1956, offering inside seating, as well as drive-thru pickup. He then opened the original Mr. Happy Burger in 1961 on the east end in Logansport. McDonald's came to town in 1969 and eventually Burger King. And it was about that time that pizza was introduced in the Midwest. Bruno's Pizza opened in Logansport in 1960, and we all loved this novel taste treat. Today, Bruno's is run by granddaughter Gina. The Sycamore Drive-In (1945), Char-Bett (1958) and B-K West (1980) also have enjoyed decades of serving the locals. Of note, the Spanish hot dog is a favorite in Logansport.

The popularity and growth of the fast-food industry is primarily attributed to America's highway building boom that started when President Dwight Eisenhower signed into law the Federal Aid Highway Act of 1956. Nearly 47,000 miles of highways eventually comprised the U.S. infrastructure.

The country's thruway system transformed America. The freeways brought an economic boom that affected industry after industry, starting with highway construction, gas and oil, and automotive.

Before long, motel chains were built along the on- and off-ramps: Holiday Inn, Howard Johnson's, Ramada Inn, Travelodge, to name but a few.

Along with all that, restaurants and shopping centers were in demand. Across the nation, we all saw it: construction everywhere you went. We witnessed bulldozers and heavy equipment moving dirt and paving the way for a roadway or interchange or a mall.

The interstate system affected the country's economy in that goods could be transported by truck from sea to shining sea. Americans had access to products being manufactured or grown across the land.

The motorways also gave birth to a faster and broader lifestyle. People could live in the suburbs and commute to work. This spurred the development of residential and commercial real estate surrounding cities across the country. For the first time, we became an automobile-oriented society. And living in the suburbs did not limit one's recreational choices since the parkways and interstates made it possible to drive what earlier was considered long distances.

As well, tourism flourished. People could drive to their destinations, and it wouldn't take forever and a day. All the small towns – with their stoplights and railroad crossings and 35-mile-an-hour speed zones from one end of town to the other – were bypassed.

Once interstates were built and multitudes of people were venturing much farther from home, a quick stop to grab a bite to eat fit the bill and was exactly what travelers wanted. The fast-food industry soared.

Today, fast food is a way of life, and it's available everywhere. Whether you're driving on a freeway, say, in one of the Great Plains states or walking through Times Square in New York, you'll have plenty of choices.

Generally speaking, food fare in America's heartland consisted of hearty meals – a lot of meat and potatoes (which I still love) with gravy.

Favorites included all kinds of beef roasts, pork, chicken and breaded tenderloin. A popular meal was chicken and thick homemade noodles in a butter sauce served over mashed potatoes (talk about carbs!). And a wholesome soup made with one's own meat and vegetables from the garden was always a hit, not to mention potato soup. My dad especially loved green beans and ham that had simmered for hours (in a deep well on the stovetop).

The farm wives had canning days where they preserved homegrown fruits and vegetables for the long winter ahead – sometimes neighbor ladies would get together and make it a joint effort.

Mother planted a garden every spring so we had plenty of fresh vegetables right through the fall. Also, Dad tried his hand at beekeeping, and we had honey straight from the hive. I still remember the full-body protective suit he wore, complete with veil, so he wouldn't get stung.

Since the Hizers ran a hatchery and raised chickens, fresh eggs and poultry were staples.

We had eggs for breakfast most mornings. Throughout elementary and junior high school, Shirley Scott and I would share eggs over easy for breakfast when we stayed at each other's house: She liked the egg yolk, and I liked the white (or was it the other way around?). Anyway, we each had a double dose of our favorite part of the egg.

During high school, my good friend Loisann Hartzler savored having eggs in the morning as that was a treat for her whenever she stayed overnight versus the usual breakfast fare of toast that her mother Maxine prepared.

For the evening meal, Dad would go to one of the henhouses and select a couple of chickens, secure them upside down on the clothesline in the backyard and chop off their head. Within a few minutes, he would dunk them for a couple of seconds in a bucket of 150-degree water for defeathering – and, wa-lah!, we had the main course for our dinner that night.

Regarding meat, it was not uncommon for a family to butcher a whole cow and/or hog once a year and rent freezer space in a local cold storage facility. I remember making the trip to Kewanna five miles up the road every few weeks to replenish our home supply. It was cold inside the storage unit, and we had to wear a winter coat even in the heat of the summer.

Going to church on Sunday mornings was a regular part of our life. We were Protestant. The denomination of the church in Grass Creek was Evangelical United Brethren until 1968, when it merged with The Methodist Church and became the United Methodist Church. When Mother was in her 90s and had to give up her house, we donated a set of mahogany candlesticks to the Grass Creek church. I'm so glad we did that. Seeing them on my visits has given me great comfort.

Sometimes a Protestant would marry a Catholic, and, in those innocent times during the mid-20th century, this was considered a mixed marriage in the Midwest. Believe it or not, all three of us kids married a Catholic.

There were lots of community gatherings, too. Every summer, church members congregated at a parishioner's farm for a good old-fashioned picnic. For many years, it was held at Roma Woods, a cluster of trees surrounded by farmland, owned by Roy and May Kumler (the word Roma is a combination of the first two letters of their respective name). Everybody brought their favorite dish, and I remember how good the homemade pies were (including Hoosier sugar cream pie – yum!). Roma Woods was also the venue for various family reunions.

A Strawberry Festival was held every May and a Corn Roast in August and a Fish Fry anytime of the year. And an Ice Cream Social was held on Friday nights throughout the summer. Another community event growing up was the Tractor Pull, a contest to determine the operator who could pull the most weight the longest distance. The competition was fierce.

And there was the ever-popular hayride. In fact, Dad invited Mother on such an outing early in their relationship one crisp evening in the fall of 1939. A few months later at the engagement party, a crossword puzzle was created with clues leading to the answer "Fred and Miriam engaged." The account was published in *The OBSERVER* for all to read. They were married the next May.

Speaking of hay, I still remember that wonderfully sweet smell of freshly mown hay when driving on the country roads in the summertime inside the car with the windows down or in the open bed of a truck. There's nothing like it.

Culver

Summers at the cottage influenced me in many ways. The summer residents of Lake Maxinkuckee would descend on Culver starting in May and came from all over central and northern Indiana. There was a large concentration of folks from Indianapolis and Chicago.

I relished having conversations with these "city slickers." It broadened my world and gave me perspective. Some came for the entire summer, and others visited just on weekends. They came from many walks of life. There were bankers, doctors, farmers, insurance agents, lawyers, teachers, and owners of small businesses and retail establishments.

One neighbor, Pete Gallette, from Grosse Point, Michigan, an affluent suburb of Detroit, was an executive at General Motors. Upon retirement, Pete moved to Culver year round and spent his time making furniture. I have a set of his handsome three-foot high mahogany candlesticks prominently placed in my living room today (similar to the set from Mother's house that we donated to the church in Grass Creek). Skip T, another neighbor, operated a beer distributorship out of Chicago and did very well.

Then there were homeowners who had become or were to become notable. George Steinbrenner's (future Yankees owner) family had a place on the lake, and an executive in the Billy Graham organization lived just a few doors north of the Hizers.

One of the descendants of the Ball Brothers Glass Manufacturing Company in Muncie, Indiana, was a frequent visitor to Culver. The plant made those glass jars that were (and still are) used to store homemade jams and jellies and canned goods that could be found in most every pantry and fridge (farm wives generally canned vegetables grown in their own garden). The five brothers who founded the company gave land, buildings and money in 1918 to the state toward a local institution of higher learning. In 1922, it was renamed Ball Teachers College in their honor.

Another neighbor, Walter Myers, founded Myers Spring Company in Logansport that became well-known for its precision manufacturing capabilities that helped spur Indiana's economy. His wife Foyvelle and Mother had the same birth date and became good friends. Note that Logansport was well-represented at Culver. About a 45-minute trip, it was an easy drive and a great place to spend the summers.

Culver sported Culver Military Academy so I was exposed to the 1,400 handsome male cadets across the way who attended summer school (a few girls were accepted starting about that time in the early '60s, and Culver Girls Academy was founded in 1971). The kids attending the academy came from around the country. They had life experiences that made me realize there was a big wide world out there, and I wanted to be a part of it. I wanted to taste everything.

There were military parades, twice-weekly dances with live music (the Big Band sound), movies and concerts all summer long.

One of the rites of passage at the academy was for an upperclassman to tell a plebe that a blind date had been arranged and that he was to meet Sally Port at 7 p.m. at a certain place on campus. The unsuspecting newbie, smartly dressed in his spiffy new uniform, would wait and wait and ask every girl who passed by if her name was Sally. They would (knowingly) giggle and say no. Eventually he learned that Sally Port was the name of the designated place to meet and that he was bearing the brunt of a practical joke.

Sally Port is the location where, several times a week, the Naval Band plays "Anchors Aweigh" along with its signature drum cadence to officially mark the end of a parade or the closing of the day. It makes you feel very patriotic.

Campbell's Boatyard (fondly known as Campy's) was the main marina on Lake Maxinkuckee and sold fuel and made engine and boat repairs. The marina also sold boats. When we bought the cottage in 1960, we purchased a used fiberglass speedboat. On June 24, 1962, Dad and Mother bought a new 16' wooden Chris Craft Ski Boat with a 325 horsepower inboard Corvette engine. They paid $1,900 for it.

That boat was my pride and joy. I became quite adept at handling and docking it (there was no anchoring due to the water depths – as mentioned earlier, it was 90 feet in some places). The wooden speedboats of that era were made of genuine teak and were beautiful. Multiple coats of varnish made the golden-brown wood sparkle.

Fiberglass boats were becoming more and more popular and would take over the market in a few short years. The last wooden Chris Craft was built in 1971. People liked fiberglass because it was easier to maintain and could be molded into shapes that couldn't be fashioned in wood. The designs fit right in with the booming economy. Some boat builders hired car designers to replicate the flashy style and features of the automobiles of the day.

Water skiing was an everyday activity, and we all became pretty proficient at it. We soon advanced to slalom skiing and kept the two skis for visitors. Even Dad skied. He liked to show off his expertise by gripping the tow line with one hand and dramatically smoking a cigarette with his other hand. Selecting the perfect ski was a big deal (they were made of wood back then). I bought a Joe Cash, named for a professional skier from Florida. Your slalom is a prized possession. Once you've found the exact fit and weight and look, you tote it around with you because you perform better on your own familiar ski. My beautiful Joe Cash (with red, white and blue stripes painted on the top) served me well for the rest of my skiing career (including in Connecticut).

There were other lakers around my age. I became good friends with a neighbor gal, Linda Sparling, and we palled around for many summers, along with the Small twins, Ed and Jim. Jamie Kimbrough was a fellow laker, and we spent a lot of time together. And then there were the Bailey boys and the Hockman brothers.

I also became acquainted with kids who lived in Culver, called townies. Sherrill Edgington, particularly, was a good summer friend. At one point, I had a crush on a boy from town, Thad Overmyer, who worked at Campy's, and I would fabricate an excuse to run the boat to the marina every day or so. (I'm surprised Campy or his son Jack didn't put their foot down since Thad was taking way too long to fill the tank or whatever else needed to be done.) I met Thad on July 4 that first summer we had the Chris Craft when he filled the fuel tank with the wrong type of gas! But it didn't take long for me to think he could do no wrong.

From day to day, we took turns as to whose boat we would take. Usually, one person at a time would ski, but we also skied doubles and even triples. We would mimic the stunts performed by the academy's Ski School. At the end of the run, we all competed to see how far we could coast and how close to the pier we could get. And the guys liked to try to land on top of the dock!

Most families around the lake had an open account at Campy's. So every few days when the gas tank was getting low, all we had to do was run the boat to Campy's, get the fuel tank filled and sign the chit. It was very convenient, and our parents were most generous (even though gas was cheap – 31-35 cents per gallon in the '60s).

Dad and Mother at the cottage at Culver, overlooking
Lake Maxinkuckee from our front lawn.

The lake bottom was sandy and, to a lesser extent, gravelly. There were few rocks, but there were some (unlike in the Northeast where rocks abound not only on land but also in the water as I would later learn).

Occasionally, the prop would get dinged up and have to be repaired, and it was Campy's to the rescue. The more common problem, though, was wrapping the prop with the polypropylene line used for towing skiers. We all had had our unfortunate experiences with that. We learned to be extra careful, particularly when the engine was in reverse.

A favorite destination was running the boat over to the academy and grabbing lunch at The Shack with friends who had come in their own boat (all the kids on the lake had a boat (or two), mostly speedboats, but some were pontoon boats and small sailing craft).

Later in life when I became a dedicated boater in Connecticut, naming one's boat was a big deal. But in the Midwest, no one followed the practice.

The Hizer cottage was a popular gathering spot. Gangs of friends were continuously stopping by. It was a choice location – up on a hill with a sweeping view of the lake. Everyone loved to come and eat and be merry and swim and ski. There were reunions and high school gatherings and visits by family and friends. Mother would bake homemade pies (a favorite was strawberry rhubarb made from our homegrown supply), set them on the buffet and try to keep them intact till later. I would say, "When I have my own home, I'll eat dessert before dinner if I want."

One time, Cynthia hosted a group of 30 for a weekend from her Girls' State delegation. Mother cooked for days before and all through the visit. Finding a place to eat a meal was nearly impossible. There weren't enough chairs. The girls were sitting on the steps leading to the upstairs. The upstairs, by the way, was an open loft with four double beds and a couple of singles (and plenty of room for sleeping bags).

The lazy, hazy, crazy days of summer (also the name of a song made popular by Nat King Cole in 1963) were filled with water activities, board games, card games (euchre was a favorite), a daily trip to the root beer stand (which added a canopy in 1962 as noted in my diary) and a movie every few nights.

Socializing with the lakers, the townies and the cadets translated into fun-packed summers.

I spent a lot of time sunbathing on the pier, getting as dark as I could with the aid of Coppertone. I spent hours reading a book, checking out who was out and about on the water that day, and taking a dip in the lake. I practiced turning consecutive somersaults underwater. My record was 13. I even swam across the lake one summer, a feat my cousins Ed and David Hines from Worthington, Indiana, still mention.

There were no cell phones or answering machines back in the '60s. If I was down on the pier when the phone rang inside the cottage, I would dash up the 32 steps and make it to the black clunky rotary phone before it stopped ringing – couldn't chance missing a call. Oh, to be young and physically able to do that again! The phone number at the cottage was Viking 2-3917. The Viking was later replaced with 84 (the numbers representing Vi in Viking) and an area code added. I always thought Viking as the name of the phone exchange at Culver was appropriate as it conjured up images of seafaring adventurers.

Another favorite pastime was to get in the car and drive around the lake. This activity must have been a popular sport as it is mentioned in my diary a number of times during the summer of '62 as something we kids did on a date, as well as a routine recreation.

The route took me from the west side of the lake where the cottage stood, north to town, past the bank and then the root beer stand (which is still there), around campus at the academy, down the east side of the lake, past Campy's at the bottom, across the south side and then north again along the twisty road leading to the cottage. Sighting a glimpse of the lake at the first curve heading north and then along the public landing always made my heart skip a beat as I took in the beautiful and familiar view. The trip took about an hour.

I especially enjoyed passing the many upscale homes on the east side. Mr. Osborn from the bank had a lovely home at the top of a rise with sloping lawns stretching to the water's edge. He died in 1981 in that house at the age of 96. Seeing these homes, whether from a car or my Chris Craft, spurred me on, and I dreamed about becoming successful enough to own a home like Mr. Osborn's overlooking a body of water.

Mother and Dad became good friends with Walt and Kay Smith, who lived in Cincinnati. Walt was an attorney in a prominent law firm located in the heart of the city's downtown area. Their son attended Culver Military Academy in the summers, and the Smiths wanted to visit him on weekends. There were few motels in the Culver area so Walt contacted Dad because they had a connection through Indiana University (Walt's older brother Lyman was a member of the same fraternity as Dad and was a friend).

That was the beginning of a long friendship with Walt and Kay.

The arrangement worked well for both families. The Smiths would spend summer weekends as guests at the Hizer cottage. On Saturday nights, we would have a filling meal, often serving steak or smoked pork from the grill regardless of the weather (there is a wonderful photo of Dad tending the grill with one hand and holding an open umbrella in the other).

Afterward, Mother would play the organ on the front porch overlooking the water, and all the neighbors would join in a singalong. She played by ear and took requests, playing most every song from memory, but she had fake books if needed (if for no other reason but to jog one's memory with the repertoire of song titles).

Just a few of the classics, many made popular during the Roaring '20s, included: "Baby Face," "Bicycle Built for Two," "Button Up Your Overcoat," "Happy Days Are Here Again," "If You Knew Susie," "Makin' Whoopee!" Another favorite was "You Are My Sunshine" (a song I have loved for decades because my husband Ray brought so much sunshine into my life). And, sometimes, I would play my flute accompanied by Mother on the organ. One of our favorite duets was "The Yellow Rose of Texas."

There were hundreds of these songs, and each had a story behind it. For example, "The Sidewalks of New York" was written in 1894 and was an immediate hit. New York Governor Al Smith used it in three presidential election campaigns. Because of its popularity, it was under consideration for a while as a New York City theme song.

Those singalongs at Culver were good times.

Fishing was a favorite pastime on Lake Maxinkuckee, whether in a boat or from a pier. Before buying the cottage, the Hizers had traveled to Park Rapids, Minnesota, every summer and spent a month at Wambolt's Camp fishing on Upper Bottle Lake. Mother and Dad would fish in the mornings and catch a variety of bass, bluegill, crappie, northern pike, perch and walleyed pike. Mother would then prepare a breakfast of fried fish and hash browns.

At Culver, the family continued with the sport of fishing. Of special note, Cynthia and her son Andrew Jubera would go to the docks at the academy at night and catch an ample supply of bluegill and perch. Alan had explained that that was where they would have the best luck because the fish would migrate toward the stadium lights that were placed up and down the piers. The prevailing southwest wind blowing across the full expanse of the lake, called the fetch, could create wave action that made for some windswept evenings.

So this was the way I spent my summers (and to think I had resisted the move to the lake during junior high school because I had a crush on the paperboy in Grass Creek – I wanted to be there to answer the door each afternoon when he delivered the paper). I now was 16 years old, and the world was my oyster. I would feel the same later on after moving to Greenwich and then Rowayton in Connecticut (FYI, Rowayton is pronounced "Row-ate-un").

During the winters, the Hizers would travel to Cincinnati every few weeks. The Smiths lived in the charming Mariemont section of town (that's pronounced "Mary-mont"). The time spent there gave me a taste of city life, and we frequented restaurants ranging from fun to fancy. The Golden Rooster was a supper club and lounge where Ronnie Dale entertained whenever he was not playing the organ at the Cincinnati Reds baseball games. Renowned for his singalongs, everyone in our group had had lots of practice singing the same tunes at the Saturday night songfests on the front porch at Culver for all those summers.

In Cincinnati, we shopped at those elegant and fashionable department stores of yesteryear – Lazarus, McAlpin's, Shillito's – that reshaped shopping habits and became the model for service and luxury. I remember having lunch in one of the fine dining rooms at Lazarus on Good Friday one year and, another time, at Shillito's Tea Room – I had been practicing table etiquette at home and welcomed every chance to demonstrate my manners in public.

McAlpin's had a unique return policy: accepting any item presented without question (occasionally even if it hadn't been purchased there). For example, an elderly lady returned a hammer (McAlpin's didn't carry hammers). She said, "I bought it here." So the clerk gave her some money. He then took the hammer to the hardware store, and the manager gave the clerk the refund. That liberal return policy helped McAlpin's make a lot of friends and generated loyal customers.

Also in Cincy, we cheered at college football games and attended lots of parties, including a Derby Day gathering every May. The Smiths had a red Cadillac convertible with white leather seats that Walt let me drive when I was in town, and I "felt like a million bucks" as I cruised around the local drive-in with the top down. Once during college, I drove through a blizzard to get to Cincy for a New Year's Eve party. I even remember the (very short) mini-dress I wore – it was made of a stiff silver material that glittered under the lights.

Back in Culver, those fun-filled summers sped by. I continued to be friends with a number of the cadets beyond high school because many of them returned for the summer during their college years to be an instructor. So there was no end to the pool of guys and entertainment.

In August of 1983, Cynthia and husband Drew Jubera flew up from Dallas, Texas, for the baptism of their month-old son Andrew. It was held in the chapel at the academy. Of note, John Costello, childhood friend pictured in the pony photo earlier in this book, drove from Chicago, where he was a priest, to officiate. Appropriately, the holy water he used in the ceremony was water he blessed from Lake Maxinkuckee. Drew's family came from Pittsburgh, Pennsylvania, and relatives from both sides enjoyed a summer weekend at the lake.

The cottage remained in the Hizer family for many more years. Life progressed: I was living and working in Connecticut and Cynthia in Dallas and then Atlanta. Living in nearby Winamac, Alan's family spent a lot of time at Culver until his kids grew to adulthood.

Every summer, Cynthia and I would find our way to the lake, and the nieces and nephews would frolic in the sun and do what kids do: water tag, water fights, diving, splashing, swimming contests, balloon fights, dunking – all in the name of fun.

One time at a family reunion, the kids, spearheaded by Alan's younger daughter Emily, secretly transformed the basement into a haunted house and charged admission.

As is normal, the kids were constantly trying to outperform each other with their antics and pranks, and the visits were filled with memories that will stay in our mind forever, the grownups and the kids alike.

Once this second generation grew up and scattered, no one was using the cottage much. In 2006, the decision was made to sell it, and I handled the transaction.

That was the end of an era, a 46-year period that was full of fun and lasting memories, but, more important, the cottage represented a place that significantly shaped my life.

The Hizer siblings at Culver: (left to right) Cynthia, Alan, Joyce.

More on High School and College

Music was the fabric that tied the growing-up years together. We kids listened to the radio all day and all night and knew the words to every Rock 'n' Roll song. We listened to the Motown sound on "American Bandstand" hosted by Dick Clark and practiced the latest dances. Teenagers across the country stayed glued to the TV whenever the show was being aired. (The popular afternoon program was picked up nationally on August 5, 1957, and ran for a total of 30 years.)

We grew up listening to Elvis Presley, the Beatles, the Beach Boys, and hundreds of other popular singers and groups.

The greatest hits from the '60s include, to name just a few: "Stop in the Name of Love" (Diana Ross & the Supremes), "The Tracks of My Tears" (Smokey Robinson), "Summer in the City" (The Lovin' Spoonful), "California Dreamin' " (the Mamas and the Papas), "Good Vibrations" (the Beach Boys), "Sgt. Pepper's Lonely Hearts Club Band" and "Hey Jude" (the Beatles), "Suspicious Minds" (Elvis Presley's final #1 hit). And then there were the ever-popular love songs that touched the heart as sung by, for example, the silky smooth voice of Andy Williams such as "Almost There" and "Hawaiian Wedding Song." I can actually remember hearing Elvis sing "Can't Help Falling in Love with You" from the movie "Blue Hawaii." I was sitting in the backseat on a double date, and we were parked at Harvey's Drive-In waiting for our burgers and fries to be delivered. All conversation stopped when Elvis started singing the song.

Whether singer or some handsome actor, the girls would swoon over their idol.

Starting as early as junior high school, there were Friday night dances and, periodically, a formal dance (the event was often referred to merely as "a formal") where the gym would be elaborately decorated with crepe paper and streamers, almost like a prom. The girls would wear a fancy dress, and the boys would present a corsage when they picked up their date. And the guy usually wore a boutonniere (usually a carnation). In fact, there was a song made popular by Marty Robbins entitled "A White Sport Coat and a Pink Carnation." For me, there would be many socials and slow dances before I met Mr. Right at the age of 30.

During the '60s, every town had a luncheonette or drugstore or some type of hangout where the kids would congregate and play favorite songs on a glitzy, full-sized, coin-operated jukebox. Often, individual tables housed a tabletop version that displayed the menu of songs, encased in clear plastic and mounted on a spindle for flipping through the selections. You could make your choices from your booth while you ate.

In the '70s, portable transistor radios became popular, and in the '80s, boom boxes reigned, featuring a cassette player in between the two speakers. Watching the infomercials and PBS specials on TV today brings back memories of happy times.

Getting away for a weekend or minivacation was common among people in the community of Grass Creek. Throughout my high school years, along with the trips to Indianapolis and Cincinnati, I was fortunate to be invited for the occasional weekend away to a host of Midwestern cities and points of interest.

Chicago was a favorite, and I wrote in my diary in 1962, "I'm almost at home there – I've been to Chi-Town quite a bit." On December 26 of that year, my friend Loisann Hartzler and I went to Chicago to visit her sister Shelby. We departed from Rochester by train. But we took a plane back and flew from O'Hare Airport to South Bend. It was very exciting. I would venture to say that was my first commercial flight.

I had flown on small private planes such as the one Everett and Rachel Rentschler owned. They were from Fulton and had a place at the lake, too. Periodically, they would take friends for a spin from the airstrip at Culver (runway length: 1,000 feet).

Years later when Dad had a heart attack, they offered to fly me home from southern Indiana where I was in college, but Granddad Hines ended up driving me there. He was well-known for his heavy foot, and he tended to tailgate. Every so often I would slam my palms against the glove compartment, bracing for the anticipated fender bender. Granddad finally told me to stop doing that, saying he was "in complete control."

Back to the story above: While in Chicago, I had written some postcards, of course. Before boarding the plane at the airport, I dropped them in one of those blue free-standing postal mailboxes. That was all well and good. It's just that I had my plane ticket in hand as well and dropped it in the mailbox along with the postcards!

I had to buy another ticket as it is against the law to tamper with the mail (I eventually did get a refund).

Years later, Frank Sinatra recorded the song "My Kind of Town (Chicago Is)," and hearing it always reminds me of the trips there during my youth.

Logansport's population in the early '60s was just shy of 20,000. The downtown area, encompassing several blocks on Broadway and Market Street, was flourishing. Stores large and small lined the streets and fulfilled the needs of the people in town and the surrounding area. It was before the influx of a lot of chain stores, and most retail establishments were owned and operated by individuals or families.

My mother was a serious shopper and frequented the department stores and shops and was on a first-name basis with most of the owners and clerks.

The Golden Rule was a well-stocked department store that carried a wide variety of products from clothes to lace tablecloths. Olsen's was Market Street's version of the Golden Rule. Bailey's Clothing Store outfitted the men around the county with high-quality and stylish clothes from head to toe and from casual to formal. The Baileys had a cottage at Culver near Campy's.

Kreuzberger Jewelers, run by Bob Burk, supplied Mother with gifts for my sister and me for decades (one Christmas as I unwrapped a gold bracelet, I said to Ray, "You just can't get too many of these."). The Hockman family, who also had a place at Culver, ran a shoe store called Modern Miss. And there was a drugstore where you could take a break from shopping and get a sandwich. Jamie Kimbrough's (a friend from the lake) father was a pharmacist who worked in the back where you picked up prescriptions.

There were lots of other retail establishments, such as Plotner's

Shoe Tree and Plotner's Style Shop and Fernbaugh's Jewelry. Bickels was the fun store where we bought our bicycles. I had a friend, Kathy Yoder, whose parents ran Pleasant Hill Greenhouse. Kesling Drugs was run by the family of another neighbor at Culver.

Barton's Business and Office Supplies was one of my favorite stores. I loved browsing the staplers and label makers and various types of paper. And it was fun to see all the latest office products, such as Dictaphones, Rolodexes and Samsonite briefcases.

Jack Barton owned the business and knew Mother well since he had a contract to maintain the manual typewriters at Caston High School. Common brands in those days were IBM, Olivetti, Remington, Brother. Jack was a delightful and inspirational guy. He made everybody feel like they could do anything they wanted to do.

Back then, you could get most any item you needed in town. But people also liked to shop in Fort Wayne, Indianapolis, Kokomo, Lafayette, South Bend and other places for greater variety.

The Logansport Mall opened in 1968 on the eastern outskirts of town (prior to that, the Eastgate Shopping Center had been built). One by one, the stores downtown shuttered their doors. Some moved to the mall and paid exorbitant rent, but most of the family-owned businesses closed for good. After that, there was not much shopping in the downtown area.

Driving distances is a way of life for most Midwesterners. Goods and services are spread out. The best hospitals and specialists are centered in the cities. From Grass Creek, for example, it is one and three-quarter hours to Indianapolis, 92 miles.

The same goes for medical practitioners who are located in many of the larger towns such as Kokomo and Lafayette, both about an hour away. But even for everyday necessities or just for dinner out, people think nothing of jumping in the car and driving to town half an hour or so away – sometimes making more than one trip a day.

And, by the way, distances in the Midwest are usually referred to in miles, not time. In the East, with heavy traffic, gridlocks and rubbernecking being the norm, destinations are measured in minutes, not miles. The reason is because it can sometimes take 30 minutes or longer to go just a few miles (and sometimes a destination that takes 30 minutes one day may take an hour another day).

After Dad passed away in 1972, Mother remarried and moved to Logansport, but she continued to attend church in Grass Creek and would drive 15 miles each way on Sunday mornings. Even after her second husband died, she continued driving that narrow Route 17 to church until she was well into her 90s. Gene Thomas, a parishioner, once told me that Mother was an inspiration to him. "If she can make the effort to drive half an hour in any kind of weather, I surely can get to church from just down the road. I really don't have any excuse."

So I grew up in an environment where, without mass transportation, driving was the only way to get around, and I could keep up with the best of them. Later in life, though, Ray took over the wheel and did most of the driving.

Ninety-two counties comprise Indiana, and each county is divided into townships. Before vanity plates became popular, the first one or two digits on the license plate represented the county in which you lived by alphabetical ranking. Grass Creek is in Fulton County, #25.

Once you became familiar with the counties and their respective number, you could identify from where any in-state car hailed. It became kind of a game when driving to and from destinations around the state, making all that time on the road entertaining. Today, kids pass the hours surfing their smartphones or watching movies.

After high school, I headed to college. I was preparing myself for the future by going through the School of Business at Indiana University. I had wanted to go to college out East. The cadets at Culver had talked about all the great schools up and down the coast, and I remembered the stories Bill Diveley used to tell about living in an eastern city (Wilmington, Delaware) when he visited us in Grass Creek during my growing-up years.

The lure of the East was calling me. But my parents said, "We pay taxes to the state of Indiana, and part of that money supports our state colleges and universities. So you'll need to go to an in-state school. After you graduate from the Indiana college of your choice, you can live anywhere you want." So I went to Indiana University in Bloomington, the main campus.

Bloomington was familiar to me because I had three maternal great aunts who lived there, and when I was in grade school, I had spent two weeks most summers visiting them. I stayed with my Aunt Esther Poolitsan. Her sisters were Naomi Hines and Isabelle Mitchell. Aunt Esther made sure we had plenty of things to do during my stay.

One of them was attending Bible School each morning for one of the two weeks. I remember her telling the story about my nonchalantly eating breakfast while she nervously stood by tapping her foot and checking her watch. Even way back then, I was not a morning person.

Joyce during the college years.

Aunt Esther's husband Chris Poolitsan, together with his three Greek brothers, owned a restaurant on the edge of the IU campus named The Gables, earlier called The Book Nook.

The Gables was a popular college hangout. The walls were covered with life-size photos of winning sports teams over the decades and other IU memorabilia. It also is where a graduate named Hoagy Carmichael wrote the song "Stardust" in one of the booths in 1927.

Carmichael went on to enjoy an illustrious musical career as a composer, pianist, singer, actor and bandleader. Classics include "In the Cool, Cool, Cool of the Evening," "Skylark," "Am I Blue?" (used in 42 movies to date in 2020), "The Nearness of You," "Heart and Soul" and "Darktown Strutters' Ball." He also wrote the song "Georgia on

My Mind" in 1930. Although a number of artists have recorded the tune, Ray Charles' version was adopted as the Georgia state song in 1979. Fittingly, Ray Charles was born in Georgia.

The Gables building today still features those oversized wooden booths, and the walls are covered with photos and caricatures of people and places with ties to IU.

Also, Bloomington was not far from Worthington, Indiana, where my mother grew up. My Grandfather Hines still lived there and, from time to time, would pop in unannounced at my door in the dormitory. He didn't believe that the rule requiring guests to register at the front desk and be announced applied to him.

On one such occasion, I was smoking a cigarette when he knocked on the door and entered my dorm room. I stamped the cig out as best I could and shoved the ashtray in the desk drawer behind me, but it wasn't long before smoke started seeping out. He didn't say a word. Granddad didn't approve of smoking, and my mother's brother and wife, Uncle Warren Hines and Aunt Ann who also lived in Worthington, used to stow their cigarettes and ashtrays in the freezer when Granddad Hines came to visit.

Just for the record, I lived in a dormitory the first couple of years and then moved to an apartment with roommates after that. And during my last semester, I lived with sister Cynthia in a house off campus.

The academic year at universities across the country was different back in the day. Fall Semester at most colleges started the week after Labor Day. We had the Thanksgiving break in November, went back to school for three weeks and then had Christmas vacation.

Classes resumed right after New Year's Day for two weeks followed by exam week. Then we had another break before Spring Semester started at the end of January. Spring Break usually fell during the first week of April, and exam week ended right at Memorial Day weekend.

Today, Fall Semester ends before Christmas, and Spring Semester ends in early May. That works better. It's more concentrated and not so chopped up, especially Fall Semester.

I had a part-time job during most of my college years so I always had my own spending money. I worked as a waitress in a friend's café and learned how temperamental some chefs can be (this particular chef sometimes took a break when every table was taken or, worse, just walked off the job). People would have to wait an exceptionally long time for their meal, and I had to try to appease them. That job was short-lived because, as was often the case, the café didn't last long.

Most of the time, though, I worked as a secretary, initially to a professor and later in an insurance agency in downtown Bloomington. And I worked the summer of 1969 at the Holiday Inn in Plymouth, Indiana, as a hostess and cashier in the restaurant. On July 20 of that year, Neil Armstrong and Buzz Aldrin landed on the moon. I was working that Sunday and remember the manager setting up a TV so the patrons could watch the historical event while they ate their meal.

My job as hostess at the Holiday Inn (14 miles from Culver) exposed me to people from across the country. One sophisticated, well-dressed lady was visiting relatives for a week. She was from Short Hills, New Jersey, an upscale suburb of New York City, and she talked about life in the East. It sounded so exciting and further whetted my appetite for wanting to move to the East Coast after graduation from college (in a mere six months).

And I met a guy, Jim Ammerman, from Whittier, California, who traveled to Plymouth on business throughout the summer. We became friends and even spent a few days in Las Vegas before I started my final semester at IU. It so happened that he took a job at Stauffer Chemical in Westport, Connecticut, soon after I moved to Greenwich, and we had fun trying out the many fine restaurants and experiencing the endless sites of interest in the place we each now called home.

I carried on the trend of taking trips through college and beyond. While at IU, a friend and I would set off in my car and drive here and there for an overnight every month or so. My car was a white GTO with black interior and a five-speed stick shift. My grandfather Charlie Hines, who lived till the age of 99½, used to say GTO stood for "gas, tires and oil." During one break, a roommate, Barbara Dalton, and I took a week and drove to Lake of the Ozarks in Missouri. And, of course, we went to Fort Lauderdale, Florida, for Spring Break and, one time, to Nassau in the Bahamas.

And I routinely made the nearly four-hour trip to Grass Creek from Bloomington to visit my parents. One time in my senior year, Cynthia and I met Mother in Indianapolis for the weekend. We went shopping at L.S. Ayres, and Mother bought me a stunning gold engraved bracelet that I still wear today. We saw the just-released movie "Funny Girl" with Barbra Streisand. We had dinner at a restaurant that had peanut shells on the floor – the latest rage.

I hoped that my next home would be where there were lots of entertainment choices and bright city lights. The book/movie *Valley of the Dolls* was popular around that time. I could relate with the central female character, a college graduate who left her Peyton Place-ish small town and headed to the Big Apple, where she hoped to find an exciting job and sophisticated men. As my graduation neared, I started putting out feelers for jobs on the East Coast. I had my sights set on the New York City metro area.

While I was learning about business from Dad as I was growing up, sister Cynthia, who was three and a half years younger, was always in the kitchen with Mother, trying out one recipe after another.

As stated earlier, at Indiana University in Bloomington, Cynthia and I lived together during my last semester. One Saturday in October, we drove to the mall and went our separate ways, agreeing upon a time to meet back at the car. Cynthia returned bearing shopping bags full of kitchen gear – from pots and pans to spices and foods (maybe even organic, as she was always ahead of her time). When asked what I had bought, my response was, "I found the perfect filing cabinet!" (That small filing cabinet accompanied me to the East and served me well for many years.) The next day, Cynthia cooked an early Thanksgiving dinner with all the trimmings.

The interests we both had way back then have stayed with us all our lives. Cynthia has had many adventures during her multifaceted life. After living in Alaska, she returned to the Lower 48 and went on to become a food writer and wrote recipe books for Time Warner, among other things. She also was hired as the food stylist for the movie "Fried Green Tomatoes" (where "the secret's in the sauce"). The project was a challenge as it was filmed in Georgia in July, and her staff had a hard time between takes keeping the icing on the wedding cake from melting.

Additionally, Cynthia wrote a weekly food column for the *Atlanta Constitution*. She organized the Farmers' Market for the organic farmers in and around Atlanta. She developed a thriving organic soap business and raised organic vegetables that she supplied to some of the finest restaurants in the Atlanta metro area. Cynthia then attended seminary and was ordained an Episcopal priest. She served the last three years before her retirement at a mission church in Navajoland in Arizona. These are just some of her life's adventures – there are many others.

My time at IU was during those tumultuous years of the Vietnam War. The threat of being drafted loomed, and the guys were worried. Some fled to Canada. There were protests and riots at colleges like Kent State and sit-ins and marches in Washington, D.C. Drugs were everywhere. There were hippies all over the country, particularly on campuses, lambasting Corporate America and the establishment.

Being a student in the School of Business, I was not affected much by these happenings, and my goal was to reach for the stars and attain the American Dream.

I give credit to our founding fathers for establishing a constitution and form of government that can withstand the strain of internal turmoil and keep our direction on track.

In the fall of 1969 at IU, time was drawing nigh – graduation was approaching (I completed my coursework in January 1970 as I had to take an extra semester to do my student teaching).

One crisp autumn afternoon during that final semester on campus, I was trekking off to class. The route took me around the old football stadium that was sunken, whereby the stands start at ground level and trickle down to the playing field far below. I was dressed in a stylish gold corduroy coat with the belt tight around my waist and the collar pulled up to my ears. I wore brown leather boots that reached my knees.

I was confident and ready for the next chapter of my life. As I made my way around the stadium, I had a vision and told myself, "Someday, I'll work in the heart of New York City in a floor-to-ceiling glassed-in office with a view of skyscrapers in every direction."

Armed with a diploma from IU as her ticket, Joyce ready to head to the East Coast and the next chapter of life.

The Move to Greenwich

In the late '60s and early '70s, it was difficult for women to break into jobs in the business world. In the days of yesteryear, most females who were in the workforce held the position of teacher, nurse, librarian, bank teller, secretary, stewardess or waitress.

My goal was to be an executive in Corporate America, preferably in the Big Apple. My parents supported that dream, but Mother, who was a teacher herself (business and music) and daughter and granddaughter of teachers (my Grandma Hines and her mother, respectively), insisted I get a teaching license as a backup. So I did that, fulfilling my student teaching requirement in Kokomo, Indiana, under a Mrs. Peggy McClung. The assignment was to end in late January 1970.

During that last semester in school, I started sending out resumes to companies and educational institutions. In mid-December, I received a phone call from the Greenwich (Connecticut) Board of Education asking if I would like to interview for a teaching position starting in mid-January in the Business Department at Greenwich High School.

My contact there was George Markscheffel, who had grown up in Wisconsin, a fellow Midwesterner from a Big 10 university. That might have carried some weight in my getting the job. Arrangements for the trip were made, and I headed east for an interview that was scheduled for December 23. Mother and Cynthia accompanied me, and we had a pleasant drive to the Ohio-Pennsylvania state line on the first day of what was supposed to be a two-day road trip.

The next morning dawned with threatening skies. By noon, the snow was falling in big, fat flakes. It wasn't long before every truck donned snow chains, and the going was slow through the mountains.

We made it to Philadelphia but had to stop. It was just too treacherous to stay on the road any longer.

The interview was set for 1 p.m. the next day so we felt we could make it on time since it normally would be just a three-hour drive.

Sure enough, the morning brought bright sunshine and cleared highways, and we arrived in Greenwich in plenty of time, checking into the Pickwick Arms Hotel at the top of Greenwich Avenue. The stately brick Tudor landmark was built in 1920 and served its distinguished clientele until the '70s when it was demolished.

I met with three people and, by late afternoon, was offered the position (I learned later there had been 35 interviewees, and selecting a final candidate had been on hold till I could travel there for an interview).

Upon accepting the job, it took another hour or so to get the paperwork in order so I didn't get back to the hotel till nearly dinnertime. I knocked on the door, and when it opened, I leaned against the doorframe in a movie star pose and announced, "I want you to know that I'm now an employee of the Greenwich, Connecticut, Board of Education!"

Mother said she had had a good feeling about the outcome since I had been gone for so long.

After the hugs and congratulations, we ventured out to dinner. In those days, traffic on Greenwich Avenue – both foot and vehicular – was directed by bobbies (this was just the beginning of my introduction to and fascination with New England's adoption of English traditions).

Not realizing that pedestrians were required to wait for the bobby to motion them at crossings, we Hizer girls started to cross the street on our way to a restaurant on the avenue. The bobby blew his whistle and waved us back. He looked at me – I couldn't wipe the grin off my face – and asked why I was so happy. I told him, and he cheered "Congratulations! Welcome to Greenwich."

Before we headed back to Indiana, I needed to find a place to live come January so the next morning I bought the local newspaper, the *Greenwich Time*, to check out the want ads. The headline read: "Old Greenwich Woman Hit by Car." I exclaimed, "That's terrible – calling someone an old woman." I soon learned that Old Greenwich was a section of Greenwich and later discovered that other towns in Connecticut are named "Old" (Old Lyme, Old Saybrook, where, in the future, Ray and I would spend time on our boat).

Mother, Cynthia and I spent the day looking for an apartment. Being unfamiliar with the area, we found ourselves lost a few times. When we accidentally got on the ramp entering I-95 in Byram for the fourth time within a 20-minute period, the toll booth operator just waved us through with a smile. (Cash and toll tickets were collected by people back then versus today's electronic tag readers such as E-ZPass.)

Not having found a place to live, we headed back to the hotel in the afternoon. We were getting a bit concerned because we were to leave for Indiana in the morning, Christmas Day (it turned out to be the ideal day to drive as there was practically no traffic).

At the Pickwick Arms, I went to the bar to get some beverages to take to the room and learned that there was an apartment available just up the way at 35 Church Street. It was on the second floor above a French restaurant named C'est Bon owned by Joe Lovetri.

The Hizer trio dashed over to the apartment, and an agreement was sealed on the spot (for a long time, I advocated that the best place to get news and information was at a bar). The only caveat was that I had to move my car (the white GTO) out of the parking lot whenever the restaurant was open to make room for the patrons. I usually parked in the church lot down the street on the corner of Church Street and the Boston Post Road because the restaurant generally wasn't open when there were church services (e.g., Sunday mornings).

The small apartment was perfect for me – not a lot of storage, but that was okay. And I still remember climbing the outside stairs in all kinds of weather (it was a black metal staircase that made clanky sounds and kind of swayed as you climbed up and down).

Back home in Indiana, Mrs. McClung at Kokomo High School

and my professors at IU bent over backwards to accelerate my schedule so I could satisfy my student teaching requirements a few weeks early.

Mother and I drove my car to Connecticut a couple of weeks later. It had a large trunk, and I had plenty of room to pack my possessions, including a stereo set and a collection of LPs, the filing cabinet I had bought in Bloomington the preceding fall at the mall and an ironing board. When it was time for Mother to leave, I drove her to Queens and LaGuardia Airport – gutsy!

I settled in easily and began my life in the East.

Shortly after I'd moved into the apartment and started my job, some guy I had met at work asked me out on a date and casually said, "We'll go into the city."

Go into the city? I was so excited!

Fresh from the Midwest, I waited to be picked up for my first trip into the Big Apple. I looked into the mirror, with a grin from ear to ear, and shouted: "Joyce Hizer from Grass Creek, Indiana, you're going to New York City!"

That was my first time there – truly a milestone.

Although I enjoyed getting into the city often, I loved living in the heart of Greenwich, and Mr. Lovetri kept his eye on me and made sure no one took advantage. From time to time, he would invite me to join him and his lady friend at the diner around the corner. And, occasionally, he would treat me to a drink or dinner at his restaurant, C'est Bon.

The building had originally been a residence that was converted, as was the case with some of the finest dining establishments in the area at that time.

Sprinkled throughout the tri-state region, these structures – often surrounded by beautifully manicured grounds – offered dining in an inviting atmosphere, often by a cozy fire in one of the many fireplaces. A mahogany-paneled bar could usually be found on the premises. In fact, "Inn" commonly was part of the name, describing the restaurant's earlier function as a place where travelers could find food and drink and a bed. Before the advent of motorized transportation, innkeepers frequently provided a place for horses as well.

Some of those wonderful old restaurants were elegant and some were quaint, but all had charm. Those that survived were renovated from time to time, combining the new with the old. One write-up I came across goes like this: "The inn was elegant and rustic, modern and colonial, open and cozy all at the same time."

Another fond memory I have about dining out in the '70s pertains to doggie bags. In those days, leftovers were cleverly wrapped in aluminum foil in the shape of animals, usually various species of birds. The creations were delightful and adorned the table during dessert. The waiters had fun making them, and the diners loved the idea of it. In contrast, today's Styrofoam or cardboard to-go boxes delivered in a brown paper bag seem mundane.

One by one, the inns are closing as did, for example, The Elms Inn in Ridgefield, Connecticut, in 2012. Two local establishments still open today are the Roger Sherman Inn in New Canaan, Connecticut, and The Inn at Pound Ridge in Pound Ridge, New York.

As the months and then the years passed, I became familiar with Fairfield (Connecticut) and Westchester (New York) counties. My pocket calendar from each of those years is packed with notations about places I went and restaurants I frequented, such as Boodles, the Clam Box, Brock's, Sassafras, Mansion Clam House, Tarry Lodge, Lock Stock & Barrel, Rosebud's, Dameon's, Emily Shaw's Inn (now The Inn at Pound Ridge), Fat Tuesday, Sneaker's, Parsley, Player's Tavern, Pellicci's, Ground Round, Cobb's Mill Inn, Modugno's, Oliver's, Country Tavern.

Most of those eateries are gone now.

I was enraptured with Connecticut and all that it stood for. I appreciated the natural beauty of the coastline and the rugged rock formations on land and water. I would wake up in the morning, look out the window and proclaim, "It's just so beautiful out here."

Oh, life was good in Connecticut.

The world was my oyster! From the flatlands of north central Indiana, I embraced every aspect of life with great enthusiasm in my Connecticut home and this new chapter of my life.

American Express Card Story
Sister Cynthia recently reminded me of a memorable evening from the 1970s. Cynthia and I were living together, and on any given Friday night, she never hesitated to suggest eating out. On this particular TGIF, we had had dinner at the Clam Box in Cos Cob.

When the bill came, I pulled out my newly acquired American Express card and presented it to the waiter with a huge smile on my face. I was as proud as could be.

You see, having qualified for a credit card – and the coveted American Express card, no less – was another milestone. Little Joyce Hizer from little Grass Creek was carrying her very own credit card and living in the fast lane. "I had arrived," as they say.

I spent seven years living in Greenwich and then Rowayton, which is where I met Ray.

There is only one public high school in Greenwich. Due to its size (~2,700 students), Greenwich High School was divided into four houses, each with a housemaster who reported to the headmaster. I thought the terms sounded so "New Englandy" versus "principal." John Bird was headmaster, and Joe DeLucia was Bella housemaster during my tenure there.

My teaching position took a surprising turn when after a year and a half, a restructuring took place and I was named department chair (officially called senior teacher). It was a full plate because I now was leader to about 10 people, several of whom had taught for a dozen years or more (and one or two who felt they deserved the promotion), and I was only 24 years old. I found I loved the administrative side even more than the teaching.

Throughout those years, I took advantage of New York City's

finest – its plays and ballets and museums and sporting events and restaurants. In fact, a lot of movies were and continue to be filmed in the New York metro area. It was exciting to see on the screen the streets and buildings and stores that I had personally visited.

And remember all the wonderful Broadway musicals of that era? One of my favorites was "Man of La Mancha." I sat in the audience watching Yul Brynner sing "The Impossible Dream," a song that greatly inspired me to reach for the unreachable star.

Teachers at Greenwich High School were often asked to chaperone field trips to places and events in New York City so I had countless opportunities to take advantage of culture in the Big Apple. And later at Berkeley, twofers (two tickets for the price of one) were readily available for the Broadway plays.

All this culture and all these events were at my fingertips, not to mention all that was waiting to be enjoyed right out my front door in Fairfield County, Connecticut. So it was beyond my comprehension when I heard the following conversation among my students at Greenwich High School.

It was a Friday afternoon with five minutes left until classes would end. My shorthand girls were all wrapped up and ready to leave, chatting away until the bell rang. One gal asked her friend, "What are you doing this weekend?"

The other girl responded, "I don't know. There's not much to do around here."

I was shocked.

Coming from rural Indiana where you most often had to create your own fun, I couldn't help myself saying, "Honey, you have no idea of what 'not much to do' means to some people in some places." I proceeded to describe a little about the entertainment offerings in Grass Creek, Indiana, in comparison.

One of my landlords held season tickets to the New York City Ballet, and, for several years, we split them. Its performance of the "Nutcracker" at Lincoln Center every Christmas season still is a must-see. And, of course, the holiday is not complete without seeing the Rockettes perform the Christmas Spectacular at Radio City Music Hall and viewing the always magnificent tree at Rockefeller Center.

Speaking of the tree, this is an interesting story. Later in life after Ray and I were married, we met boating friends George and Lyn Lillie, whose sailboat was named Scotch Mist. George worked at Rockefeller Center and was involved in the selection of the Christmas tree every spring for the following holiday season and the plans surrounding the big event. It was fun learning from where the tree would be coming and all the details long before the information was announced to the public. (After George retired, Ray and I no longer were privy to the inside track about the seasonal tradition.)

George said every tree chosen had to be one that had a limited life and would have been uprooted anyway. And transporting the Norway spruce each time to New York City was a story in and of itself.

After all the pomp and circumstance of the holidays, Rockefeller Center donates the tree to a worthy cause. Since 2007, that charity has been Habitat for Humanity. In January of each year, the tree is milled into lumber and gifted to the nonprofit for use in building homes for the needy in the state from which the tree came.

Getting into New York City was easy, a mere 50 minutes by commuter train or by car (40 miles). Even watching the news on TV was exciting. The network channels would show dramatic aerial views of the city and play uplifting music that made my heart soar to realize this was all part of my life.

From my base in Connecticut, I took advantage of every opportunity to expand my travels. I explored the Northeast by car. I toured Boston. I took a share in a ski house in Vermont for a couple of winters. I spent a month in San Francisco one summer. I took trips out west and skied the Canadian Rockies. Many of these trips were taken with my roommate Lorraine C.

And one Christmas, I visited sister Cynthia and her husband Pat Dixon, who were living in Kenai, Alaska.

One of my fondest memories of that trip was driving down the Kenai Peninsula about 80 miles to the coastal town of Homer and buying half a dozen Alaska king crabs right off the boat from a fisherman.

The crabs were huge and took up the entire back of the white Toyota Land Cruiser. Each crab leg was long and spidery, about three feet, so each crab had a span of about six feet from leg tip to leg tip.

King crabs have six walking legs, one large "killer" claw and one small "feeder" claw. The best meat (rich, sweet and juicy) is the merus, which is found in the upper section of the walking leg from the knuckle to the first joint. The main body cavity, or carapace, at the center is generally not for eating.

We took the crabs home and stowed them in a bathtub full of water to keep them alive until we could cook them.

Because of their size, we could boil only one at a time. We put the crab into a galvanized steel tub about three feet in diameter and placed it on the stovetop. Using all four burners, it took about 30 minutes to bring the water to a boil, 30 minutes to cook the crab, and another 30 minutes to clean and prepare it for consumption. We didn't finish until about 4:00 in the morning.

Alaska king crab was abundant in the Kenai area. Practically every gathering we attended during my stay featured appetizers and entrées made with crab.

I ventured to Europe several times starting that first summer after landing the job in Greenwich. Everyone, it seemed, was heading across the Pond during the break, and I caught the fever. I was to join friends for four weeks after they were finished in late July with their summer commitments here. But I felt that if I was making the trip, why not go for a longer period of time? I went ahead of my friends and spent a month on my own. (Note: We all purchased quantities of travelers' checks rather than carrying lots of cash. Credit cards were not the customary method of payment.)

On that first sojourn to Europe, I toured London and surrounding points of interest. I then took the ferry from Dover, England, to

Calais, France, and picked up the train. I had purchased a Eurail pass that allowed unlimited travel all over the Continent.

I made it as far north as Copenhagen, Denmark, and took a boat ride to Malmö, Sweden, eventually wending my way south to Florence and Venice in Italy. A couple of times, I took a night train and slept on board. And I had good luck hitchhiking. It was safe to do that back then.

One afternoon while in Amsterdam in the Netherlands, having promised to write a letter to my parents detailing highlights of the trip to date, I went in search of some writing paper. I found myself on a street where there were people all around, and the residents (females) were very friendly. I said hello to one gal, who invited me into a sitting area inside. I had a lovely chat with her. She gave me some stationery, and I was on my way, not realizing until afterward that I had been in the Red Light District, renowned for its brothels.

A few years later when I rented a house on Yarmouth Road on Bell Island in Rowayton, the landlady, in an attempt to portray a nautical theme, had installed a red light on one side and a green light on the other side of the front door. The thing was that plantings and other paraphernalia around the porch mostly covered the green light, and people on the street could see only the red light. Remembering my experience in Amsterdam, I opted not to turn the front lights on for fear of sending the wrong message to passersby.

The whole travel experience was great. I had to learn how to get around in a foreign country where English wasn't always spoken, figure out the currency (each country had its own monetary system at that time versus the euro today), find a place to eat and sleep every day, become familiar with the bus and train systems, find the tourist attractions in each city and, in every way, learn the ropes and manage on my own.

Here's an example of learning the ins and outs of traveling. I was in Copenhagen and was wending my way to see The Little Mermaid, a statue of the famous character in Hans Christian Andersen's popular fairy tale. It took me all morning to get there using mass transportation. The next day, I decided to take a four-hour bus tour of the city. The Little Mermaid was just one of about 20 stops.

I met up with my friends in Salzburg, Austria, and we had a wonderful month exploring and sightseeing. After the trip, several people at Greenwich High School said I had matured a great deal over the summer. I probably had.

Friends said traveling alone in Europe was pretty gutsy and maybe not safe. But I hadn't let that stop me. There were people my age everywhere, and it was easy to join up with them.

I wanted to see the world, and there was a lot of world still to see. The following summer, I convinced my parents to join me on a trip to England for five weeks. I acted as tour guide and actually mastered driving on the left-hand side of the road. Dad used to say, "How ya gonna keep 'em down on the farm (after they've seen Paree)?" This was a popular World War I song that epitomized my desire to take it all in.

Dad had a dry sense of humor. For example, he used to say that a farmer is a person out standing in his field. (Now that is a "corny" joke.)

Some people said I had nerve. I guess maybe I did have a little bit. Not long after moving to Greenwich, I read in the newspaper that Elvis Stahr, former president of Indiana University and at that time president of the National Audubon Society, had been admitted to Greenwich Hospital. Being an IU alum, I thought it would be a fitting gesture to pay him a visit. He graciously thanked me and said it was not often a complete stranger took the time to wish him well in person while in the hospital. I (innocently) answered by saying he wasn't a stranger – I had heard him speak at IU events when I was on campus in Bloomington.

That quiet directness is a trait I've carried most of my life. When a situation called for confrontation, Ray or Cynthia or a colleague would back away and say, "Have Joyce do it." In fact, Ray avoided personal confrontation and reverted to the written word whenever possible. So in a non-threatening manner, I would serve as the front person. I would have made a good poker player because I've mastered the skill of keeping a straight face through it all.

But my choice normally was to remain silently in the background and do the best job conceivable. Some colleagues called me a high achiever. That may be true, but I was not looking for the limelight. I am soft-spoken and have a steady-at-the-helm demeanor. Some have even honored me by calling me humble. Important character traits to me are honesty, integrity and confidentiality. I have also always tried to give credit where credit is due and not usurp someone else's efforts. And I think complimenting people goes a long way. I have tried to abide by these principles every day.

I had some good direction along the way, too. Several people took an interest in me and helped me make good decisions throughout my life. It started with my parents. As a teenager having to make a decision, Mother and Dad would say: "Make a list of the pros and cons of each choice. Then you can see if any particular one stands out." Today, we can develop a decision matrix on our computers that quantitatively evaluates a set of choices.

After moving to the East and being 20-something and living and working in a whole new world, Ann Liston took me under her wing. She was a friend of Lois Cherdron's from Indianapolis, a close family friend as mentioned earlier. Upon being widowed, Ann had gone to work at Northwestern Mutual Life Insurance Company and done very well. She was highly regarded there during her career, and the company named an award for her: the Ann Liston Award for Excellence in Ethical Standards. Ann lived in Bedford, New York, and we shared many dinners together. When she attended my wedding a few years later, I arranged for her to dance with my grandfather Charlie Hines in an attempt to do a little matchmaking (it didn't work out).

Many people in the Midwest have a distinct accent. In some of the southern hill towns especially, the accent is particularly evident and sometimes is referred to as a twang. One of the factors contributing to a Midwestern way of speaking is the way vowels (a, e, i, o, u) are pronounced. The vowels are often spoken as long vowels instead of short vowels.

A long vowel is where the vowel sounds like the letter name; for instance, the first "a" in "spatial." But the Midwesterner would pronounce the "e" in "special" like the first "a" in "spatial." An example of abusing the short vowel is the pronunciation of "git" for "get" or "tin" for "ten."

There are many other words that are pronounced differently from region to region. For instance, "caught" in the East would be pronounced as "cot" in the Midwest. Pronouncing "warsh" for "wash," adding the "intrusive r," is a common example of what's called the Midland dialect.

Then there are the words and phrases for which Midwesterners are famous, such as the use of "pop" versus "soda," "soda pop" or "Coke" and "you guys." That would be pronounced "youse guys" in certain boroughs of New York City and "y'all" Down South.

And, of course, it's good that different regions throughout America have retained colloquialisms rather than becoming homogenized. Just to name a few: In the Midwest, it's "sack" but "bag" in the East. In Indiana, it's "purse" but "pocketbook" in Connecticut, "garage or yard sale" there and "tag sale" here, and "hose" there versus "stockings" here.

The word Hoosier, which means being from Indiana, has an unclear origin. Adopted in the 1840s, there is no universal agreement on the derivation of the word. But one of the most popular is that it's a slurring of the greeting "Who's here?" in Appalachian English to become "Who'sh 'ere?" and finally "Hoosier."

I was determined to perfect my speech and would spend hours in my apartment reading aloud in an attempt to refine my elocution and inflection. And I had lots of opportunities to practice as I roamed the classroom dictating to my shorthand students at Greenwich High School. The room was on the top floor of the old high school building on Field Point Road in the downtown area, and I could see Long Island Sound through the expansive windows. We moved to the new high school location on Hillside Road in the fall of my first full year of teaching in 1970.

The practicing paid off, and I ended up with basically no accent – like many commentators in the media. Every once in a while someone would tell me I had a lovely speaking voice, and I would consider it the ultimate compliment.

I was very aware of the accents of people in the East – it was all part of the aura of New England. I was thrilled when I heard someone say "caah" when they were referring to "car," following John F. Kennedy's Bostonian gold standard of pronunciation where the "r" is dropped at the end of a word. Or it might be dropped within a word such as "pahk" for "park."

Sometimes an "r" is added at the end of a word ending in "a," such as in "agendar." And friends in Rhode Island would say "pawk the caw" and "teacheh" instead of "teacher," where "er" is pronounced "eh" (the "r" is dropped). The rules for these pronunciations have evolved over the centuries and are called non-rhotic and rhotic varieties. A wealth of research has been conducted linking speech patterns to social class.

There was one occasion not too many years ago when Ray and I had run our boat from Cuttyhunk and were staying at Peter Hicks' private dock on Point Judith Pond in Rhode Island. We were having dinner with Peter and his wife Kathleen and John and Annie Spence, all of whom are Rhody natives. Peter told a joke, and everyone laughed but me. When asked why not, I said, "It took me so long to translate your accent into plain English that I missed the whole point."

Over the years, I refined my ability to distinguish the various accents from specific states or regions: Maine, Massachusetts, Rhode Island, the Bronx, Brooklyn, Long Island, not to mention Canada. A number of people in my circle are Brits and speak with a lovely British accent.

U.S. states or regions have their own speech characteristics. For example, Long Island is pronounced "Lawn guy Land" (with a hard "g") if you are a native Long Islander. If you're from Brooklyn and speak Brooklynese, it's "shore" for "sure," "I dear" for "idea" and "out ta" for "out of." And if you're from Maine, it's "dee ah" for "deer" and "yip" for "yes."

Tom Power, a dear friend from my Greenwich days, grew up in Brooklyn and had the quintessential Brooklyn accent. I always think of him when I hear someone pronounce "bottle" as "bott ole."

A bad habit lots of people have is the overuse of filler words in their speech, words such as "ah," "like," "so," "um," "well" and "you know." (Growing up, I used the latter "you know" way too much according to my brother Alan and had to discipline myself relentlessly to break the habit.) Using those words incessantly diminishes our credibility and distracts from our message, and people just tune out.

During those years at Greenwich High School, I took courses during three summers at Indiana University to earn a master's degree in counseling (the state requirement at that time was that a teacher had to be matriculated in a master's degree program after three years on the job). In those years, I made road trips, usually by myself, back and forth from Connecticut, covering 817 miles in the 16-hour drive to Bloomington. I would stop for the night in the vicinity of the Pennsylvania-Ohio state line.

One year, the spring rains had been relentless, and much of the Northeast experienced flooding. Summer school at IU was starting, and I didn't want to drive on the interstates where high water caused traffic jams for miles, and people were stranded for hours. Alan surprised me by flying to LaGuardia and accompanied me on the drive back to Indiana.

After crossing the Tappan Zee Bridge on the Hudson River, we stopped for coffee at a McDonald's. I was driving my car #2, a tan Monte Carlo with vinyl top, and Alan spilled his scalding hot coffee in his lap. He couldn't get the seat belt off fast enough and burned his behind. There had been a recent lawsuit against McDonald's for the same type of incident, and Alan said maybe he should sue, too, because it was so painful. The rest of the trip was uneventful, and I made it to Bloomington in time for my first class.

Alan, being five years older, had always looked out for me. He liked his cars and had a collection of beauties over the years. In the spring of 1962, he bought a bright red Corvette convertible that he spent hours washing and polishing. I have a framed photo of Alan and his Corvette taken at the cottage. Every time I look at it, it reminds me of when we were young and carefree and had our entire life ahead of us.

Later, his red Porsche 911 Carrera was his pride and joy, and he worshiped that car. At every opportunity, he would take me for a joyride.

Alan with his Porsche 911 Carrera at public landing on Lake Maxinkuckee in Culver.

He boasted about going from 0 to 90 miles an hour in seconds, and he would take those right-angle turns with wheels screeching (there was little traffic on the country roads back then, and it was relatively safe to drive fast).

While at IU during my last summer in the master's program in 1974, one of my electives was marketing communications. My research report for the course was on the expected wide usage of credit cards. I started my presentation by holding up a wallet that housed 20 or so credit cards in individual plastic pockets. I raised my arm toward the ceiling and let the cards fall to my knees, exclaiming: "This is the way of the future! Everyone will be carrying a wallet full of cards." At that point, few people carried a credit card. Purchases were paid for by cash or check. The idea for carrying such a card came about when a well-to-do businessman took a group of clients to dinner and, embarrassingly, ran short on cash.

The first charge card was the Diners Club card introduced in 1950. It was a cardboard card and, after one year, was accepted at 28 restaurants and two hotels in New York City by 20,000 cardholders. They could make charges that were to be paid in full at the end of the month.

In 1958, American Express came out with a plastic card that allowed a cardholder to make purchases at a variety of establishments in the travel and entertainment industry instead of just at restaurants and hotels. After five years, 1 million people worldwide carried the American Express card.

The banks got involved and initiated consumer card programs that allowed cardholders to extend credit beyond a month for a nominal interest fee, truly becoming a credit card. The bank cards were accepted at a network of citywide stores that linked city to city to allow national access. Still, the masses did not carry a credit card.

There were few, if any, multi-purpose cards for general use like we have today where you can charge most any item on one card – from groceries to clothes to gasoline to furniture to airfare and even to taxes.

During the '70s, each store or brand started offering its own card. So it wasn't long until it was common to be carrying a couple of dozen cards – just as predicted. All the department stores jumped on board, and a dedicated shopper would need to lug a ton of cards on any shopping trip. Likewise, each brand of gasoline offered a card, and people would carry four or five cards so they could always find a gas station that would accept their card. That also was the era when automated teller machines first made it possible to withdraw cash without having to go inside a bank.

The final requirement for my master's degree was to complete an internship. Mine was at a boys' reformatory in Indianapolis, and I drove there and counseled juvenile delinquents two days a week.

My eyes were opened when I realized that there was such a difference in people's goals and culture. These kids regarded success as pulling off a robbery and not getting caught. After this experience, I was even more convinced that my lot in life was in business.

After three years as department chair at Greenwich High School, opportunity knocked again. I was named academic dean of The Berkeley School, a two-year proprietary college in White Plains, New York (now called Berkeley College). The school had five campuses in New York and New Jersey, White Plains being the largest.

Larry Luing and his executive team owned and ran the business most of my years there (Berkeley was part of ITT Corporation when I first started, and I took the job partly because I thought it might be a way to break into the corporate world, but ITT divested its education division soon after I joined Berkeley). Bob Maher was director of the White Plains location, and Josephine Longo headed up admissions. Warren Schimmel oversaw academics at all five campuses.

Marketing was a major thrust of the organization, and we hosted countless functions in the local communities and attended conferences throughout the region to establish relationships and goodwill.

On occasion, I was a speaker or led a breakout session. Wining and dining and promoting the Berkeley name were important activities, and our events were always first-class affairs. From the beginning, I was propelled into a flurry of activity and loved every minute of it.

Although I was thriving in my job, I still had my sights on entering the business world. A few years after I joined Berkeley, I enrolled in the master of business administration (M.B.A.) program at the University of Connecticut in Stamford and started taking evening classes, thinking an M.B.A. degree might be my ticket into Corporate America.

As an employee at Berkeley, I was able to take advantage of the tuition reimbursement benefit, which paid for most of the cost. And then, two years later, I met Ray. In fact, he audited my final course in the program so we could attend classes and study together and wouldn't have to be apart all those hours.

My time at Berkeley proved to be invaluable over the long term. In addition to duties surrounding hiring and evaluating instructors, shaping curriculum and leading the academic arm of the school in general, I attended numerous conferences locally and throughout the East.

My pocket calendar from 1976 notes at least a dozen meetings in Westchester County and northern Jersey and, regionally, as distant as Lancaster, Pennsylvania (in the Pennsylvania Dutch Country), and Rochester, New York (little did I know I would return year after year to Rochester for press checks).

One of those conference venues was Grossinger's, an old, elegant resort in the Catskills in upstate New York that, in bygone days, catered mostly to the Jewish community in New York City who expected top quality.

New Yorkers would flood to the mountains during the summer to get away from the heat. There were games and activities from dawn to dusk and fine kosher dining and entertainment at night.

Those hotels became a boot camp for aspiring humorists, and many went on to become household names. Here are just a few of the "Catskill comedians" who clawed their way to the top of the heap, serving their stint and paying their dues away from the madding crowd and bright lights of the Big Apple: Sid Caesar, Milton Berle, Groucho Marx, Jerry Lewis, Red Buttons, Rodney Dangerfield, Don Rickles, Jack Benny, Danny Kaye, George Burns, Woody Allen, Joan Rivers, Larry King, Peter Sellers, Billy Crystal, Gene Wilder, Phil Silvers, Jerry Seinfeld.

The classic 1987 movie "Dirty Dancing" with Patrick Swayze was inspired by those resorts. All the Borscht Belt hotels are gone now – even the buildings have been demolished.

Another Berkeley perk was attending the Milliken Breakfast Show. It was held in the Waldorf Astoria's Grand Ballroom in New York City every spring from 1956 to 1980. The meal was served early, and the show for retail buyers and garment manufacturers started at 8 a.m. with a star-studded Broadway cast performing a musical comedy.

Then glamorous chorus girls would model that year's fall fashions. Forty backstage attendants would make sure all 250 costume changes were fitted to perfection. Afterward, attendees were whisked to 7th Avenue (the Garment District) to make their purchases.

It was a marketing extravaganza. Over the course of a couple of weeks, 25,000 retail customers were treated to a private Broadway performance and fashion show extraordinaire.

Another experience while at Berkeley exemplifies a lost era. I was at a conference in Atlanta, and our group had dinner at a restaurant where a costumed waiter stood watch by the table the entire evening, attending to each guest's every need. The table was adorned with the finest of china and crystal and sterling silver, including a chilled salad fork and plate. A fresh glass replaced the original one with each refill. The waiter lighted the cigarettes. Candles burned everywhere, and, between courses, there was dancing to the live orchestra.

Such grandeur!

In Westchester County, I was asked to represent Berkeley at fundraisers and other special events on a routine basis and was proud to have Ray as my escort.

Berkeley was on the quarter system so there was a graduation every 12 weeks, but the June ceremony was the largest. The three other events were held in the ballroom of a local establishment, such as the White Plains Hotel.

The June graduation, however, was held in different places on a grander scale. For example, one time it was held on the Marymount College campus overlooking the Hudson River in Nyack, New York. Another time it was held at Madison Square Garden in the city.

As academic dean, I presided over the ceremony and presented each graduate with a diploma. Ray was in awe the first time he watched me addressing all those proud parents and friends, wearing my own cap and gown.

The faculty and administration wore a black cap and gown. The colored hood identified the school where the academician had graduated and the highest degree earned.

After leaving Berkeley, I discarded my garb, thinking I wouldn't need it again. Wrong! Every year at Halloween, I wished I had it back because it could have served as the basis for all kinds of costumes, the most obvious being a witch.

Prior to our wedding, it seemed like every time there was a raffle at some fundraising event or party (including the yacht club festivities in Rowayton), we won a prize. Ray said it must be a sign that our life together was going to be lucky.

At a wedding shower prior to August 6, 1978, Josephine Longo, a friend and colleague at Berkeley, proposed the following toast: "May the most that you wish for be the least that you receive."

About the time Ray and I were married, Berkeley was named recipient of a prestigious award, and several of the top people were invited, along with their spouse, to spend a long weekend in Boca Raton, Florida, in the fall to accept the award and to be honored.

Ray and I stayed at the Boca Raton Hotel & Club. Our room faced east and overlooked the Intracoastal Waterway and the Atlantic Ocean through floor-to-ceiling windows. The sunrises were spectacular, and the full moon rising over the ocean was stunning. We were wined and dined the entire time in the finest of restaurants and had a fabulous five days.

Afterward, Ray said he realized how lucky he was to have won my heart (and that he had). Life together was not only going to be good, but it was bound to include some pretty exciting adventures as well.

It was on the plane ride back to New York that October that Ray announced he was stopping smoking. And he never had another cigarette.

Bell Island Back in the '70s

I met Ray in 1977 when I was living on Bell Island, the Rowayton peninsula that juts into Long Island Sound. Its two beaches, winding, narrow roads and stone walls give it a Nantucketesque atmosphere.

Cynthia was living with me, and we were moving down the hill from Yarmouth Road to South Beach Drive for the summer. I loved the beach and waterfront views and had managed to arrange for a summer rental directly on the water. It had been a long, drawn-out deal to accomplish. Everyone said it couldn't be done, but I had found a way.

South Beach on Bell Island – where Joyce and Ray met, and it all began.

The old, dilapidated beach shack was owned by an elderly lady who was becoming senile. I visited the landlord in her ramshackle house up by the Merritt Parkway, trying to convince her to lease the house to me for the summer.

After several meetings over many weeks, the lady reluctantly agreed. She had me write the lease and required that the entire summer's rent be paid in cash in advance along with a hefty deposit. In the end, I stayed there two summers and loved every minute of it. I claimed the front bedroom and was lolled to sleep each night by the calming sound of the waves splashing on the beach across the street, just a stone's throw away.

During those years, the '70s, many of the homes on Bell Island were owned by people who came for the summer only. The residents arrived on or around Memorial Day weekend and left in early to mid-September. That arrangement was familiar to me after having moved to the lake at Culver every summer during my youth.

The rest of the year, many of the houses were rented to groups of singles. There was a house of guys who worked at IBM and at AT&T and at Xerox and at other Fortune 500 companies in the area. There was a house of bachelors who were investment bankers just getting started on Wall Street. There was a house of pilots who flew for Eastern, Pan Am or United Airlines. There was a house of gals who were nurses or teachers or librarians or secretaries or stewardesses, respectively.

The entire island was dotted with residences housing all these young professionals who loved hosting and attending parties. (The term "yuppie," standing for young urban professional, was made popular a few years later in the '80s.) Today, like in the '70s, many Rowaytonites own more than one home and leave for the winter, but they do not rent their house out during the off-season.

Some of those then singles still live in Rowayton because they couldn't bear to leave, including me. Woody Woodworth has a pocketful of colorful stories from that era. He was one of those fun-loving bachelors from the house of pilots (he ended up marrying a flight attendant, Andrea). He went on to serve Rowayton as a member of various civic organizations. Today, his hair is white, and he wears the red suit and white beard as he co-pilots the fire engine all around town every Christmas season on the Santa Run.

And I must mention Bill Tims. He grew up on Bell Island and lived with his mother just a few houses away and was a teacher back in the day. He became a real estate broker and is known throughout the area for his waterfront listings. He's still living on Bell Island and can often be seen tending to one of his coveted automobiles.

For most of those years, Dr. Henry Gloetzner and his wife Lois were our neighbors on Yarmouth Road, and they kept an eye on the girls next door/across the street, offering to help us in any way they could. Andy D'Alessio was another neighbor who always had a smile on his face and a cheery hello.

I lived on Bell Island – moving in and out for the winters and then spending the summers there, too – for five years. It was a special period with lots of fun times. Later on when I chose a name for my business, I selected Bell Island Enterprises because of the fond memories and, most important, because that's where I met my beloved Ray.

Ray loving the boating life from the cockpit of Aquila.

It was moving day that Memorial Day weekend in 1977. I took a carload of boxes down to the beach house overlooking South Beach and walked into the living room to find Cynthia entertaining a very handsome man (he reminded me of Robert Redford with his windswept blondish hair). Cynthia said, "Joyce, this is our neighbor, Ray. He rents a year-round beach house two doors over."

Ray was just the nicest person you could ever meet, and we all hit it off.

So Ray became the guy next door who took the Hizer girls, and an occasional friend, sailing all summer long on his boat, Aquila, a 35' Dickerson ketch. Back at the dock after a sail, Ray would sit in the cockpit or down below in the main salon and regale everyone with stories about the sea. One fun joke he told went like this: "When you're away, I'm restless, lonely, bored, dejected. Only here's the rub, my darling dear, I feel the same when you are here." – S. Hoffenstein

Ray was employed at IBM in White Plains and worked at 1133 Westchester Avenue, which was located – as luck would have it – almost directly across I-287 from Berkeley on West Red Oak Lane, where I worked. Our offices were less than 20 miles (about 20 minutes) from Rowayton. We started commuting together whenever our schedules permitted. We enjoyed each other's company, and it was convenient to dash home from work and head out together for an evening sail.

The happy days of summer sped by. Ray and I caught the latest movies and played a little tennis and took lots of walks on the beach across the street. He was just so easy to be with.

We often met for cocktails after work and shared dinner overlooking Long Island Sound. Once in a while on a Saturday or Sunday, we would venture into Rowayton and have a leisurely breakfast at Cap'n Henry's on Five Mile River (which later became Rowayton Seafood Restaurant) or dinner at Higgins (later renamed Five Mile River Grille and then River Cat Grill and currently called Sails). It was a fun-packed season.

As high summer morphed into late summer and early fall, we went sailing every weekend under the soft autumn sun and gentle afternoon sou'wester. And during the week, we grabbed every good afternoon and went for a sail after work. Later, we would head back to the dock at dusk or in the dark and then share dinner and the rest of the evening together.

I moved back up the street to a house on Yarmouth Road along with Cynthia and another roommate named Kathy. The house was owned by Mrs. O'Shea from Scotch Plains, New Jersey, and I lived there for two winter seasons.

In late September, I took vacation time during the quarter break. I spent the weekend sailing with Ray on his boat and then left for a short trip. I drove to Wilmington, Delaware, and stayed with Bill Diveley from my Grass Creek days and his wife June, who took me to the outlets for lots of shopping. Then I headed to Washington, D.C., to visit some friends I had met through work at Berkeley. I returned to Rowayton on Sunday in the late afternoon and spent the evening with Ray.

It was the last week of September, and we were having a great stretch of soft sunny days, and Ray and I went for a sail every day after work that week. The good weather continued on into early October. A couple of times when the forecast was exceptional, we took a half day off from work, trying to grab every last day of the season.

I loved being with Ray. And it was thrilling to go sailing with him every time we could squeeze in a few hours on the water. It was all so magical.

And that marked the beginning of the realization that there was something very special about our relationship. After a summer of getting to know each other and becoming friends, we just clicked.

In fact, Cynthia had said in late summer, "Joyce, if you gave Ray half a chance, he just might be interested in being more than friends." Maybe that opened my eyes. On more than one occasion, Cynthia has had great insight into my life and has given me a nudge toward moving in a direction or making a decision.

By mid-October, Ray and I knew we were meant for each other. After the Decommissioning party at Wilson Cove Yacht Club (WCYC) on the 16th, Ray parked his car, a little red Fiat (that always was on the blink), in front of his house on South Beach Drive, put both hands on the steering wheel, looked over at me and said, "Joyce, I think I'm falling in love with you."

We vowed to spend every evening together from then on regardless of our work or other commitments. We just loved being together.

We became engaged over Thanksgiving weekend. My mother and stepfather had just left for Indiana after spending the holiday with Cynthia and me in Rowayton (my dad had passed away six years earlier at the age of 62 from cardiovascular disease, and Mother married longtime friend Glen Reid a few years later).

Ray and I were at his beach house on that sunny Sunday afternoon, enjoying a fire in the fireplace. We were sitting in the living room, with the beach and Green's Ledge Lighthouse in view through the large front window. Ray looked at me, took my hand and said, "Let's get married!"

I said YES! right away.

Two weeks later in December, we went into New York City to celebrate our engagement. We went to The Plaza Hotel and had a drink in The Palm Court followed by dinner at the Benihana Japanese Steakhouse.

The restaurant had opened 13 years earlier and was the first of nearly 100 locations. It was a fun dining experience. With the patrons sitting around a rectangular teppanyaki grill, a highly skilled chef entertained us with theatrics and intricate knife work while preparing the meal, dazzling our eyes, as well as our taste buds.

We decided on August 6 as our wedding date.

We flew to Indiana for Christmas so Ray could personally and officially ask Mother for permission to marry me. We had dinner at Chanteclair, a French restaurant in Indianapolis that had a strolling violinist who played "Till There Was You" when Ray gave the signal (from that moment, it became "our" song).

Chanteclair was elegant with its brown-rose décor. The food was heated tableside and served sizzling hot by an attentive waitstaff. And best of all, the translation of Chanteclair from French into English is "rooster" – how appropriate since I had grown up on a chicken farm and hatchery!

In mid-January, we went into New York to the Diamond District and selected an engagement ring. We picked it up the following weekend and had a celebratory dinner the next night in Rowayton with Cynthia and her friend Jim Haswell.

In late January, I purchased a plane ticket to Indianapolis, planning to attend Granddad Hines' 90th birthday party and show off my ring, but the celebration was postponed due to the Blizzard of '78. His birthday was January 31, and Grandma Hizer's was the 29th. Mother always said my birth on the day in between was an act of diplomacy.

In May, Mother and my stepfather came east for my graduation from the M.B.A. program at UConn. All of us, including Cynthia, drove to Storrs and had a cold lobster picnic on the campus green. After the ceremony, we stopped in Essex and had dinner at the Griswold Inn. Little did Ray and I know that Essex would serve as our base later in life when cruising the Connecticut River and surrounding waters.

Also that spring, we started looking for a house to buy. Then, like now, year-round rentals were virtually nonexistent so renting was not an option. There was no doubt that we wanted to stay in Rowayton – with its beach- and boat-driven lifestyle. Even hearing the soothing sound of the Green's Ledge Lighthouse foghorn was all part of the charm.

The housing inventory was low at that time, but we found our house on Rowayton Avenue and made the deal. Betty Berry was our realtor. She worked in the Paul P. Dauk Associates real estate agency here in town.

The closing was set for September 29. As usual, I had to vacate my winter rental on Yarmouth Road in May. So until we could move into our home, we rented a room at Ed Ernst's house on Drum Road for showering and stowing clothes and spent most of our time that summer on the boat.

We signed the contract for the house the day before the wedding. "It was a busy weekend!" we often commented, referring to the tasks of finalizing the paperwork pertaining to the purchase of our house and hosting our rehearsal dinner – with the wedding and all its festivities to follow in a few short hours. Some of the forms had to be notarized, and Lou Froelich at Rowayton Hardware didn't charge a fee, saying it was a gift to the bride and groom. Thanks, Lou.

Our rehearsal dinner the night before the wedding was held at Wilson Cove Yacht Club, where we feasted on fresh lobster. Afterward, we adjourned to the Ramada Inn in Darien (Connecticut) where the wedding party was staying and danced away the night.

I left earlier than most of the others, saying, "Goodnight. I've got a big day tomorrow!" Even though I tried, I didn't sleep much. I was so excited and couldn't wait to marry Ray. And I did something that was and is rare: I woke up at 6 a.m. and couldn't get back to sleep. To kill time, I wrote some thank you notes for wedding gifts that had already arrived.

We were married on August 6 at the United Church of Rowayton. The founding pastor, the Rev. Donald W. Emig, was away on vacation so could not perform the ceremony, but he found a good substitute, the Rev. Donald B. Holmes, who got the job done.

The reception was held at Roton Point, a private club in town with majestic views of Long Island Sound.

The day was sultry, and there was a thunderstorm late in the afternoon. They say rain on your wedding day brings good luck, and it must have with us.

We spent our wedding night on Ray's sailboat, Aquila, on a mooring in Ziegler's Cove (nicknamed Ziggy's). And we spent our honeymoon cruising Shelter Island, a boater's paradise at the east end of Long Island nestled between the twin forks. Cynthia had made a sizable red and yellow burgee with "Just Married!" in large letters that we hoisted up the mast, and the kids giggled "Congratulations!" as they sailed by the mooring.

Cynthia and I laughed often about how she found Ray and introduced me to him. She has kidded all along that she is still waiting for her finder's fee. (Just for fun, I sent her a check in 2020, but no amount of money could ever settle that debt.)

Of note, the beach house I had rented for two summers went on the market earlier that year, and Ray and I put a bid on it but lost out in a silent telephone auction.

Ray – the Love of My Life

It was a fairy-tale life and a marriage made in heaven. Ray and I were devoted to each other and never tired of being together.

As Ray was leaving for work one morning early in our marriage, I said, "Ray, I want you to know you'll always find a safe haven here at home." I went on to say that whether one is at work or just out in the world, there will be times when a person gets beaten up. I told him that no matter what, home would always be a place filled with love and support – a refuge.

Every time one of us left the house, we would give each other a two thumbs up, wishing the other Godspeed on the outing. I endearingly called him "my love" several times a day (pronounced "m' love"): "Good morning, my love," "What's up, my love?" "How are you doing, my love?" "See you later, my love," "Goodbye, my love," "Goodnight, my love."

I just had so much love to give.

We kidded each other and said, "You're the best in the county." Now that's quite a compliment since Fairfield County, and the metro region in general, has a huge population filled with accomplished individuals in every walk of life.

To commemorate our pet phrase, I found a shop in Valhalla in Westchester County, New York, and had "Best in the County" inscribed on a blue ribbon. It was proudly displayed until it turned purple after many years of being exposed to sunlight.

I defended Ray fiercely. He would excuse it and say, "You're just young and crazy in love." Bob Maher, director at Berkeley, asked me about a year after the wedding how I liked being married, and I answered, "I didn't know life could be so good." When I was working at General Electric (GE) about 10 years later, someone asked, "Are you married?" My response was "*very* married."

We went on to enjoy 41 years of bliss. People would ask how we could spend five weeks on the boat and not get on each other's nerves. The response was always, "We just love spending time with each other."

As I pursued my career goals, Ray supported me in every way and embraced my dreams and aspirations. He was my anchor. With a solid foundation of love, drive, skillset and confidence, there wasn't anything I couldn't accomplish.

Our love was deep, and we were inseparable. He made my heart sing. I would say, "He's just so easy to love." Without a doubt, we were soulmates.

One couple, Rich and Chris Bonosky, sent a sympathy card after Ray passed away that said, "We always think of 'Ray and Joyce' or of 'Joyce and Ray' because the two go together. You have always been a unit." And our periodontist and friend Gerry Strassberger, in expressing his sympathy, said, "It's sad because you and Ray were so good together."

Maybe it was because of the age difference (15 years) that we cherished every day we had together. Life was good.

Even when you know it's good, though, you don't realize how much until it's gone.

Ray was known to say, "You can't have your cake, eat it and sell it on the side," meaning you can't have it all forever, but we had it all for more than four decades. I often wished I could give Ray some of my life expectancy if it would extend the years we had with each other.

About the time he turned 85 years old, I started praying to God every morning to keep Ray safe and well. He wasn't failing – just slowing down a bit. I was preparing for the normal ailments that go along with aging into the 90s, but that wasn't to be. God had other plans. No one will ever know if my prayers bought Ray extra time.

Boating

Boating – it's thrilling, it's challenging, it's exhilarating, it's exhausting, it's relaxing, it's calming, it's all these things and more. It can be fun, it can be terrifying, it can be expensive and it can be addictive.

And there's nothing like it in the world.

In my opinion, there's nothing more enjoyable than being on the water. When nature behaves, it doesn't get any better: blue sky, sparkling water, a gentle breeze, the warmth of the sun on your face, ideal temps and the beauty of the scenery.

Being on the water makes you forget your troubles and allows you to take it all in and appreciate the moment.

The water changes constantly, and it is mesmerizing to watch the surface change color and mood as clouds scoot by and the sun ducks in and out.

I never tire of watching the prop wash as it blends into the horizon where surface meets sky. And the familiar and soothing sound of the engine gives comfort.

Seeing navigational aids in the water and landmarks on shore become visible through the mist and fog is a phenomenon that never gets old.

These are some of the things that boaters enjoy during the season and dream about all winter long.

Sailboat, powerboat, large or small boat, it doesn't matter as long as you can be on the water. It's a world unto itself. It's a hobby that becomes a way of life.

Day trips are great.

Cruises are even better. At the end of the day, when you are at anchor or on a mooring, the stars twinkle brightly, and the moon shines fully. As you lie in your bunk, you fall asleep to the sound of the water lapping against the hull. You are filled with tranquility and peacefulness, and all's right with the world.

Over the 41 years we were married, we primarily had three boats: Aquila, a 35' Dickerson ketch sailboat (1978-1982); Intrepid, a 36' Grand Banks trawler (1983-1998); and Blue Heron, a 36' Northern Bay downeast lobster yacht (2001-2020).

We kept our boat in a slip at Wilson Cove Yacht Club in Rowayton for most of those years.

On August 6, 1978, Ray brought to the marriage two items in particular: 1) a little red Fiat that broke down or fell apart even when it was merely sitting in the driveway and 2) a sailboat.

Our first boat, Aquila, a 35' Dickerson ketch.

The boat (whatever boat we might have had at the time) was, and continued to be till his dying day, a force that guided Ray's every decision. That fierce drive dictated the direction of our lives. Fortunately, I had spent summers on the lake at Culver and loved boating almost as much as Ray did so I was a good and willing partner.

The goal was to spend as much time as possible on the water. Ray kept saying, "If I had a boat with an inside helm and was sheltered from the elements, we could be out on the water even more."

We came up with the idea of renting our house during the summers and putting that money toward the purchase of a boat with an inside steering station.

It was a great arrangement. We spent a few nights a week at the dock and a few nights at Ziegler's Cove or some harbor on Long Island. And the yacht club and marina endorsed the plan because there was a presence on the dock to deter any nefarious activities.

Our house was in the Rowayton Beach Association (RBA) with its own private beach on Long Island Sound and a view of Five Mile River across the street. It was a sought-after location that attracted tenants. We ended up renting for the summer months for close to 10 years and living aboard the boat, taking a five- or six-week cruise every season.

We found the boat of our dreams in 1983: a three-year-old 36' Grand Banks that had lots of amenities that allowed for easy living aboard. We ran the boat from Lake Champlain in Burlington, Vermont, down the Hudson River to New York City and into Long Island Sound. It was exciting to maneuver the many locks and lift bridges on the Hudson.

It was during those years that Ray decided to get his captain's license. He took a course and studied diligently. He then passed the exam administered at the Battery Park Building in New York City and met all the requirements for a captain's license from the U.S. Coast Guard in November of 1987. He toyed with the idea of chartering our boat but, in the end, decided not to do so. After Ray earned his captain's license, I referred to him as "O Captain! My Captain!" (vis-a-vis the poem by Walt Whitman) and declared him "captain of my soul."

We named our Grand Banks Intrepid and were the proud owners for nearly 15 years. We spent all our free time enjoying the local waters of the Sound, as well as cruising the East Coast.

Let's talk about boat names. Naming one's boat is akin to naming a child – it's a matter to be taken seriously. The name has to be a good fit and have meaning.

When Ray bought his sailboat, it was named Aquila, a constellation represented by the figure of an eagle. Since it supposedly is bad luck to change the name of a boat, he kept the name.

Our second boat, as noted above, was named Intrepid. During the summer of '81 on Aquila, we ran aground and hit Ram Island Reef in Fisher's Island Sound. So the next boat name had to imply being sturdy and impenetrable.

Our second boat, Intrepid, a 36' Grand Banks.

The final boat we owned was named Blue Heron because the boat went through the water gracefully like a blue heron in flight, and we saw blue herons along the shore in harbors up and down the coast.

So selecting the name of one's boat is a big deal. When I was editor of the Wilson Cove Yacht Club newsletter in the '80s, I had a standing column (titled "What's In a Name?") on how it came to be that members had selected their boat name.

There are some great stories. One boat was named Someday Came in recognition of achieving a long sought-after goal, in this case enough success to enable the owner to purchase a particular boat brand and size.

I remember the days when I was hauling eggs in my Corvair

in Grass Creek a lifetime ago and fantasized about living out East with the man of my dreams and having a successful career, shouting "Someday!" Someday Came would have been an appropriate name for me to select.

Long Island Sound is a tidal estuary of the Atlantic Ocean, lying predominantly between the state of Connecticut to the north and Long Island, New York, to the south. From west to east, the Sound stretches 110 miles from the East River in New York City to Fisher's Island Sound or the Race in Block Island Sound. The widest point is 21 miles. The distance is seven miles from Rowayton to the closest point across the Sound on Long Island.

Rowayton is 40 miles east of New York City. The latitude and longitude coordinates are 41 degrees N and 73 degrees W. More than 20 million people live within one hour of Long Island Sound.

On weekends all season, we would run across the Sound to Oyster Bay, Northport, Lloyd Harbor, Eaton's Neck, Port Jefferson or several other ports of call and spend Saturday night aboard. We had a mooring in Ziegler's Cove in nearby Darien so we would return on Sunday afternoon and spend the night in the charming cove, heading back to the dock before work on Monday morning.

Ray took all his vacation days at one time during the summer so we would spend five to six weeks at Shelter Island, located between the twin forks at the east end of Long Island, New York.

Passing through Plum Gut and entering Gardiner's Bay with Shelter in the distance was considered (by us) the gateway to vacationland, and we would hoist whatever beverage was in hand (early on it likely was a beer and later on a soda or water) and make a toast to a wonderful cruise. During the trip, we would make stops at all the popular ports of call, including Stonington and Block Island.

We loved our time at Shelter.

We would have lunch at The Dory and dinner at Ram's Head Inn. We would anchor for the night in one of our favorite harbors – West

Neck, Coecles, Dering, Three Mile.

One of our passions was watching the sunset from the boat, often a breathtaking experience. We would laugh and say our biggest problem was running out of ice. If that happened, there was "trouble in paradise."

Those were such carefree days.

We met lots of people – islanders, as well as boaters from all over the region. We became good friends with Bud and Natalie Fox, who lived near West Neck Harbor.

Our tender was a 13' Boston Whaler, and the name T/T Intrepid was painted on the side in bright red letters (standing for "tender to" Intrepid). We towed the dinghy up and down the Sound every season. It was the perfect boat for scooting around the harbors especially where there were no speed limits.

The Whaler served as a ski boat as well, and I was known to provide a good show for boats at anchor. I had been a pretty good slalom skier in my youth and never completely lost my touch. We also used the Whaler for gunkholing in and out of coves and harbors around the Norwalk Islands in our local waters and for patrolling Five Mile River as part of Ray's responsibilities as harbor superintendent.

Beyond Shelter Island and Block, we threaded our way eastward. We frequented Newport and discovered quaint Cuttyhunk Island and even made a trip to Maine in those early years. Cuttyhunk is the outermost of the 16 Elizabeth Islands and is situated between Vineyard Sound off Martha's Vineyard and Buzzard's Bay.

A decade later when Ray retired, Cuttyhunk became our base, and we would stay there tied to a piling for two or three weeks at a time. One of the highlights was to climb Lookout Hill – the highest point on the island and a naval lookout during World War II – on a clear day where you could see forever. It is one of those rare mountaintop experiences that literally takes your breath away.

Another destination was a weekend at West Point in the fall. We would run the boat west in Long Island Sound to New York City, navigate the sometimes turbulent currents at Hell Gate, head up the Harlem River and then enter the Hudson River at the Spuyten Duyvil swing bridge. We would chug north and pass under the Tappan Zee Bridge and then make our way up to West Point, where we would catch a football game on Saturday afternoon.

One year we had to cancel our trip to West Point due to work commitments, and Ray said it was an opportunity lost forever. Once the moment is gone, it can never be recaptured: You may have tomorrows but never yesterdays. His Great Neck High School class motto was "carpe diem," and Ray tried hard to "seize the moment" every day.

As you can imagine, boating friends like to keep in touch, especially when cruising. Ray and I made it widely known that we manned our VHF radio every morning from 10 a.m. till 10:15 a.m. so people could contact us.

Joyce and Ray aboard Intrepid at Cuttyhunk Island.

We had lots of time to read. No matter what port we were in, we both read a lot of books. Ray had a voracious appetite and usually had three books going at once. And I read all the time. Two nautical stories we both enjoyed are *The Perfect Storm* and *The Light Between Oceans*. We each kept a log of books read.

At Shelter, we made it a point to catch the book fair at the Shelter Island Library every summer and would get an ample supply of hardcovers and paperbacks that would fill every nook and cranny on the boat. Loaded with several bags of books, we would hitchhike back to the harbor. Someone always gave us a ride.

Being a reader, Ray appreciated the written word in many forms – from books to poems to sayings. Our friend Lyle McGuire had a saying engraved on a piece of beautifully varnished mahogany and presented it to Ray as a gift one year. "Boating is not inherently dangerous, but, like the sea, it is terribly unforgiving of carelessness, indifference and neglect." Adaptation of quote by Captain A.G. Lamplugh, aviator.

Whenever we were cruising, I made it a point to call my mother every week or so, and the calls generally lasted about an hour. Before cell phones were commonplace, Ray and I would scout out the phone booths at every port of call.

When my nephew Andrew Jubera was born, I was informed of the happy occasion while standing in a phone booth in East Hampton, New York, in Three Mile Harbor. The date was 7/11 (what a great date for a birthday!), and it was hot in the direct sun. I asked Mother for the phone number at the hospital so I could call Cynthia. I didn't have pen and paper so I wrote the number in the sand with my toes.

I spent many hours in phone booths over the years, with Ray patiently waiting in the wings (or walking the docks). It was possible to make calls to landlines on the VHF radio on the boat, but anybody could tune in and listen to the conversation. Mother didn't like that, saying it was like the party line of old. So I made it a point to find a phone booth. Mother, who was a renowned knitter, made an afghan exclusively for the boat that features an image of the WCYC burgee with its distinctive blue and orange colors. I still have it.

History of Wilson Cove and Wilson Cove Yacht Club

We kept our boat in a slip at the yacht club in Wilson Cove in Rowayton for most of our 40+ years of boating. I researched the background of the cove and penned the history below. It was published in the roster/membership directory and posted on the club's website.

In the 1920s and 1930s, the northernmost portion of Wilson Cove was a shallow tidal basin used primarily by commercial boats.

One such activity was harvesting ice – big business before the advent of refrigeration. Ice from ponds and lakes in the local area was transported from the cove to Oyster Bay for sale on Long Island and New York City.

On the return trip, ships would head for Wilson Cove bearing coal for distribution in Fairfield County.

Prior to that, the cove was used, among other things, as a naval storage base during World War I. Once the ships were loaded, they set off for France to provide guns, ammunition and other war supplies to the troops.

The east side of the cove, now occupied by Norwalk Yacht Club, at one point served as a steamboat landing. A spur of the New York, New Haven & Hartford Railroad ran along the eastern shore to the south end of Wilson Point.

Ice, coal and farm products in the railcars were transferred to the boats docked there. Also, an oil transfer station and tank farm for Standard Oil Company hugged the shore along Wilson Avenue.

The name Wilson dates back to 1825 when Lewis O. Wilson became owner, as dowry from his bride, of the property where Wilson Cove Yacht Club sits today.

Wilson was in the textile business in New York City. A robber baron who eagerly participated in high-stakes deals was owner of hundreds of acres of prime property around Wilson Cove and the surrounding area. He enjoyed the best that life offered but died a pauper alone in a rundown hotel in Norwalk in 1892.

The Norwalk Yacht Club clubhouse was originally located on the west side of Wilson Cove along Bluff Avenue. The 1894 Victorian with dock is still there and now is a private residence.

Also situated on the west side of the cove, just south of Wilson Cove Yacht Club, is the original Rev. Thomas House. It now is part of the Thomas Place Condominium Group of homes.

The Thomas House was originally built on Wilson Point. However, it obstructed Wilson's view of Long Island Sound. So the house was moved to the opposite shore by pushing it across the ice one winter when all of Wilson Cove was frozen solid.

Eventually, commercial use of the cove ended, and the inner part of Wilson Cove was dredged. The excavated material was used as landfill for the existing building and parking lot. A barge was brought in and served as the foundation for the present mast shed.

One of the early owners of the land was the Lunette Burchard estate that sold the property to Daniel Toomey in 1922, who started a marine construction business.

Upon Toomey's death in 1945, the property was sold to John and Cecilia Spangle, also for marine construction use. They later installed docks and finger slips for recreational boating.

At some point in the late 1950s, it was determined by City of Norwalk officials that the Wilson Cove marine business was running a commercial operation in a residential zone and was in violation of the zoning regulations. The town fathers then stipulated that the business could continue at that location if a social group became affiliated with it, and Wilson Cove Yacht Club was born.

In 1959, 12 of the yard's patrons established Wilson Cove Yacht Club, each donating $10 to start the treasury. The first commodore was elected in 1962. That is when Betty Ann Smith made the Cocktail Flag that is still used today and is hoisted to signal that the bar is open. Her husband and subsequent commodore Dick Smith fired his cannon at every Commissioning and Decommissioning ceremony, eventually donating it to the club.

The property has seen several owners since the Spangles: Bob Anderson, Toste Moller, Grove Ely and now Clute Ely. On two occasions, the club attempted to buy the property: in the mid-1970s and then again in the late 1990s. In both cases, the club was unsuccessful.

Wilson Cove Yacht Club leases the clubhouse from the owner. Over the years, it has been redecorated for the pleasure of the members.

Yachtsmen come from the tri-state area and are delighted to keep their boat in an attractive, protected cove with easy access to Long Island Sound.

Wilson Cove Yacht Club

WCYC was a big part of our lives. Ray joined the club in 1974. He served as commodore in 1982, and we were active members for decades.

I was publicity chairman and editor of the club's newsletter, *Wilson Cove Soundings*, for many years. I now serve as historian, as happens when you get older and have longevity in an organization.

As part of the preparations for the club's 60th anniversary activities in 2019, I was able to retrieve – with the help of some very able and helpful fellow boaters – some important artifacts from the club's history. We found 16 years of rosters. We located 22 scrapbooks that are loaded with party invitations and newspaper clippings and photos of celebrations and cruises and rendezvous.

Joyce and Ray aboard Intrepid at Wilson Cove Yacht Club.

And from the 1980s, we found eight of the 10 years of newsletters. I wrote the article below for the club's website. The newsletters provide a sense of the fun and camaraderie Wilson Covers enjoyed during those years.

WCYC Brings Back Newsletters from the '80s
By Joyce H. Meurer, Historian, Member since 1974
Spring 2019

As part of WCYC's 60th anniversary celebration [in 2019], we are pleased to present archived issues of *Wilson Cove Soundings*, the name of the club's newsletter 30 years ago.

We urge you to read every word of every issue. You will get a taste of what Wilson Cove Yacht Club was like in those days.

It was a vibrant group of boaters who loved to be out on the water and who lived life to its fullest ashore. Most parties drew 100+ people, and a good time was had by all – all year round.

Aside from the Commissioning and Decommissioning ceremonies, we had a Super Bowl party in the winter. We had a Commodore's Champagne Brunch in March at a local yacht club. We had fitting-out lunches and a paint party in the spring. We had dock parties. We had barbeques. We had lobster fests and clambakes. We had a summer cruise, generally to Shelter Island and Block Island with stops at popular ports.

And nearly every weekend, there was a planned or impromptu rendezvous at a nearby harbor. Oyster Bay was a favorite, and a raft-up was made up of as few as three or four boats or sometimes as many as 25 to 30. In the fall, we drank Pink Panther rum punch with steaks from the grill and also held a hurricane party. Outdoor get-togethers lasted well into autumn until Old Man Winter came knocking on the door.

Members spent a lot of time together at these gatherings and on the docks. The weekend fun started on Friday after work with cocktails on someone's boat or in the clubhouse. Lots of people would sleep on board their boat that night, and the camaraderie continued through Saturday and Sunday.

If we didn't go to a harbor or yacht club or didn't have a scheduled event at the club, we Wilson Covers made our own party, often going to dinner en masse at a local restaurant and telling lots of tall tales.

In those days, the Christmas party was combined with the Annual Meeting, held at a premier yacht club the first Saturday in December. Everyone arrived all decked out for the holidays at 5 p.m. for a rousing meeting and recap of the season, complete with trophies and gifts of appreciation. Then we dined and danced until the wee hours of the morning. It was a gala event that commemorated another great year of boating at WCYC.

Because of the active participation and a common love of the sea, we all became friends – it was like one big, happy family. The newsletters from that era reflect the comings and goings of the members' personal and boating lives: those who had kids graduating from high school or college; those who had become grandparents; those who had been to intriguing vacation destinations; those who wanted to sell used boating gear; those who might be looking for a new boat.

There are stories about members' boating backgrounds and memorable experiences on the water in our local area, as well as afar.

There are profiles of some of the past commodores. There's an entire series on "What's In a Name?" depicting how one came to the important decision of naming the boat.

Scattered throughout the issues are all kinds of boating tips, cruising secrets, recipes for hors d'oeuvres in the cockpit and dinners in the salon, and a myriad of other nautical information and advice.

Oh, we did have fun!

Recently, I resumed handling the club's communications, including producing the roster and writing frequent eblasts and a monthly newsletter. I currently serve as historian and vice commodore, due to become the next commodore.

Tide Calendar Story

It was the 1984 Christmas holiday, and Ray and I were sitting at the kitchen table looking at the '84 tide calendar for the month of

December that hung on the wall. We had just returned from Rowayton Hardware, where we had gone in search of the next year's tide calendar but had been informed by the owners, Lou and Lois Froelich, that it no longer was available.

Ray looked at me and said, "Now there's an opportunity." Living near the water meant you kept an eye on the tides every day, and the calendar was a household necessity. Everyone in town felt the same way. Ray always had excellent ideas, and I was good at executing – we made a great team.

I jumped at the idea and, along with building my corporate communications business, spent the next 10 months pulling together all the facets to make the Bell Island Enterprises Long Island Sound Tide Calendar the best product on the market.

A designer was hired to give it a professional look. I visited print shops all over Fairfield County seeking to find quality printing at a fair price.

But most of all, I knocked on doors from Stonington, Connecticut, to the Bronx and the entire north shore of Long Island, convincing business owners – marinas/boatyards and boat dealers and boat repair shops and bait shops and seashore restaurants and fish markets and insurance agencies and hardware stores – to purchase my tide calendar and sell it or use it as an advertising piece.

The inside front cover could be customized for each merchant's business, and I collected an arsenal of nautical artwork from local artists from which to choose. Ray would come home from working at IBM and say, "You have all the fun!"

The Long Island Sound Tide Calendar was an immediate success.

It is filled with all kinds of pertinent information. The attractive 11" x 8½" size provides space to make the numbers big enough to read easily and still leave room for making notes.

Each day lists the high and low tides. The tide cycle is approximately six hours so there generally are two high tides and two low tides each day (one day each week, there are only three tides due to the timing).

The height of the high tides is listed as well. The average high tide height in Rowayton is 7.2 feet.

Phases of the moon are shown. Every two to three years, there is a blue moon, which means there is a second full moon within one calendar month (blue moons are not blue, by the way – "a blue moon" is an expression meaning every few years or not very often). If a full moon falls during perigee (see definition below), it's called a supermoon.

There is a double blue moon, meaning a blue moon occurs twice within one calendar year, three to five times per century. This usually occurs in January and March when there is no full moon at all in February (called a black moon). The most recent double blue moons occurred in 1999 and 2018 (and in January 2018, both full moons were supermoons as well).

The next double blue moon will be in 2037.

For many years, I consulted with the Hayden Planetarium in New York to verify the astronomical information.

The greatest gravitational force comes when there is either a full moon or a new moon.

Apogee and perigee are noted on each month. The moon circles the earth in an elliptical (or oval) path. Apogee is when the moon is farthest from the earth, which means there is the least gravitational force, thus resulting in a lower tidal rise and fall. Perigee is when the moon is closest to the earth, which means there is the greatest gravitational force, thus resulting in a higher tidal rise and fall.

When the moon is in perigee in combination with either a full or new moon, the height of the tides can rise an extra two feet (to 9.2 feet or so) in Rowayton. Likewise, when the moon is in apogee in combination with either a first or last quarter moon, the height can be as little as 5.9 or 6.0 feet in Rowayton.

Other features of the calendar include times of sunrise and sunset and a chart of high tide variations at 30 harbors on both sides of Long Island Sound (the north shore, for example, from City Island in the Bronx to Stonington, Connecticut, near the Rhode Island state line).

One hour is added for Daylight Saving Time so the reader doesn't have to remember to do so.

Over time and due to popular demand, I expanded the choices and offered three versions, as well as produced specialized tidal charts for individual businesses. For many years, one insurance company in Norwalk, J.M. Layton & Co., ordered 7,000 calendars annually to be distributed to its customers, as well as to libraries and schools and organizations all over Fairfield and New Haven counties.

Ray headed up the shipping department, and he and I would spend several days each December packaging calendars to be shipped via UPS and the postal service.

I became known locally as "the tide calendar girl" – the go-to person for tidal information. I would get phone calls from both sides of the Sound from mothers when newly engaged daughters were planning their wedding by the water.

And whenever a storm and flooding were predicted, I would get (and still do) a flurry of phone calls from Rowaytonites asking if they should move their cars to high ground. I've had fun producing the Long Island Sound Tide Calendar for decades: At last count (in 2020), it was 34 years.

Ted Kennedy Story

For many years, Ray and I served on the race committee for the Corinthians, and I was the official timekeeper. One summer, we were invited to participate in the Mayor's Cup in the waters surrounding Liberty Island and the Statue of Liberty in New York.

Before the race, there was a skipper's meeting.

On the way back to the race committee boat, we female members were delighted to see that Ted Kennedy's beautiful classic wooden sailboat was tied up to the face dock at the end of the pier. I suggested that the group walk down and take a look at the boat.

As we approached, Ted noticed we were wearing race committee garb (white blouse/tie, blue blazer, khaki slacks).

Always quick to recognize opportunity and rub elbows with the right people (like any successful politician), he invited us to tour his boat. His sister Eunice also was aboard and was quite gracious.

Just like the magnificent exterior wooden hull, the down below was beautifully appointed. As my friends and I stood in the cockpit ready to disembark, we wished him good luck in the race. Ted was an excellent sailor and very competitive, and he won that day.

Abacos Story: "It will all become apparent."
Most every vacation that Ray and I took centered around a boating or beach venue. In January 1991, we rented a small house in the Abacos in the Caribbean for a week. The cottage was situated atop a hill with a panoramic view of water in all directions. We also chartered an 18' runabout.

When we were checking out the boat in Marsh Harbour in preparation for heading to Elbow Cay, Ray asked where the compass was. The marina owner, Scott Patterson, said, "You won't need a compass."

Then Ray asked for a chart of the local waters, and Scott said, "You won't need a chart." Ray said, "It's pretty shallow in some places out of the channel. I don't want to go aground." Scott responded, "Don't worry. It's all sand. If you go aground, you won't hurt the engine or the hull."

Ray was leery, but we had no choice but to get under way. Scott raised his arm and pointed to the east and said, "Just head that way until you get close to shore, and then it will all become apparent. Don't worry, be happy, mon."

And it did become apparent.

In the ensuing years when something was uncertain or vague, we always reverted to the philosophy that "it will all become apparent." And, generally, that was the case.

Another of Ray's favorite expressions when the way was not clear was to say that the person's two feet were "planted firmly in mid-air."

On our trip home, Scott asked if we would mail some letters for him when we were stateside, and we were happy to accommodate him. He said it would take about two weeks for delivery if mailed from the Bahamas versus a couple of days from Florida.

Now there's more to this story.

Prior to arriving in the Abacos, I had planned to get my week's supply of cigarettes and scotch (Winston 100s and Johnnie Walker Red were my brands, respectively) at the airport in Florida – so I hadn't taken any.

Upon arrival at West Palm Beach, I was sorely disappointed to find the duty free shop closed. Ray said, "Don't worry. We'll get supplies in Marsh Harbour or Hope Town."

After the short flight to Great Abaco Island, Ray thought we should proceed directly to our rental house before it got any later. It had been a long day already so we decided to skip food shopping at the only real supermarket in the vicinity. We went straight to the marina, loaded the luggage onto the charter boat and headed across the harbor (where it all did become apparent).

We finally arrived at the dock, offloaded the gear, hiked up the hill and settled into our abode. We walked to Sweeting's Grocery and Liquor Store to get provisions but learned that the market was out of cigarettes and no longer carried liquor.

We learned, too, that in that part of the world, most establishments are closed on Sunday.

So here we were on vacation for seven glorious days on an island in the sun – and, for the moment, I had no cigs and no scotch.

As we all do when desperate, we get creative.

I discovered there was a restaurant in the nearby Abaco Inn where I could purchase the needed inventory to tide me over till Monday.

We had a delightful week exploring the many islands and beaches in our runabout. There were occasions when we were the only boat anchored in a remote cove.

And there's one other vivid memory from that trip: Every morning at first light, we were rudely awakened by the resident rooster crowing "cock-a-doodle-doo" that resounded for miles. A notation in the guest book read "Strangle the rooster!"

We agreed wholeheartedly.

More on Boating

Having retired in January 1992, Ray was eager to move ahead with his plan to spend more time on the boat.

By then, my career was well-established, and I was able to work from the boat via cell phone, fax and overnight delivery. So we were footloose and fancy free and weren't tied to my office, and we spent a huge amount of time boating.

In the fall of 1995, we ventured south to the Chesapeake Bay and spent a year exploring the dozens of harbors and creeks the area has to offer.

It was great fun, and the crab cakes there are the best.

We made Oxford, Maryland, our base, a charming yachting center on the Eastern Shore. We frequented the Robert Morris Inn and splurged on fresh rockfish topped with crabmeat. We were featured in an article in *Pleasant Living* magazine, a Virginia-based publication about life in the Chesapeake, describing our adventures and lifestyle aboard Intrepid.

By this time, Ray was ready to embark on his greatest dream of all – transiting the Intracoastal Waterway to Florida and back.

Based in Virginia at that point, Intrepid was commissioned for the trip, and we headed south in October of 1996. It took about a month, running nearly every day from first light until mid-afternoon.

We had wonderful experiences and met interesting people at every stop. Each cruiser had a boat card (like a business card) printed that we all passed out to fellow boaters along the way. It was fun.

After boarding boat after boat and making comparisons, Ray realized that to be more comfortable, we needed a bigger boat. He said he wanted one that, specifically, had a separate shower and was beamy enough so he didn't have to turn sideways to walk through the main salon.

Ray also hoped to get a boat that didn't have so much brightwork. He spent, on average, 14 full days each spring sanding and varnishing the rails and trim and window frames and steps to the bridge on our Grand Banks.

He would work on the woodwork on weekends starting in March and grab every suitable day until finished, usually in late April. We had had a custom canvas cover made by Fairclough Sailmakers when we bought the boat, and it would get toasty warm on a sunny spring day under the cover.

Ray enjoyed varnishing, but all that wood began to be too much to maintain. He was good at it, but, occasionally, a sag or two would develop. Bryan Lawrence, a fellow Wilson Cover, always excused it, saying, "Well, you can't see it from Cos Cob." (Cos Cob is a section of Greenwich, Connecticut, where I had lived and worked when I first moved east.) It became a phrase we used often when something wasn't perfect.

After an intense search for another boat, we bought a three-year-old Grand Banks 42 the next summer (1997) in Vero Beach, Florida, that met all the criteria on Ray's list.

We spent another year on and off the new boat, also named Intrepid, in the Sunshine State, flying back and forth to Connecticut every few months. On one flight when I was heading south to join Ray, the plane was close to Cape Canaveral, and we saw, just for a couple of seconds, a shuttle hurtling through the sky that had been launched from Kennedy Space Center.

Ray and I joined St. Augustine Yacht Club, which was part of the Florida Council of Yacht Clubs. Members are entitled to visit any of the 30-some yacht clubs up and down both coasts and to dock and dine at each facility. Between the Florida yacht clubs and those in the Northeast, we enjoyed dockage and dining at more than 100 clubs over the years.

I became adept at handling the lines and could lasso a piling even in a stiff breeze. I had played softball as a kid (pitcher and captain of the team), and my pitching skills have served me well throughout life.

In the spring of 1998, we ran the boat from Florida to Annapolis, Maryland. We had decided the 42 Grand Banks was more boat than we needed for our future boating plans. We listed it with a local broker, and it sold a few months later.

In search of the next vessel, Ray set his sights on a downeast boat. He was enthralled with the lines of the downeast design and was more than excited about the higher speed. Ray had tired of cruising at seven knots on Intrepid. "The older I get, the faster I want to go," he said on many occasions.

For a number of reasons, we decided to go back to a 36' boat for cruising Long Island Sound and New England. A Maine lobster yacht was a good choice because those boats are sea-kindly (they're made for running in the ocean and are known for their dry, stable ride) and fast (the sweet spot on Blue Heron was 17 knots, but we generally ran at 12 knots – still, nearly twice the speed of the original Intrepid).

After having had boats with a white hull, we liked the idea of a dark hull, as are so many downeast boats. A dark hull retains heat both inside and outside more so than a lighter-colored hull, but that wasn't much of a concern. In New England, there are a lot of dark-hulled boats in comparison with the South.

Our third boat, Blue Heron, a 36' downeast lobster yacht.

Ray scoured the market for months but could not find any boats for sale that were relatively new. So he made arrangements to have a custom downeast boat built, a Northern Bay. A Spencer Lincoln (of Lincoln-Duffy fame) design, John Hutchins at Downeast Boats and Composites in Penobscot, Maine, produced the fiberglass hull, and Pete Buxton of Buxton Boats in Stonington, Maine, was retained as builder and finisher. It took two years and 13 trips to Maine to get Blue Heron built and splashed.

We would leave Rowayton by car in the morning and stop for lunch at a park overlooking Lake Quannapowitt just north of Boston in Wakefield, Massachusetts, sharing a Grampa sub we had picked up at White Bridge Deli at the Darien-Rowayton town line.

We would drive the remainder of the several-hours' ride to Belfast the first night and take a room in a motel with a view overlooking Penobscot Bay. The next morning, we would drive the last one and a half hours to Stonington, located at the bottom of Deer Isle, and consult with Pete Buxton.

The drive down the island itself is a delight, passing through quaint towns with picturesque vistas of water and islands and hills and pine forests in the distance.

In July of 2001, we traveled to Stonington for the final phase of the boat building. It took three weeks for all the finishing touches to be completed so we took advantage of the specialties that Deer Isle has to offer – lobster, fresh fish entrées and fish burgers at a local diner, homemade donuts and blueberry jam, to name but a few. When the boat was ready, we had the best trip of our life running Blue Heron to Connecticut with stops at Boothbay and Portland in Maine, Scituate, Massachusetts, and Stonington, Connecticut.

We loved running Blue Heron for the next 20 years and always took a summer cruise.

In later years, we traveled in tandem with Alex Mackintosh and his mother Ann on their boat Loch Moy. Blue Heron's hull is aristo blue and Loch Moy's a bright red. The two boats made a pretty picture as we paraded in and out of the harbors. Our favorites included Cuttyhunk, with stopovers at ports on Vineyard Sound, Hamburg Cove on the Connecticut River and, of course, Shelter Island.

Ann was quite a trouper. She lived to the ripe old age of 102 and was an avid boater right up to the end. Ray and I had been friends with Ann and Alex since the late '70s and had had a lot of fun together. Always the lady, Ann loved her glitzy clothes and colorful jokes.

They had had interesting lives. Ann and her husband Don were living in Java (now Indonesia) in the early 1940s when the family was taken as prisoners of war for three years by the Japanese during World War II. Ann always said attitude was the gating factor of whether one survived or not. Just a few short years after the war ended, Ann contracted polio and lived with limited physical abilities most of her life.

She didn't let adversity stop her and was a model for always demonstrating perseverance. Despite her disabilities, she still made it down the ramp and dock, supported by her cane, to board Loch Moy and was able to maneuver the steps up to the flybridge.

When cruising, another favorite stopover was Point Judith Pond in Rhode Island. We would tie up at Peter Hick's dock and spend a few days seeing the local sights. We also made it a point to eat lunch and dinner every chance we had at Old Mountain Lanes (called Lanes for short) in Wakefield. It served fish right off the boats and was among the freshest and best we'd ever had. It is a unique eatery because it is a coffee shop in a bowling alley, of all places!

On these summer cruises, we would invariably see Ted and Janice Strauss aboard their sailboat Eagle's Wing. They had been members of Wilson Cove Yacht Club from 1980 to 1989.

They then joined Saugatuck Harbor Yacht Club in Westport, Connecticut, and we've remained friends all the years since. We would be in Coecles or Three Mile or Hamburg Cove, and they would come to our boat in their dinghy named Feather. Ray would take the line from Janice and say, "Welcome aboard," and we would catch up on all the news since the last visit.

Ray always was crisp and clear when making plans (on or off the boat) so people understood what was to happen. Janice once put it in perspective, saying, "One always knows where you stand with Ray. He is very direct and clear. It makes things easy."

As well as cruising, we enjoyed being on board at dockside at Wilson Cove Yacht Club, especially on a foul weather day. In total, we spent approximately 100 days a season under way or at the dock or on the mooring.

We spent every good weather day either at our mooring in Ziegler's Cove or anchored off one of the Norwalk Islands and frequently ran across the Sound to one of the lovely Long Island harbors.

Ray with Blue Heron in background in Hamburg Cove
on the Connecticut River on a crisp sunny day.

When it was time to head back to the house, Ray was famous for saying, "Ready to head for the barn?" (That must have been a carryover from when he worked on farms as a teenager.)

Ray captained the boat until age 86 when he was diagnosed in the fall of 2018 with the cancer that took his life 10½ months later. Running a boat until the mid-80s is unusual as most people give up the sport in their 60s or 70s at the latest.

We never understood why so many people sold their boat upon retirement once they had all that free time. But they just got tired of coping with the elements and the continual maintenance and expense.

Not Ray! Boating was his passion till the end.

Much more could be said about our lifetime of experiences on the water, but that's another book. I kept meticulous records of our cruises, but many of the logbooks and journals were ruined in Superstorm Sandy in 2012.

Blue Heron was put on the market and sold in July of 2020 to Pete Buxton, who had built the boat, and his wife Sue.

It was the perfect ending to the story as they will take care of and cherish Blue Heron as much as Ray and I did.

After the closing, Pete, Sue and I ran to Ziegler's Cove, picked up Blue Heron's mooring, and made a champagne toast to the new owners and to Ray's memory. As mentioned earlier, Ray and I spent our wedding night on a mooring in Ziggy's all those years ago so it was an appropriate setting to mark the end of our boating days together.

Two days later, Pete and Sue left for Stonington, Maine. They took some of Ray's ashes and secured them in a jar in the main salon so he could look through the cabin windows and enjoy the ride eastward one last time, called the twilight voyage.

They left from Norwalk Cove Marina. I stood on Calf Pasture Beach and watched them traverse Norwalk Harbor out past Goose Island and Peck's Ledge Lighthouse. Through the binoculars, I watched the boat steaming east until Blue Heron was just a speck on the horizon.

The first stop was Clinton, Connecticut. Of all the harbors Pete and Sue could have chosen, Clinton is where Ray had kept his sailboat for a couple of seasons before he and I met. So it was most fitting that he was able to revisit his old stomping ground.

The next leg of the trip took them through the eastern end of Long Island Sound, Fisher's Island Sound, Watch Hill Passage, Block Island

Sound, Point Judith and finally Cuttyhunk.

Pete and Sue scattered some of Ray's ashes in the Cuttyhunk area, and the baton passed from captain to captain. Sue texted me during the runs, reporting on where they were located and what the sea conditions were. I felt as if I was aboard and making the trip with them. When they reached Stonington, Maine, the boat had come full circle.

Shortly thereafter, Pete and Sue scattered more of Ray's ashes in their local waters so his presence would be felt at their home port.

They took the remaining ashes and permanently mounted them in a small container in the main salon so Ray would always be on his boat.

Chesapeake Bay Cruise

As I was writing this chapter on boating, I gathered all the references at hand such as logbooks, journals, itineraries and diaries (as mentioned earlier, some of the records, unfortunately, were destroyed in Superstorm Sandy). I laboriously compiled the information into a rather extensive appendix (approximately 100 pages) of our cruises over the years from Maine to Florida.

In the end, I decided not to include the appendix. It made the book quite long, and I felt all that minutiae might not appeal to readers. In so doing, however, much of the flavor of our cruises and visits to the many charming and interesting ports of call was lost.

To rectify some of that, I've attached my notes from our cruise to the Chesapeake Bay as an addendum to this boating chapter. I hope the description of the daily activities and events will convey at least a smidgen of the pleasure we derived from our boating adventures.

Yacht Intrepid Logbook/Journal
Rowayton to the Chesapeake Bay, September 1-October 11, 1995

Ray and I ran our Grand Banks 36 Classic to the Chesapeake in September of 1995.

Grand Banks is a brand of high-end pleasure yachts called trawlers.

Because of the hull design, they are not fast boats. Top speed generally ranges from 7-10 knots, much like the fishing boats they resemble. Unlike the commercial vessels, these boats are known for their quality craftsmanship and handsome teak woodwork and decks. They are built with many amenities for long-distance cruising.

A semi-displacement hull, our boat was powered by a single 120 horsepower Ford Lehman diesel engine. At 1700 rpm's, our normal speed over the ground was 7.3 knots.

Our draft was 3.8 feet, meaning we needed about four feet of water to stay afloat and avoid going aground.

One of the major challenges of cruising the Chesapeake Bay is the shallow water. The average tidal rise is 1.0 foot to 3.0 feet (whereas, in Rowayton on Long Island Sound, the average tidal rise is 7.2 feet, and the range is 5.9 feet to 9.2 feet). We had our share of passages whereby we held our breath and then sighed with relief as we threaded our way through the skinny waterways of the Chesapeake.

Upon discovering Oxford, Maryland, and its charm, great boating and conveniences, we decided to make it our home base.

Following is an accounting of our cruise and happy days spent on board Intrepid on the Eastern Shore that year.

September 1, Friday, Rowayton to Port Washington, N.Y.

It was a beautiful cloudless, relatively windless day when we left Wilson Cove in the late morning. The forecast for the next week was for sunny days and light southerly winds – a perfect weather pattern for making a run in the Atlantic Ocean along the New Jersey coast.

Prior to departing, we had been advised by many people not to transit the waters along the New Jersey Shore in any kind of east wind. While it can be done, it is a rough and uncomfortable ride on a boat like ours.

With regard to the wind, we try to run on days when it is blowing less than 15 knots.

The direction and speed of the wind are important factors when making decisions about passages.

On that spectacular day in September, we were filled with great hope and anticipation as we embarked on our adventure to one of the most coveted cruising areas in the country.

We ran west on Long Island Sound to Port Washington in Manhasset Bay. The 3.3-hour run was smooth, and we picked up a mooring at Knickerbocker Yacht Club upon arrival.

Manhasset Bay is near where Ray grew up in Great Neck, New York, and he learned to sail there. So we were in familiar territory.

Our plan was to catch the outgoing tide early the next morning and traverse the East River past Manhattan and head for the Atlantic Highlands. However, by evening, the wind had turned northeast. The forecast was revised, and the weathermen were predicting 15 knots or more out of the northeast for the next several days.

So we hunkered down in Port Washington to wait out the wind.

September 2, Saturday, Port Washington, N.Y.
Morning dawned with the wind out of the northeast as forecast, and the two-day outlook was for more northeast wind.

Since we were in Port Washington and had time to kill, we telephoned some of our relatives who lived in the area to see if they would like to go for a boat ride. Everyone already had plans for the day so we spent the afternoon poking around Little Neck Bay.

At 6 p.m., back in Manhasset Bay, we checked the weather. Lo and behold, the forecast had changed again. The wind was to be out of the southwest starting late in the afternoon of the following day.

Note: The wind stayed out of the south/southwest for our trip down the Jersey Shore and up the Delaware Bay into the Chesapeake. We certainly got a break in the weather.

September 3, Sunday,
Port Washington, N.Y., to the Atlantic Highlands, N.J.
We slipped the mooring at Knickerbocker Yacht Club at 6:35 a.m. and headed for the East River. It was a windless morning. We glided

past LaGuardia Airport as jets took off, roaring above our heads.

Maneuvering a favorable current underneath the Triborough Bridge and through Hell Gate, the loran read 15.2 knots over the ground. We felt as if we were flying! Our normal speed over the ground was 7.3 knots. The only other time we had topped or even approached 15 knots was during our passage through the Cape Cod Canal on a cruise to Maine in the early 1980s.

The East River and the Manhattan skyscrapers glimmered in the early morning sun. As we sped along, we waved to joggers, but no one waved back.

Automobile traffic on the East River Drive was light, and it was exciting to see New York City waking up.

As we passed Lower Manhattan and Wall Street, we waved and called out "buy low, sell high" in remembrance of the renowned financial wizard Bernard Baruch, who made those words famous (and which Ray quoted to me on one of our first afternoons on the beach on Bell Island when we first met).

Once past South Street Seaport, the Staten Island ferry boat slips and the Coast Guard's Governors Island, we entered the Upper Bay with a view of the Statue of Liberty in all her majesty. We could not spot all the floating aids to navigation shown on the chart, but we managed to weave our way safely past all the large cargo ships anchored in the Bay.

The waters turned choppy as we passed beneath the Verrazzano-Narrows Bridge and entered the Lower Bay. The wind was out of the southeast, and there were a lot of early morning sport fishermen speeding hither and yon.

The Lower Bay was larger than we had imagined it would be, and it was difficult to pick out the many floating aids to navigation. Even the "red right returning" rule used on waterways throughout the Americas didn't help much. There were too many channels converging, and it was hard to keep the respective buoys straight.

Our electronic chart, combined with radar, was a great help in identifying and leading us to our marks. This electronic support proved to be valuable even though we always had the paper charts in front of us.

As we approached the Atlantic Highlands, the waters of the Lower Bay became rough but then flattened out as we ran behind the shelter of Sandy Hook.

The mooring area in the Atlantic Highlands is protected by a long breakwater and was busy with dozens and dozens of boats buzzing about.

We picked up a private mooring that had been offered to us by an acquaintance on a sailboat moored at Knickerbocker Yacht Club. He had said he didn't use it much, and when we picked up the lines, we found them completely covered with slime and barnacles. (Yuck!)

The run from Port Washington to the Atlantic Highlands took 4.3 hours, and we arrived at 10:50 a.m. Secure on the mooring, we settled in for the rest of the day. I spent the afternoon getting a head start on a project for a client, and then we both relaxed and reviewed the charts for our trip to Barnegat Inlet. Studying the charts for the next run is a daily task when on a cruise.

The view of the Manhattan skyline with the Verrazzano-Narrows Bridge in the foreground was magnificent, particularly after the sun had set.

September 4, Monday,
Atlantic Highlands, N.J., to Barnegat Inlet, N.J.

We left early in the morning for our first run in the Atlantic Ocean down the Jersey Shore.

The sky was clear, and the wind was light. The wind picked up a bit in the afternoon, but it never blew more than 15 knots out of the southwest.

Rounding Sandy Hook, the waters were choppy due to the current running out over the 20- to 30-foot depths and the early morning fishermen in their runabouts.

Most of them scoot around in 18- to 25-footers powered by

outboards. We like them. They always are there and are the first to come to your aid if you need help. We found that to be true years ago when we went up on Ram Island Reef in Fisher's Island Sound.

The run to Barnegat was delightful – an easy passage in the open waters of the ocean. About seven miles out, we used our recently installed cellular phone (a popular new item) to call Al Gillen, a friend of ours who runs a 24' Black Fin, twin-engine recreational fishing boat out of there. He and his wife Sue Ann – with two small children, each one fast asleep on an engine box – came out to meet us and led us into the inlet.

It was Monday of Labor Day weekend, and it seemed like every boat in Barnegat Bay was running in and out of the narrow waterway at top speed.

No one slowed down. One 60' sport fisherman came barreling out, throwing a wake as high as our bridge. He did, however, slow down ever so slightly when he saw us plodding along amongst all the fast boats, wallowing in their wakes.

Boats were passing us to the left and right in both directions. It was furious. Since we were so slow – running at a steady six knots – they just scooted around us.

At the same time, the surf was breaking on the rocks of a submerged breakwater on our starboard. The water and foam spewed six to eight feet in the air as the surf broke along the rocks.

The waves also were breaking on the sand shoals on either side of the channel leading into the inlet. The channel is clearly marked with red buoys on the starboard and green buoys on the port, but we were happy to have someone show us the way in this first time. Thank you, Al.

Once inside, the scurrying about of boats at top speed did not stop until we entered a quiet anchorage called Meyer's Hole. The Gillen family came aboard for a visit, and we talked about local boating and offshore fishing.

Afterward, Ray and I had a lovely evening on board among the sand dunes, listening to the low roar of the ocean's surf and soothing sound of Barnegat Light's foghorn with the almost full moon lighting the sky. We vowed to come back to this lovely anchorage someday, but we never did.

September 5, Tuesday, Barnegat Inlet, N.J., to Cape May, N.J.
We were up bright and early and weighed anchor at 6:50 a.m. On the way out, unlike yesterday, we had the inlet all to ourselves, and it was easy running. We headed for the sea buoy off Barnegat and set a course for Cape May.

We were running from the lower helm station in the cabin versus up on the bridge as we often did when in unfamiliar waters or rough sea conditions (there's more motion up above). That habit stems from Ray's sailboat days when the only choice was to steer from the cockpit. Even though you don't have the advantage of the panoramic view from high up, it's easy to gage the water.

By around 9 a.m., our southerly course put the eastern sun right at eye level. (Note: The main salon has large windows all around – nearly a 360-degree view to the outside.) The sun was so blinding we closed the curtains on the port side for a couple of hours. It was rather comical to be running in the Atlantic Ocean with the draperies pulled!

The wind was south southwest at less than 10 knots but picked up to 15 knots by the afternoon.

Never once did we take water over the bow during our two-day transit of the Jersey Shore. We had a two- to three-foot chop on the surface, and the surf was running about four to six feet.

Most of the time, we were one-and-a-half to two miles offshore, and it was easy to read the wording on the water towers displaying the name of each town we were passing. There are plenty of buoys so navigating from mark to mark was effortless.

Throughout the day, we noticed that the electronic charting and global positioning system (GPS) were showing the courses in a true, not magnetic, heading so we had to adjust for that.

Additionally, intermittently, our speed over the ground dropped from 7.3 to 6.8 knots, then jumped up to 8.1 knots, proving that selective availability of GPS is a fact. It also made it clear to us that one cannot totally depend on GPS and electronic charting. These navigational devices are new to the recreational boating market and are not perfected yet. No doubt they will be before long.

Despite this instability, we continued using these devices, and they were helpful when cruising in unfamiliar waters. We also ran the loran, which is much more stable than GPS. We did not have differential GPS.

Radar, on the other hand, was always stable. We felt we could depend on it to show targets that were aids to navigation, other vessels or landmasses. We also used loran to track thunderstorms, but, so far, we hadn't had any of those on this trip.

We did bring a paper *Rand McNally Road Atlas* with us so we could get our bearings from the water. And, by the way, when the storms did come, weathermen identified warning areas by county name so the paper maps were a big help in tracking bad weather. (Note: Thunderstorms in the Chesapeake can be fierce.)

Arriving in Cape May late in the afternoon, we took a slip at Utsch's Marina at $1 a foot. It had the least expensive diesel fuel so far: 79 cents a gallon.

We washed down the boat. This is an important chore to do after every run if possible. It's desirable to get the saltwater off the exterior surfaces to protect the finish (salt residue is also sticky and gets on everything). If you're not in a private slip, you have to find a place to put on water (such as a town dock). We also filled the two water tanks. We carry 120 gallons in total, which lasts about four days if we're careful (that includes normal cooking and cleaning up, flushing the head, taking daily showers, etc.).

Our second day of running on the "outside," as they call it, had been a delight.

We had dinner on board and slept well.

September 6, Wednesday,
Cape May, N.J., to Chesapeake City, Md.

It was another lovely day. We left before 7 a.m. and had the Cape May Canal to ourselves as we headed for the Delaware Bay.

As we entered the Bay, the waves were short and steep off our starboard bow. It would have been a long day if that had kept up, but it didn't. The water smoothed out, and it became a millpond as we moved up the Delaware Bay. We were bound for the Chesapeake and Delaware Canal, commonly called the C&D Canal.

It was easy to spot the marks in such clear weather and smooth water plus the buoys were close to each other as we headed northwest. We were running against the current all day. We arrived in Chesapeake City at 4:34 p.m.

All the guidebooks advise favoring the right side of the entrance to the small anchorage in Chesapeake City. Thus we kept to the far right – and promptly went aground!

We had misjudged the current, which carried us farther to starboard than we had expected. So we sat there 100 feet off the shore, watching workers weld together sections of a steel bulkhead they were installing. Nobody waved to us or acknowledged our presence or our misfortune. Groundings must happen all the time.

After a while, a large powerboat passed by in the canal. It was throwing a huge wake as it slowed down to go by some boats tied up to the bulkhead in front of a restaurant.

As the wake rolled into the harbor entrance where we were aground, it lifted our boat up and off the shallow bottom. As each succeeding wave shifted the boat, we were able to inch our way into deeper water.

We circled the small harbor and selected a spot to lower our 33-pound Bruce anchor. We let out some scope and tried to back down on the anchor.

The mud was so soupy that the anchor would not hold. Finally, we decided to let out all 90 feet of our 5/16-inch chain and hoped the wind would not blow more than 15 knots. It didn't – the wind was light and variable all night. That was lucky because the anchor came right up the next morning, indicating that it had never dug in.

The grounding and poor holding ground were a disconcerting start to our navigating the thin waters of the Chesapeake and the accompanying sludge encountered in some places. The water depths in the Bay are generally much more shallow than in Long Island Sound and most of the northeast coast.

That was our worst experience (although we would have white knuckles entering and leaving some of the creeks later in the cruise), and the holding ground improved greatly in some places in succeeding days. Annapolis, on the other hand, posted notices stating that the holding ground in its local waters was generally poor. We would have to be careful and check out one harbor at a time.

September 7, Thursday, Chesapeake City, Md., to the Sassafras River

Weighing anchor at 8:45 a.m., we officially entered the Chesapeake Bay at Welch Point at 9:27 a.m. We maneuvered to the edge of the shipping channel to get as far away as possible from the huge freighters that were passing by.

We steamed past the mouth of the Bohemia River on our way to the Sassafras River, where we encountered our first field of crab pots. These fields are clearly marked by orange and white buoys that read "crab lines."

Workboats were everywhere. The fishermen, called watermen in the Chesapeake, harvest crabs, fish and oysters. These distinctive boats, called deadrise, have a V-shaped bow and square stern and are designed to navigate the choppy waters of the Bay. Stacks of crab pots are transported in the big open cockpit.

We went up the Sassafras River and anchored outside the entrance to Turner Creek and had lunch on board. Then we continued up the river to Georgetown with its many large marinas and hundreds of sailboats and powerboats at docks and moorings.

Returning to Turner Creek, we anchored just outside the entrance. We were reluctant to enter the narrow channel leading into Turner Creek after our grounding at Chesapeake City. We set the anchor in good holding ground and spent a quiet, moonlit night in the Chesapeake.

September 8, Friday, Sassafras River, Md., to Swan Creek, Md.
Out of nowhere, we heard the sound of engines and shouting. It wasn't even first light, and the watermen were already starting their day. They came within two feet of our boat, and we worried they would bump into us. But they were pros and knew how to handle their boats. The lobstermen in Maine are up early, too. They roll out of bed at about 3 a.m. and are setting traps an hour later.

We left the Sassafras River and headed for Rock Hall, which is adjacent to Swan Creek. Both places combined have at least nine marinas and are home base to hundreds of sailboats and some powerboats.

Note that these waterways can be quite large. A creek in the Chesapeake can be as wide as any major river elsewhere in the country.

We went into Swan Creek because it has moorings and room to anchor. Rock Hall has only slips. We picked up a mooring at Swan Creek Marina and had lunch on board.

Nobody came out to ask us to register as is customary in our home waters. So we dropped the mooring and puttered over to the dock. We finally were able to hail someone, who said, "Just pick up any mooring and come ashore to register." People in this part of the country are very easy-going.

We put our new 11' Avon inflatable dinghy in the water for the first time and secured the also new 8 horsepower Evinrude engine. Everything worked great.

I had been working on a project and needed to fax material to a client. The marina was happy to accommodate us. We stayed on the mooring in Swan Creek two nights so I could complete more projects.

On Sunday, we rented bicycles and rode into Rock Hall. Our lunch at the well-known Waterman's Crab House was as good as everyone said it would be.

We came back to the boat and moved to the anchorage for the night.

September 11, Monday, Swan Creek, Md., to Queenstown, Md.
We left Swan Creek mid-morning. Queenstown, just off the Chester River, was only a few hours' run.

Inching our way (it was shallow) into Queenstown Harbor, we pulled up to the town dock. Here, as at most of the town docks on the Bay, is where the watermen keep their boats. They sell the bushels of crabs and other bounty they catch each day to a buyer who waits at the dock in a white refrigerated truck.

We walked into the village three blocks away in search of a pay phone, as we would do every day or so (phone booths were scattered about in every town). We had signed up for a new phone messaging service that used a beeper to alert us of voicemail, which we accessed by phone.

Cellular phones were relatively new, and we had one on board (it was big, black and clunky). Ray had installed it in a case above the helm station so you had to reach up and dislodge it. Believe it or not, we still have the same cell number today.

We limited our usage of the cell phone because it was expensive. Costs ranged from 45-75 cents per minute plus other charges based on parameters such as within/out of a caller's network and the service provider's home territory. So we used public landlines whenever we could.

Queenstown is a miniature village with a post office, bank and Potter's Pantry, which served a delicious lunch of grilled cheese and tomato sandwich with homemade chicken noodle soup – all for $2.50. Even the noodles were homemade!

We explored the charming, quiet community, loving every minute of the peacefulness. In many ways, it was like Shelter Island. Queenstown seemed to be a sleepy little burg tucked away in the middle of nowhere. So we were surprised to learn that the highways were just a few blocks from downtown, and busy, civilized life was just around the corner. In fact, Annapolis, the state capital, is 18 miles away, generally a mere 30-minute drive by car.

Back to the town dock, we crept our way out of the channel later that afternoon and anchored in Queenstown Creek. Ray was still up on the bow, and I was at the helm when the phone rang. That was one of our first incoming calls on the cell phone. It was so strange hearing a phone ring when on board. I just stared at it and exclaimed, "The phone's ringing!" And Ray said, "Well, answer it!"

The caller was Sharon Prince from American Home Products Company. The reception was crystal clear, and we discussed some upcoming projects. What a wonderful invention this cellular phone was going to be! It would alleviate having to go ashore and walk sometimes several blocks to find a phone booth.

We were one of two boats anchored in the protected waters that night. The moon came up on cue, and we had another lovely and restful evening under the stars.

September 12, Tuesday, Queenstown, Md., to Annapolis, Md.

At 5 a.m., the watermen already were out running their crab lines. They, again, had come very close to the anchored pleasure boats even though there was plenty of space in the creek. This was becoming a morning ritual, and we were getting used to it. We no longer panicked when it appeared as if they were going to hit us. The watermen are skilled helmsmen (some just get a kick out of putting a little fear in us yachties).

We also noticed that there were no sandy beaches. This is farm country, and the grass and trees come right down to the water's edge. And, if the wind is right, one occasionally gets a whiff of horse or cow manure in the anchorages.

With eyes glued to the depth indicator and chart, we departed Queenstown Creek at a snail's pace. Our white-knuckled fingers finally relaxed once we made it through the skinny water (the water depth in some places was just under four feet so we figured we only had a couple of inches to spare without hitting bottom).

Our destination was Annapolis. America's Sailing Capital turned out to be quite a change from the pristine countryside and quiet anchorages we had been experiencing.

We made a toast to each other as we passed under the expansive and magnificent Chesapeake Bay Bridge (going under bridges on a boat is awesome – in the true sense of the word). We stayed well to the side of the main shipping channel to give plenty of room to the large freighters that go thumping up and down the Bay.

As we approached Annapolis, the water became choppier, and we threaded our way into the anchorage and picked up a mooring.

The town has 40 moorings in the main harbor, which practically takes up all the space. It is a small harbor with marinas and boat slips along every inch of the shoreline. There are more than 30 marinas in the surrounding area. And, of course, the U.S. Naval Academy is right across the waterway.

The entire basin in the main harbor is bulkheaded, which means the waves bounce around from shore to shore with no place to go (the "bathtub effect"). With so many boats coming and going, the water is never still, and our boat rocked constantly. Even the boats tied up in slips were being moved about by the wave action. Sailboats fared a little better because of their hull design, but the trawler types like us rolled all day and all night. We hardly slept.

Ashore, Annapolis is a delightful town with an ample supply of high-quality restaurants, shops, marine stores and charming hotels. And right in the middle of town, it was fun watching all the beautiful boats taking a spin through Ego Alley and the captains proudly showing off their pride and joy.

I was expecting FedEx packages, which were being shipped to me in care of the Annapolis City Marina. The people there were happy to assist and were most accommodating, as was everyone with whom we came into contact at the marinas and docks on the Chesapeake. It's a friendly part of the world.

September 13, Wednesday,
Annapolis, Md., to Leeds Creek near St. Michael's, Md.
Because of the constant rocking in the harbor, we were happy to be leaving Annapolis. We waited for my FedEx packages, which arrived at 11:30 a.m. We then slipped the mooring and headed for Leeds Creek near St. Michael's, another major center of boating activity.

We spent the night in Leeds Creek, which is across the Miles River from St. Michael's. We were the only boat in the anchorage, which is spacious enough for more than 50 vessels. We had a relaxing afternoon and evening. The holding ground was good, and we slept well.

September 14, Thursday, Leeds Creek, Md., to St. Michael's, Md.
The next morning, the watermen, as usual, were running their lines at 5 a.m. We pulled anchor at 9 a.m. and motored a mile and a half across the Miles River to St. Michael's Harbor, which is quite small.

We tied up at St. Michael's Dock Marina. The people were extremely helpful in taking our lines and securing the boat and were courteous in general. When the FedEx packages arrived the next morning, a dock person actually delivered them to our boat.

A lot of the marinas give transients little mementos. Here, we were given a package of mauve-colored cocktail napkins displaying the marina name. And a complimentary copy of *The Wall Street Journal* was dropped off every weekday morning and *The Washington Post* on Saturday. Diesel fuel was $1.09 a gallon.

It turned out that we stayed two nights there while I worked. Kay was happy to have an excuse to dink around the harbor to an office with a fax machine, sending copy to my clients.

Downtown St. Michael's is only two blocks from the marina and boasts a good supermarket. And the laundromat did our laundry for $12 (plus the normal cost to operate the machines and purchase detergent). That was a very good price. In fact, we found the price of most items to be a little lower than those at home.

St. Michael's also has some fine restaurants (we ate at the Crab

Bar) and clothing stores. It is a charming little town of about 1,000 residents and well worth a visit.

September 16, Saturday, St. Michael's, Md., to Oxford, Md.
We left St. Michael's at 9 a.m. and headed out of the Miles River to the Chesapeake Bay and down to the Choptank River, which leads to the Tred Avon River and Oxford.

Our destination was the Oxford Yacht Agency, the Grand Banks dealer in the Chesapeake. As we entered Town Creek in Oxford, we saw a sign on a big building that read "Oxford Boatyard and Yacht Sales."

We pulled up to the end of the dock and, with the help of the dockmaster, secured the boat. We put on bow, stern and spring lines and rigged several fenders to keep the boat off the pilings. Then we washed down the boat since we had had a wet run that day (heavy seas that splashed as high as the bridge at times and coated the entire exterior with salt).

After about an hour, all snug and secure, we walked up the dock to the office to register – and learned we were in the wrong place! The Oxford Yacht Agency was farther down Town Creek almost to the end.

Reluctantly, we untied all of our good work and headed down the waterway. As we approached, we saw a sign at the end of a private dock: "Overnight Dockage." We asked the person standing there if that was his dock. He said it was and that his fees were much lower than dockage at the yacht agency next door.

We tied our 36', 24,000-pound trawler to the south side of the dock. The other side was home to a 54', 64,000-pound trawler named Esprit built by the owner of the dock, Dale Denning.

It was a great arrangement, and we decided to make this dock and Oxford our home base for cruising the Chesapeake. Throughout the season, Dale rents dock space to friends and transients, and we became a slipmate to a variety of sizes and types of boats while we were there. And we would become longtime friends with Dale and his wife Kay.

September 17-October 11, 1995, Oxford, Md.
Oxford is a quiet, laid-back town with a population of 750. Yes, it is small. But it has many amenities and is a refuge from the busy and bustling outside world. It features tree-lined streets, immaculate historic homes and waterfront parks. Throughout the village, striking views can be seen of the Tred Avon River, Town Creek and the Choptank River.

The Oxford-Bellevue car and passenger ferry that crosses the Tred Avon was established in 1683 and is the oldest privately owned ferry in the country.

Oxford has the usual shops for essentials but also boasts a few unique retail establishments: A bicycle shop sells gourmet foods as well as bikes, a confectionery shop offers steaks and other frozen entrées, and the Oxford Market, an all-purpose grocery store, features homemade pies ("to die for") on the weekends.

There are a number of boatyards plus the Grand Banks dealership and the Tred Avon Yacht Club. Various other marine-related businesses are scattered about. Surrounded by water, the entire town has a nautical feel to it.

The building that houses the Robert Morris Inn was bult in 1710. It opened as an inn in 1800. Today, it is the oldest full-service inn in America. Morris, a signer of the Declaration of Independence, slept there as did George Washington and other dignitaries of the time. Ray and I frequented the restaurant and feasted on rockfish topped with crabmeat. The crab cake recipe is a deep secret that is not divulged to anyone.

Easton is 10 miles away and offers every convenience of a city.

In this happy environment, Ray and I spent about four weeks taking day trips and anchoring overnight in the local rivers and creeks. Of note, we were anchored in Edge Creek listening to the final day of the infamous O.J. Simpson trial when the Not Guilty verdict was rendered by the jury on October 3 of that year.

We took a trip to Solomons Island and ran the full length of the Patuxent River and anchored in St. Leonard's Creek.

A friend, Eileen M, drove our white Cadillac (with blue leather interior) to Oxford so we were able to get supplies and explore the Eastern Shore of Maryland by land, as well as by sea.

One rainy day (not good for boating), for example, we drove to the Delaware coast and watched the surf and smelled the salt air. In Ocean City, Maryland, we visited Assateague State Park. The famous wild horses were magnificent. Parkgoers were warned to keep a distance as the horses are, indeed, wild.

We scouted 10 boatyards in the area for a place to store the boat for the winter and decided upon a marina in Georgetown.

There were many good times socially, meeting locals and hosting friends from home. All the while, I continued to meet my deadlines with clients. It was a busy and pleasant time.

Let me say a word about my work. As you will have noticed, it was an effort on both our parts to plan our schedule around my projects. But this was a small price to pay in order to enjoy the lifestyle we had chosen: spending a lot of time on board and exploring points of interest on the waterfront.

I didn't want to give up the business I had worked so hard to build and from which I reaped so much gratification. Likewise, we didn't want to forgo long-distance cruising. So we were able to work out a plan that allowed us to accomplish both goals.

That meant working from the boat during our trips and planning around deadlines since we were gone for such long periods of time. If I were taking a one- or two-week vacation, I would have just blocked out the time. But to be unavailable for six-week stretches would have meant my clients would have had to look elsewhere for their editorial support. So our plan worked, and we both were happy with it.

We had a wonderful time navigating the Chesapeake Bay and many of its estuaries that fall of 1995. And this was just the beginning. Someone said it would take a few seasons to visit all the rivers and creeks and towns and places of interest.

Eagles, ospreys, herons, crabs, turtles, gulls, swans, geese, ducks and other species abound all over the region. We saw lots of blue herons – our boat's namesake – sporting their beautiful blue-gray feathers as they patiently stand in the shallows awaiting their prey. On the negative side, the waters also can be abundant with jellyfish and sea nettles to the point where you don't want to go for a dip.

Here is a portrayal written by our friend Lyle McGuire depicting a stay aboard Intrepid: "One summer on the Chesapeake Bay, we anchored in a quiet creek for the night and watched the full moon rise through the trees. Waking at dawn, I watched deer glide through the mist on one riverbank, while a bald eagle on the other bank rose slowly and majestically into the sky. These are the kinds of memories being with Ray and Joyce made possible."

· We loved the distinctive screwpile lighthouses (so different from the lighthouses up north and, specifically, Green's Ledge as shown on the back cover – called a sparkplug structure).

It can get rough in the Bay partly because of the many estuaries that feed into the main body of water. It's easy to get fooled because the Bay is shallow and often looks so innocent. As is the case anywhere, you have to pick your days for running.

Usually Ray was the captain, and I was the navigator. But, occasionally, he would get seasick. So he'd hand the helm over to me and retreat to the aft cabin, where it is less rocky. Since I never get seasick, I'm able to handle the bounding up and down or slogging through the water without any problem.

After spending six weeks on board, we drove to Rowayton on October 12. We spent a few days setting up a meeting for IBM in New York City. A week later, we returned to Oxford and ran Intrepid to Georgetown, where we decommissioned the boat for the winter.

Back home, we left on November 1 for Europe to set up meetings for IBM in Paris, Amsterdam and Vienna with Ray's former manager and our friend Lyle McGuire.

Speaking of Lyle makes me reminiscent of another incident on Intrepid. This boating chapter would not be complete without the

Cape Fear River story. So I'm going to tell it here – twice (You'll see: "It will all become apparent!").

Cape Fear River Story

We were on the boat in Hampstead, North Carolina, on our way to Florida. Lyle and Mary Pat McGuire joined us for a few days. Our itinerary was to traverse the Intracoastal Waterway in the Wilmington area with a destination of Southport, North Carolina. There, we would take a lay day and spend time on the beach at Bald Head Island. By the way, the lighthouse there, Old Baldy, is the oldest standing lighthouse in the state, having opened in 1817. The lighthouse helps guide ships past the treacherous shoals at the mouth of the mighty Cape Fear River. Predecessor lighthouses date back to 1794.

Our route took us through a portion of the lower river. The waterway is so wide there that large powerboats can run at high speeds and not imperil other vessels as long as they keep their distance. However, not all captains are courteous, and some ignore proper boating etiquette. Running at full bore and leaving large wakes can cause problems – and we can personally attest to that.

One such "stinkpot" was barreling along on a course heading straight toward us (called a collision course) and wasn't about to give way (even though we had right of way). At the last minute, the skipper veered off but was much too close. His gigantic wake rocked our boat unmercifully. We were thrown about the cabin, and everyone lunged for something – anything – to hold on to until Ray could get the helm under control and the boat righted itself.

Infuriated that our lives and the boat had been needlessly endangered, Ray grabbed the mic to the VHF radio and, on Channel 16 for the world to hear, shouted, "Is there no law and order on the Cape Fear River?" (Note: Channel 16 is a marine radio frequency designated for international emergency and distress calls.)

Now here's another version of the same story as told so eloquently by Lyle at Ray's memorial service.

"We joined Ray and Joyce on the Intracoastal Waterway in North Carolina. The weather was spectacular: blue Carolina skies and a soft ocean breeze. Dolphins rode the bow wave as we entered the Cape Fear River at Wilmington.

It was idyllic, serene, calm.

A perfect day.

Then a cabin cruiser on steroids came roaring past, throwing a huge wake. As Intrepid bucked and rolled, the usually soft-spoken Ray grabbed the radio mic and yelled, 'Is there no law and order on the Cape Fear River?'

The always mannered and even-keeled Ray had reached his limit thanks to a hooligan on the Cape Fear."

Another friend, David Snyder, was Ray's assistant when Ray was harbor superintendent of Five Mile River. Having worked together for years, David often referred to Ray as having a steady-at-the-helm nature. But that was not the case on an autumn day in North Carolina on the Intracoastal Waterway.

Back to our Chesapeake Bay cruise: Following our assignment in Europe, we would return to Rowayton and carry on business as usual through the winter, eagerly anticipating spring and a full boating season on the Eastern Shore.

With dozens and dozens of nooks and crannies just waiting to be explored, spring couldn't come soon enough.

Our hope was that the flowers would bloom and the grass would turn green a little earlier in the Chesapeake than in Connecticut.

Work Highlights

From an early age, I knew I wanted a career in business. So when the time came, I majored in marketing at Indiana University.

In those days, the late '60s, females in business were uncommon and opportunities rare. As stated earlier, most women who were in the workforce worked as a teacher, nurse, librarian, bank teller, secretary, stewardess or waitress.

In my senior year at IU, for example, I had an interview with a representative of an oil company for a position in marketing. At the end of the session, the recruiter looked at me and asked, "Why are you interviewing with us? There aren't any women in our company except for secretaries."

My parents supported my desire to do something beyond the norm but insisted I get a teaching license as an insurance policy. That acquiescence diverted my journey by a dozen years, but, eventually, I found a way to realize my aspirations. Many years later, my lifelong friend Loisann Crimmins, née Hartzler, and her husband Herd visited Ray and me in Marco Island, Florida, and Loisann proclaimed, "You always knew what you wanted to do."

Having landed the job at Greenwich High School and then becoming department chair after a year and a half, I had gained valuable skills that qualified me for administration. A few years later, I accepted the position of academic dean at the Berkeley School in White Plains, New York.

One reason I took the job was because Berkeley was part of ITT Corporation, and I thought it would be a foot in the door to Corporate America. In fact, once asked while at Berkeley what my professional aspiration was, I answered "to be an executive in a major corporation." The retort: "But you already are."

But Berkeley was not my end goal. I wanted to work with top

management in a multinational corporation with offices in skyscrapers in cosmopolitan cities.

In the meantime, I had a pretty good position at Berkeley. However, ITT divested the education division soon after my arrival, and Berkeley became a privately owned school again. In that leadership role, though, I honed innumerable skills that would be useful in any organization. I just had to break out of the education career path – easier said than done.

I pursued looking for ways to launch into the corporate world. Not a week went by that I didn't send out a resume or make some calls. I entered into discussions with one corporation to manage its companywide administrative assistant program, which would have been a good fit, but that didn't pan out.

One evening over dinner, Ray was telling me about the advertising campaign he had been working on for months with Geer DuBois, one of IBM's ad agencies in the city. He said, "It's all done except for Dr. Z's review." Dr. Z was a professor at Columbia University who was hired on an ad hoc basis to review IBM's ads to make sure they were grammatically correct. I immediately said, "I can do that!" Once I realized there was a niche in business for some of my strongest skills, I recognized there was a career path right before my eyes.

Here's just a little background on that. In high school, my mother taught business subjects, including typing and shorthand. Being the teacher's daughter, I had to achieve higher standards to earn the same grade as other students so that Mrs. Hizer wouldn't be accused of showing favoritism. So I worked hard and became quite adept in typing and shorthand.

Learning to keyboard properly avoids the hunt and peck form of typing. The touch typing system is the most common, whereby the student places all eight fingers on home row and keeps them there as a springboard to reach adjacent keys, always returning to home row and never visually looking at the keys.

The key for each index finger has a raised dot or bar so one can locate home row by touch, avoiding the need to look at the keyboard.

Computer keyboards today still feature a distinctive mark on the "f" and "j" keys to aid in finding the proper position.

To demonstrate how effective the system is, Mrs. Hizer would tie a bib from the back of her neck to the top of the typewriter, covering the keyboard while she typed.

Mother loved being a teacher and went beyond the call of duty to help her students. This incident exemplifies her desire to conquer a challenge: On the first day of school one year, a young man walked into her classroom and said he would like to learn to type. He was hesitant because he had lost part of a finger in an accident.

Mrs. Hizer said that was not a problem and devised a program that allowed him to master the skill. He was forever grateful, as were many of her former students. In fact, as a kid and as an adult, time and time again I heard Mother's former students telling how their typing skills had helped them in life.

In college, I took typing and shorthand as part of the requirement to get a teaching license and degree in business education and excelled in both courses. My typing was fast and quite accurate – I rarely made an error, and I always spotted a typo. Shorthand came easily to me, too, and I attained the highest scores.

One of the typing and shorthand instructors at IU was Esther Bray. On the first day of class, she distributed the outline for attaining an A in both subjects and then proceeded to test the students. My scores showed that I was in the A category already, and I was pleased. But Mrs. Bray said I had to raise those scores by 10 points in order to get an A. I didn't think that was fair, but I ended up pushing myself beyond what I thought possible and making the grade.

Mrs. Bray was one of the first female professors in what is now the School of Business at IU and played an influential role in encouraging female students to pursue great professional achievements. She was committed to sparking ambition in young women, with the intention of helping them become strong and successful and understand they could control their own fate.

She was named Woman of the Century by the *Herald-Times* in 1999, a daily newspaper in Bloomington, home of Indiana University. Mrs. Bray was married to William G. Bray, 11-term congressman in Indiana. She was a living example of the virtues she tried to instill in her students. I thank Mrs. Bray for being the trailblazer that she was and promoting high aspirations in so many young people.

My cousin Ed Hines' daughter, Sarah Mullins, has thanked me numerous times for helping to pave the way for young professionals in the business world so that women her age have been more readily accepted than in earlier times. I'm always quite moved when she talks about my contribution in that regard. Sarah has a lot of flair and is an up-and-comer. She holds a top executive position in a company in Indianapolis specializing in the swanky destination management business. She will go far (she already has).

The chairman of the department at IU was T. James Crawford (renowned author of typing textbooks). I remember how he kept his students abreast of his daughter's trials and tribulations during her high school years. Dr. Crawford said he carefully screened her dates (I, too, remember how embarrassing that was) because he wanted to be certain that the young men would be respectful to his most prized possession. I saw Jim several times after moving to the East because we both attended some of the same conferences, and he was the guest speaker at some of Berkeley's promotional events.

While at IU, I would type reports for my courses. If I did make an error, I could use the popular correction paper to cover the typo and retype the word correctly. But I chose to retype the entire page so it was flawless. For a while, my brother attended IU at the same time, and he took full advantage of my keyboarding skills for his reports (even though he could type, too. In fact, his skill of typing kept him off the battlegrounds and safely in an office when he was in the Army in Vietnam.).

Regarding shorthand, people often understate the skills that studying the subject builds.

It requires learning a written language based on sounds and combinations of letters of the alphabet, words and phrases. It encompasses listening, remembering, recording in this new language and transcribing accurately a pageful of pen strokes into English. And most important, using shorthand sharpens one's grammar skills. Of the two commonly used systems, Gregg shorthand is considered more efficient and easier to learn than the Pitman system.

In shorthand, the student is taught proper sentence construction – all about nouns and verbs and parts of speech and complete sentences and sentence fragments and parallelism and all the rest. Then the student is taught rules of punctuation and style. Combining all this results in a solid command of the English language.

As an aside, Billy Rose, songwriter/lyricist and impresario, theatre/nightclub owner and Wall Street investor who amassed a fortune, studied shorthand under John Robert Gregg, inventor of the Gregg system of shorthand. Rose could type well over 100 words a minute and take dictation at 180 words a minute. Gregg arranged for teenager Rose to make presentations demonstrating these skills and show how they could aid in achieving a successful career. In addition to being sought-after skills in business, reporters and journalists were encouraged to develop the ability to get words down on paper quickly. Shorthand was one way to accomplish that and was popular with people wanting to follow that profession.

Because of his competencies, Rose landed a job in Washington, D.C., as head stenographer for the War Industries Board under Chairman Bernard Baruch, American financier who became advisor to three presidents. After the end of World War I, Rose pursued his interests in show business. Baruch became a lifelong confidant and advised Rose on many of his investments.

Rose is credited with writing the music and/or lyrics for approximately 400 songs, including "Me and My Shadow," "It's Only a Paper Moon," "That Old Gang of Mine," "More than You Know" and "I Found a Million Dollar Baby (in a Five- and Ten-Cent Store)" to name but a few.

Today, shorthand courses are not as common as in the past as the digital age has more or less replaced the subject with newer, less complicated and easier-to-learn systems and technology.

A side benefit from teaching shorthand (and typing) was that I became a master in using a stopwatch (to time different dictation speeds and typing tests). This skill was very useful years later when I served as official timekeeper on the race committee at Corinthian and yacht club sailboat races. I could be counted on to start races and call finish times to the second.

And, by the way, all during my childhood and adolescence, Mother was correcting her own kids' grammar — at home and sometimes in public. I complained on more than one occasion, saying, "It was annoying" or "… embarrassing," but that training did leave its indelible mark.

Mother also drilled into us phone etiquette. Example: The phone rings. I say, "Hello?" The caller asks, "Is Joyce there?" I answer, "This is she" (not her). Cynthia and I have the same inflection in our speech, and even Mother couldn't always tell one from the other, and callers often had to get clarification. And if anyone in the family asked, "Where's it at?" Mother would respond, "Behind the at" to make her point (cannot end a sentence with a preposition, particularly "at").

I went on to teach typing, shorthand and business English at Greenwich High School. And at Berkeley, I was in charge of structuring the curriculum for these core subjects, along with several others. Included in every course taught, I instituted a lesson on the proper way to shake hands, as I felt it was a valuable practical skill.

My dream to build a career in the corporate world never waned. Armed with three academic degrees, experience and drive, I struck out on my own. Having spent years studying the fundamentals of the English language, I had become a master of grammar by then and could spot a typo a mile away. With sentence construction top of mind, I found I was diagramming sentences when listening to people speak (and silently correcting their grammar!).

I had a stint in market research and advertising and then began to pick up clients on an ongoing basis for copyediting projects. One of those companies was General Electric at its corporate headquarters in back country Fairfield, Connecticut, about 30 minutes north and east of Rowayton just off the Merritt Parkway.

It was a win-win situation: An arrangement was worked out whereby I could work there every day I wasn't obligated elsewhere. So I was able to take time to grow my business and still maintain a steady revenue flow. Aside from my basic skills, I was acquiring new ones. I became familiar with the business lingo and gained experience in producing brochures and a myriad of marketing collaterals. I was expanding my skillset and building a reputation as a respected copyeditor.

To add to my roster of clients, I looked for opportunity at every turn. Living in the New York metro area provided endless leads through a strong and comprehensive network of contacts, and I left no stone unturned. I went to the library and researched names of companies and specific people in a position who might need my services (today, that can be done at home on the computer). I sent dozens and dozens of letters to potential contacts. I spent hours on the phone every week trying to make inroads into the hundreds of companies of all sizes located throughout the metro area.

It paid off. Within a year, I had more work than I could handle. And it wasn't long before I could predict my schedule of projects a year out. The hardest part at the beginning was to convince people they needed my services. Once I completed work for them, they said they couldn't sleep unless I had reviewed their copy and given it my blessing.

I wanted the wording and grammar and style and punctuation – everything – to be perfect and wouldn't sign off on a project until I was 100% satisfied with it. This drove some clients crazy, but, in the end, they were happy I hadn't let anything slip through the cracks. For several years, I worked on projects with Joe Marshall from IBM. At the end of one assignment (at 3:30 in the morning), I said, "I'm happy with it." Joe retorted, "Well, if you're happy with it, I'm ecstatic!"

My skills were recognized, and, over the next three+ decades, I had the pleasure of working with highly respected companies and individuals.

I have often said: "Some people call me a proofreader because it is an easily recognizable function, but my services include so much more than that."

Specifically, I would reorder clauses for proper syntax. I would strive for clarity by reworking sentences so they read well and flowed into the copy. I would review for proper grammar. I would fact check every statistic and statement. I knew every rule of grammar and style – and the exceptions – and applied them to the copy. I watched for the duplication of words and inserted an appropriate substitute (I pursue relentlessly until I find the perfect word). I corrected any misuse of words (for example, common errors are the usage of "compared to" instead of "compared with," use of "anxious" when "eager" is intended, and the treatment of "comprise" and "peruse").

Another common error is the misuse of "proven" and "proved." Use "proven" as an adjective and "proved" as a verb. For example, "Our company has a proven track record," and "He has proved himself again and again." I pointed out redundancies (e.g., using "in addition" and "also" in the same phrase or sentence). I quickly recognized first versus second preference spellings. Consistency was my middle name. Regarding copy, it had to be right in every way, every time.

Back in Grass Creek in junior high school, I had taken Latin, taught by a prim and proper Miss Murphy (all the kids thought the "old maid" was ancient, but she probably wasn't). In fact, she organized a field trip to see "Ben-Hur," the 1959 movie starring Charlton Heston that won a record 11 Academy Awards that year (including Best Picture and Best Actor). 1959 also was the year that Alaska was admitted as the 49th U.S. state, and Charles de Gaulle was inaugurated as the first president of the new Fifth Republic in France.

One of the far-reaching benefits of studying Latin is that you learn word roots. One study shows that 30% of English words are derived from Latin. Having an understanding of the language is useful in a number of disciplines: art, law, literature, medicine, music, philosophy, science, theology. Latin fell out of favor in the 1960s, and most schools discontinued offering the course.

Having studied Latin was a tremendous help for me, particularly in my projects with the pharmaceutical companies.

I loved my work and was fascinated with vocabulary. I spent hours just browsing the dictionary, becoming familiar with new words. A friend once said, "Every time I'm with you, I learn a new word or two." The TV program "Wheel of Fortune" has been on the air since 1975, but Ray and I didn't start watching it until just a few years ago. It's a game show based on the spelling and usage of words and phrases. In the comfort of my living room, I always do pretty well.

As mentioned above, I had studiously learned all the rules and exceptions to the rules pertaining to grammar, punctuation and style. There are several respected style guides, principally among them: *The Elements of Style* by Strunk and White, *The Chicago Manual of Style*, and *The New York Times Manual of Style and Usage*. I became familiar with them and could accommodate a client if the company style was predicated on one of those style guides. But the reference used most often by corporations across the country is *The Associated Press Stylebook*, and I advise following that style whenever possible.

For a large or ongoing project, it often helps to create a style guide for that specific assignment for ease in maintaining consistency. Regarding favored dictionaries, most companies consider *Merriam-Webster* the "Bible," but I prefer *The American Heritage College Dictionary* because it includes hundreds of usage notes with examples that make the treatment of words crystal clear.

As the years go by, I am concerned that the bar is being lowered when it comes to the general public's knowledge of the vernacular. I have said many times, "Proper speaking skills and writing competency across the board are getting worse."

Work Highlights

One of my pet peeves is the misuse of the proper usage of the article "a" versus "an." The rule is simple: Use "a" before a word that starts with a consonant sound (plus "w" and "y"); use "an" before a word that starts with a vowel sound. Just remember, it's the sound that determines which article to use, not the actual letter (including silent letters).

A common mistake is the usage of "an" before "historic." It should be "a historic" because the "h" is pronounced (versus, for example, "honest" where the "h" is silent). You wouldn't say "an history book."

To make it simple, I've created a tutorial.

Proper Usage of "a" versus "an"	
"a" Precedes Consonant Sound	"an" Precedes Vowel Sound
a gnawing	an accountant
a historic	an apple
a history	an articulate
a knot	an enviable
a knowing	an essay
a national	an essential
a physics	an herb
a pneumatic	an honest
a psalmist	an hourly
a psycho	an important
a reddish	an insurance
a unique	an M.B.A.
a unit	an ointment
a wise	an opening
a withdrawal	an RV
a wonderful	an SUV
a yacht	an umpire
a yam	an understanding

There are always some in-vogue expressions that the in-crowd likes to use that, many times, abuse basic grammar rules. Right now, ending a sentence with a preposition tops the list ("we need to know where we're at" instead of using proper grammar and saying "where we are"). The other egregious error is using the second preference or British spelling of "toward" ("towards"). It hurts my ears to hear these mistakes being spoken everywhere I turn.

Another common error is noun/verb agreement ("there's hundreds of people interested" instead of "there're hundreds of people interested").

From news commentators and sports broadcasters to those who answer help questions on the phone, so many people massacre the English language, and their elocution is lacking. John Livingston, pastor of our church, is an exception. I've told him how much I appreciate his mastery of the language, not to mention his articulation and delivery. John's messages are always moving, and he parlays words into inspiration and action. He tells parents that they can give their children two legacies: roots and wings.

Ray was always by my side throughout those years of long workdays. Being in the communications field, he taught me many lessons along the way that improved my work. For example, he said, "Always start with the headline, whether you're writing or speaking. Then describe the subject. Then summarize what you just said. And be succinct."

I worked on that all my life. Another basic Ray taught me was the KISS principle: Keep it simple, stupid (term thought to be coined by Kelly Johnson). He also said it's easier to write about subjects you know best.

Aside from tips and guidance about work, Ray took care of the shopping and cooking so I would have more time at my desk to satisfy my clients' needs.

Sometimes when he was on his way out to do some errands, he would kid me and say, "Don't forget to clean in all the corners," knowing full well I would be working in my office and not cleaning the house.

He also gave me moral support, as well as assistance with the computer and operations – he was my ops guy.

Wherever we were, Ray was able to set up a makeshift office so

I could meet my deadlines – from the rental house in Florida for 10 winters to the temporary quarters in two Rowayton locations after Superstorm Sandy to the boat all summer long.

After Ray passed away, I struggled to figure out all the tech stuff.

Full Spectrum of Projects and Clients
My clientele has included many Fortune 500 corporations, as well as medium and small businesses and design houses. No matter the size or importance, I have valued every single company and project.

Early on, Xerox and General Electric were steady clients. The Xerox building was located in downtown Stamford, Connecticut, and featured a striking bright red sculpture on the front lawn.

In those days, many corporations were vacating New York City and relocating their facilities to suburbia and, often, purchasing sprawling tracts of land spread out in pastoral country settings. Executives were drawn to the suburbs because of lower tax rates, good schools and family-friendly towns.

IBM moved its base of operations in 1963 from New York City to undisturbed open space in the country. The facility sits majestically atop a hill in Armonk, New York, a hamlet in Westchester County 37 miles north of Midtown Manhattan. And GE, after exiting New York City in 1974, was headquartered for 42 years near the Merritt Parkway in Fairfield, Connecticut, nearly 50 miles from Midtown Manhattan.

The current-day trend is back to the city – young people want to work and live in a vibrant urban setting. GE moved its headquarters to Boston in 2016, selling its 66-acre property to Sacred Heart University. When I was working on-site at GE in the mid-'80s, the two six-story buildings (three stories above ground and three below) spanned the beautifully maintained grounds. It was a thrill to drive up to the entry gate and present my pass and a privilege to park in the employee parking lot, eat in the employee cafeteria and shop in the employee store.

VCRs had just become popular. I would rent a machine (about the size of a suitcase) complete with several movies and drag all the gear down to the underground parking garage to my car. Then Ray and I would binge on movies all weekend – titles like "Top Gun," "Back to the Future," "Star Wars," "Scarface," "The Shining" and "Ghostbusters." We ended up buying the "Top Gun" videotape (and later CD) starring Tom Cruise and watched it at least a couple of times a year every year thereafter. And we never tired of watching the 1972 film "The Godfather."

Aside from the usual corporate communications projects, there were a number of one-of-a-kind assignments. One of my first notable special projects was working on the biography of Richard Perkin, co-founder of the Perkin-Elmer Corporation, headquartered here in Norwalk, Connecticut. The company was a leader in the precision optics business and, among other highlights, built the optical components for the Hubble Space Telescope.

To celebrate the company's 50th anniversary, Dick's wife Gladys was interested in publishing his life story and the founding of the company. A *New York Times* reporter was hired to do the research and write the story, interviewing people across the globe who had known Dick.

Gladys contacted longtime employee Tom Fahy, who agreed to take what had been written and get it ready for production. I was brought in to help make that happen. I had the pleasure of meeting with Gladys at her home several times. The book was published and was well-received.

Another interesting project I worked on over the course of a few years in the mid-1990s was the biography of William Simon, who served as treasury secretary under President Richard Nixon. A colleague from IBM, Kendra Bonnett, was handling the assignment and interviewed about a hundred people who had known Simon. My role was to edit the transcripts. Interviewees ran the gamut from top government officials such as George Shultz, who served under four presidents, to Wall Street tycoons to Simon's personal friends, many

Work Highlights 165

of whom were household names.

My clients spanned the world of industry and commerce. Not long after starting the business, my motto became "R&R." That didn't stand for "rest and recreation" as one would expect – it stood for "repeat business and recommendations."

Joyce in her office in Rowayton.

For a while, every time I landed a new client or huge project, Ray would go out and buy a lottery ticket to celebrate, but we never won a penny. Cynthia had lived in Atlanta for many years by then and said the southern expression for something extremely good happening in one's life is "landed in cream." I made a toast using that idiom many times.

So R&R is how my business grew. I would do work for one client, who would recommend me to colleagues and friends. When that client was promoted, I was recommended to the successor. And if the original client took a job at a different company, that person would spread my name around the new organization. For example, Jon Diat, one of my clients who did very well, was with four different Fortune 500 companies during his 25-year career. He is retired now and runs his boat out of Sag Harbor, New York, every chance he gets and writes a weekly fishing column for *The East Hampton Star*. And by the way, one of his neighbors is *the* Jimmy Buffett.

From the beginning, there always seemed to be one anchor company that monopolized my time. First it was General Electric, and then it was IBM and then Wyeth and then FTI Consulting.

In each case, my workload for that particular client was nearly a full-time job in and of itself. I was continuously juggling projects in order to meet deadlines as other clients would send assignments simultaneously. The anchor company generally had an arrangement with me whereby my contacts would ask me to support a specific division or divisions of communications at headquarters. Then they would send a notice of my availability to the communications people at locations across the country and, in many cases, the world. So people around the globe would contact me directly to do work for them.

I never knew what project from which location might come in on any given day, but the one sure fact was that an assignment would come in from someone. There were countless times when I had 15-20 projects in the queue. It was not uncommon to clock a 90-hour week. And I generally worked 60-70 hours a week, month after month, not to mention the occasional all-nighter.

Due to the continuous heavy workload, I was always on the lookout for someone to help me. But until fairly recently, I was unsuccessful in finding a person who had the knowledge base and business experience to meet the standards my clients expected. Late in my career, I had occasion to work with Sharon Steinhoff from J.P. Morgan, and she had the skillset and work ethic that I needed. She subsequently left the company. We have collaborated on a number of projects, and I value her input. And thank you, Sharon, for your comments on this memoir.

So, yes, there were sacrifices made in building the business. In fact, my teenaged niece Julia Hizer once asked me if it was possible to have a successful career and raise a family at the same time. I said a lot of women do that. Although extremely capable, Julia chose not to pursue a career outside the home. She and her husband Jason Wagner live in Cincinnati and have five children, and Julia is home schooling them.

After working a dozen hours on any given day, I would close the office anywhere from 9 p.m. to 11 p.m. I would spend the remainder of the evening with Ray, warm up the dinner he had prepared earlier, watch some TV (maybe a ball game) and then relax for an hour reading a book before calling it a night, generally around 1:30 a.m. (early on, it was more like 3 a.m. when I might have had a particularly heavy workload and had to work even later than normal).

I read all kinds of books but especially enjoyed stories about men and women making it to the top. According to my log, I averaged reading 40 books a year. That's about 1,500 books during my adulthood. But Ray read more than twice that many. We both have been ardent supporters of Rowayton Library.

Here's a quick side story that illustrates Ray's passion for reading. His first job after graduating from college was with Walden Book Company, headquartered in Stamford, Connecticut. In those days, book companies rented space within department stores. Ray's job included setting up exhibits in retail establishments around the region.

One particular day, the president of the company asked Ray to ride along to visit one of the stores (I think it was Macy's). During the conversation, the top executive asked Ray how he liked his job and why. Ray's response wasn't what one would expect – extolling his virtues and detailing his successes – he merely said, "I love to read."

Even with a heavy workload and long days, there was time for pleasure, specifically television in the evenings, and Ray and I followed a number of TV programs. During the '80s, '90s and early '00s, some of our favorites were "Cheers," "Hill Street Blues," "LA Law," "Seinfeld," "Law & Order," "NYPD Blue," "Friends," "Frasier."

Ray would head upstairs to bed around 11:00, and I would watch the news and then a late-night program. I enjoyed, of course, Johnny Carson on "The Tonight Show" and still remember Bette Midler's farewell to Johnny on his last show when he retired in 1992, singing "One More for My Baby (and One More for the Road)." I then became a fan of Jay Leno. I also watched "The Late Show" with fellow Hoosier

David Letterman. The little gap between his two front teeth always reminds me of my cousin Ed Hines, who has a similar dental feature and actually has been mistaken for the late-night talk show host.

Early on at Bell Island Enterprises, we had converted one of the upstairs bedrooms overlooking Rowayton Avenue to the west into an office for me (Ray took the other corner room facing west for his office). Mine was a good-sized space with eight windows that lent an open-air feeling with a view of Five Mile River. So being ensconced in my office all day wasn't too confining because I had the sense of being outside. Up and down the street, I could watch the comings and goings of people taking a stroll or walking their dog. And on the river, I could watch boats going out and coming in. It's still that way – except my view of the river has been diminished due to more and bigger houses being built.

Ray was always trying to make my work environment better. He experimented with an assortment of lamps to make it easier for me to read the fine print that I often had to review. He had me try out different office chairs. He was always coming home from Staples or some office supply store with a surprise.

I never seemed to tire and normally would work through the day without taking a break, which tended to interrupt my concentration. Ray and I had a house joke about one of my favorite pastimes. If I was bone tired and just couldn't face reviewing another page, I would reconcile the bank statements for a little light reading.

From the beginning, I kept detailed records of our expenses and income and constructed a balance sheet and asset valuation every month along with a full roster of quarterly and annual summaries and analyses. I liked knowing where we stood financially, and it was relaxing to compile the numbers.

After I had the statements ready, Ray and I would go over them and analyze our financial situation. We were a great team: I was the detail person, and Ray saw the big picture. Money management was important to both of us. From the time I started working way back in Culver, I took the first 10% of my paycheck and deposited it in a savings account.

Regarding my revenue, on any given day of the year, I would add up my hours (I've always charged by the hour) on all the open projects and add that amount to the accounts receivable total and determine my year-to-date revenue. Whatever the total was, I would compare it with the amount one year ago, two years ago, five, etc., and try to figure a way to beat those numbers.

I was always in competition with myself and set quotas. That also enabled me to project year-end income so I would get the numbers right for the estimated quarterly income tax payments.

Yes, the days were packed full. With such a rigorous work schedule, I have always had trouble empathizing with those I considered to be slackers and have had little patience or tolerance when those same people complained about how much they did or how hard they worked.

It was during my time with IBM (in the '90s) that I realized my aspiration of having an office in Manhattan, albeit part time. The publications group with whom I worked in White Plains, New York, was relocated to New York City for a period of time. I was thrilled when my nameplate was mounted on the wall and I applied for my ID badge for the New York City location.

Prior to and after that, I met with clients across the city, and a view of skyscrapers was not uncommon. I had attained my dream – working in New York City in an office with glassed-in windows from floor to ceiling – the dream I had envisioned one autumn day at Indiana University as I walked around the old sunken football stadium in that gold corduroy coat and those brown leather boots and exuded confidence and excitement about my future life.

Life was good, and I was happy.

Most companies maintained a cafeteria for employees. GE's was the best. But the food was good at Xerox and IBM, too. When I was single, lunch served as my main meal. Way back at Greenwich High School and then Berkeley, the food was excellent at both institutions.

And don't forget those free lunches at the State Exchange Bank in Culver, Indiana, oh! so long ago.

After getting married, dinner became the main meal, and Ray and I would share the day's activities over a fine repast. Until the latter part of my career, we would eat in the dining room most every night with a dozen candles burning, and we, literally, wore out our china and crystal (a replacement set of china was purchased after about 20 years). Over time, we acquired nautical artwork (mostly from the Mystic Seaport Museum) that features special lighting to complete the dining ambience. We also had a ship's model of Aquila and Intrepid custom made that added to the atmosphere.

Many of the projects were for clients based in London, and I became well-versed in British English. Because of the time zone difference, I sometimes had to work crazy hours. Let's say the client sent a project at the end of their workday and needed it back the next morning. At 5 p.m. in London, it is noon here, and at 9 a.m. the next morning in London, it is 4 a.m. here. So, when necessary, I would work into the wee hours to meet the deadline.

I had been a night owl since high school so this schedule was not a hardship (just don't ask me to get up at sunrise!). I served customers all over Europe and a few in Asia. I loved working with my clients, and they always treated me with the highest respect.

Through the years, the client list grew, but I also lost some companies – sometimes because of a restructuring or change in the business plan but primarily due to a merger. For example, I had developed a long-term relationship with Champion International, but it was acquired by International Paper Company in 2000. I had worked with Wyeth (earlier named American Home Products Corporation) since 1988 until it was acquired by Pfizer in 2009.

A number of my contacts at Wyeth retired when the acquisition was finalized, and I was saddened to see the entity fade away. I had worked with Rich Feldheim and his team on the annual report for 22 seasons, and we had become friends.

Four companies had been a client of mine for more than 20 years: JPMorgan Chase, Morgan Stanley, Russell Reynolds Associates and Wyeth. The people changed during that period, but the companies remained loyal.

Along with my M.B.A., I had a master's degree in counseling. I never officially practiced, but I felt the skills learned enabled me to work with clients (and people in general) more effectively. Here are a couple of takeaways: First, the training teaches one to become a better listener. That's invaluable – understanding what the other person is really saying, not what you want them to say or think. John Livingston, our pastor at church, told this story one time upon officiating a wedding. Just before the ceremony started, the groom said: "John, you've been married a long time. What's your secret?" John thought for a moment and then replied: "Being a good listener."

A second lesson is the suggestion to strike the word "should" from one's vocabulary as it is judgmental and often causes defensiveness (for example, "You should have done x" versus "I wish you would have done x").

The clients represented the full gamut of industries. Most were large conglomerates that are household names. In addition to IBM and other tech corporations, there was a heavy concentration of pharmaceutical companies (Wyeth, Merck, Pfizer, Mylan Labs, Endo, Amgen, among others) and investment banking organizations. I have worked with Morgan Stanley for more than 30 years. And I have worked with JPMorgan Chase or a predecessor company for more than two decades, most of those years with a designer named Gerben Hooykaas. And I've teamed up with communications specialists at Citigroup for 15 years. After so long, these colleagues become friends as well.

I always believed that every company was important regardless of size and that every project deserved the same high level of dedication.

Mostly, I work out of my home office in Rowayton, which Ray called Bell Island Enterprises World Headquarters, but I worked on-site or attended meetings all over the metro area, specifically New York City.

On many a morning, I could be seen racing along the platform to catch the commuter train with nary a minute to spare. Grand Central Terminal itself is an institution. It was thrilling to be among the throngs scurrying past the Information Booth and the famous clock on top, heading to the office or an appointment.

And the return commute was just as exciting. With no cell phones, there would be long lines at the bank of phone booths with people calling home with their ETA. A conversation might go like this: "Hi, there! I'm taking the 5:44 and will arrive at 6:34. What's for din-din?" I waited my turn to call Ray so he could come fetch me.

Rather than being dropped off and picked up, many commuters drive to the station, often purchasing a "station car" just for that purpose. Getting a seasonal parking pass, however, can be a scramble. There are never enough spaces so it becomes competitive.

Every September, heads of state and government from around the globe meet in New York as part of the United Nations (UN) General Assembly to discuss international issues. Due to the security measures necessary when these high-profile dignitaries are in town, many streets are closed to the public to accommodate escorts and allow these world leaders to move freely about the city.

As a result, congestion on the remaining streets is heightened. Average speed can drop to under four miles an hour. The dates that the UN General Assembly is in session are considered Gridlock Alert Days, and alternative modes of transportation are highly encouraged.

One such September, I was working on-site at a client location about 30 blocks from Grand Central Terminal. There were, virtually, no taxis around so I walked the distance in the morning (in my high heels carrying a heavy briefcase). At the end of the day, I desperately looked for a taxi. I just couldn't face walking another 30 blocks back to Grand Central. But there was not a taxi in sight.

Out of the blue, a young, energetic person came up to me and asked if I needed a ride. I looked around and saw that he was the driver, or puller, of a rickshaw (a two-wheeled passenger cart to be pulled by a person on foot). I said "YES!" to this gift from heaven.

It was delightful. This kid squeezed in and out and weaved between idling cars and cabs sitting in gridlock all the way to 42nd Street and Park Avenue. It was a breeze – and fun!

At Christmastime, corporate headquarters and office locations throughout the area spare no cost when it comes to decorating inside and outside. My heart would skip a beat as I proudly entered those buildings, wearing a fashionable business suit, silk blouse and high heels (before the days of "business casual") and carrying one of my many handsome leather briefcases. It was a thrill to see all the men and women dressed in their best corporate attire. I loved dashing into those office buildings and all that that represented.

I was living my dream.

I also had the privilege of traveling a fair amount to manage certain aspects of a conference or to handle a specific responsibility.

One of my favorite trips was to an IBM recognition event held in Palm Springs, California. Included among the entertainers brought in for the week were Bill Cosby, K.T. Oslin and Roger Williams. I happened to see Williams in the lobby one morning and had the opportunity to tell him how much I had enjoyed his show the night before. In fact, I have a photograph of the two of us.

Another time, I had flown into LaGuardia and was heading to Baggage Claim, where I spotted my surname on the placard being held by the limo driver. He was a handsome young man with blond hair and blue eyes, wearing a gray uniform complete with cap. He said he had a surprise for me: I would be traveling to Connecticut in a stretch limo at no extra charge.

On the ride home, he put on a CD featuring Linda Ronstadt accompanied by the Nelson Riddle orchestra. The chauffeur said he had been hired to drive around New York City the previous evening and had played this popular album and served champagne to the guests. I thought that sounded very romantic, and I bought the CD and enjoyed

Ronstadt's music for years. One of my favorites was "Someone to Watch Over Me," and I thanked my lucky stars I had my beloved Ray in my life. He was always there waiting and welcoming me home.

Joyce dressed for work – a wardrobe packed with business suits, silk blouses, high heels and, of course, the requisite leather briefcase.

The jobs covered the entire spectrum of the written word. Many of the assignments were for top-level executives (including chief executive officers (CEO) and board of directors) who became personally involved. I worked on projects ranging from product brochures, external newsletters, press releases and employee publications to whitepapers, training materials, surveys, benefits plans, management transcripts and executive speeches.

At Russell Reynolds Associates, for example, I reviewed hundreds of whitepapers and surveys over a multi-decade period.

But annual reports, 10-Ks and proxy statements became my specialty, and I always referred to the period January through April as my "busy season," akin to an accountant's "tax season."

In later years, I became involved in the copy for company websites. And through it all, I helped many a corporation develop a style guide that was distributed companywide and became gospel to its employees. On more than one occasion, I led an on-site grammar seminar loaded with everyday tips on grammar, style and consistency.

Over the last decade, corporate responsibility reports have become in vogue, and every company is expected to publish one. Pulling together an organization's accountability surrounding charitable contributions and sustainability has kept me busy in the off-season.

As mentioned earlier, I worked on dozens of one-of-a kind projects. Through the years, a number of clients produced a publication detailing the company's history. They were always beautifully done and took months to put together.

At JPMorgan Chase, I was asked to assist in producing an art book that features photos of the company's art collection housed in facilities around the world. It's a handsome coffee table size and contains 340 pages of stunning photographs and art descriptions. I was also involved in finalizing the copy for the bronze plaques that are mounted outside each entrance to JPMorgan Chase's 10 dining rooms on the top floor of the company's world headquarters. I like to say that my words have been "set in stone."

Once in a while, I even get mentioned in the credits or acknowledgments or on the masthead. That is rare, though, and I am content not to be in the limelight or to be singled out (Ray was the same way). Additionally, I have reviewed copy for a couple of people who self-published, including Lynn Slavin, who wrote a book about anticipatory grief.

Design houses have been another source of leads, and I worked with a number of notable and highly respected design firms in New York City and in Fairfield and Westchester counties.

Early on, I did a lot of work for Jack Hough Associates here in Norwalk and then Context when Tom Morin started his own firm. Tom's book *Threads of Influence* was well-received in the design world, and his works were donated to Yale University and are housed in the Haas Family Arts Library.

Kurt Gibson, principal at Inergy Group, once said, "After about 20 years in the design business, you have done it all. There isn't a project out there you haven't seen. It's our job to create a fresh new look every time." After so many years in the field, I, too, have worked on about every kind of project that exists in corporate communications. Kristin Gibson, Kurt's wife and co-principal of their firm, and I go back a long time. Ray introduced us in 1993 when we were working as contractors for IBM at COMDEX, a computer expo trade show that was held in Las Vegas every year from 1979 to 2003.

When asked what traits have contributed to my success, I answer "a good memory."

Throughout high school and college, it was brought to my attention that I possessed unusually strong memorizing skills. In fact, this entire book was mainly written by putting on paper events that I was able to pull from my mind. That capability has served me well in my work. For example, if a certain statistic is mentioned on page 10 and then referenced incorrectly on page 90, I would be expected to catch the error.

Part of the secret is working in a quiet space. Whether in my office, on the dock or on location at a press check, I often wear earmuffs to mute sounds so I have complete concentration.

Other important traits include stick-to-itiveness and patience.

The annual report is a top priority for a public company, and, from the beginning, as stated above, I spent the first quarter of each year inundated with reviewing annual reports, 10-Ks and proxy statements. In many cases, I was asked to accompany the team on the annual report press check. This was beneficial because, inevitably, there would be changes to the copy, and we had to get it right. Generally speaking, a mistake in the annual report could mean the loss of one's job. So, as Ray would say, the FUD factor meant business for me (FUD stands for Fear, Uncertainty and Doubt).

These press checks were most often grueling. The closer it was to press time, the longer the days. It was not uncommon to work 18 hours straight, grab three or four hours' sleep and then work another 18 hours. By the time the week was over, our days and nights were turned upside down.

But it was exciting.

Spanning my career, I have reviewed hundreds of annual reports. But I always felt every project was critical – from copy for a coffee mug (the first project for FTI Consulting) to the annual report for the Fortune 500 company printing a million+ copies.

I never left anything to chance. Fact checking is an important part of my services, and, in addition to grammar and style, I would research every fact on every page.

Press Checks

Let's talk about what happens on an annual report press check.

Printing plants in and of themselves deserve some commentary. They generally are large structures situated in an industrial park of a city or out in the boondocks where real estate is less expensive. Note that although the printing facility usually is located far from the madding crowd, the annual report review team stayed in a luxury hotel in town, which made the sojourn more appealing.

And we had the opportunity to have dinner out at some very fine restaurants – usually at the beginning and/or end of the trip. Every city had a few standouts, and we tried them all. One of our favorites was Ruth's Chris, where they serve the best cuts of beef sizzling hot on a 500-degree plate.

Most plants house several presses that are used for various kinds of print jobs. For just one annual report, two or three different presses might be used for the various types of paper selected or the size of the run; for example, slick glossy paper for the magnificent photographs in the shareholder letter and marketing section, heartier stock for the covers and newspaper stock for the financial section.

Then there are various presses used for the number of pages, called signatures, always in multiples of four. A typical signature is

16 pages, but this can vary by press size or width of the paper. The bindery requires that a signature consist of at least four pages, and that's why there sometimes are one to three blank pages at the end of a publication.

For long books, a signature of more than 16 pages is common, say 32 or 64 pages. A 16-page signature can be divided into four units of four pages or two units of eight pages for the shorter sections, again printed on varying stock.

The paper often comes in large rolls, sometimes chest high.

Printing plants also contain customer lounges. Each company is assigned a large room or suite of rooms with desks and chairs, easy chairs and chaise lounges, and a kitchenette. Food is brought in, and there is a ready supply of sodas and snacks. During downtime, the group might play music or watch a movie. One printing company in California actually had a slot machine and pool table in the customer lounge.

The lounge becomes "home" for the group for the duration of the press check. I always requested my own office or private room so I could concentrate in a quiet place and be away from conversations, ringing phones and noise in general while working. I would pack a carry-on suitcase filled with essentials for the week, including earmuffs, magnifying glass, reference books and dictionaries, background materials, previous rounds of edits, a metal pica ruler, red pens, paper, Post-it notes, Sharpies and a whole host of other office supplies. I even took a high-intensity lamp because the lighting at the printing plants and hotel rooms (yes, I read in my room sometimes when the others had a break) was not always good.

The printing process has evolved over the years and is faster and less cumbersome these days. In fact, there is significantly less printing being done due to the Internet. But back in the day, it was quite involved.

The first phase was to finalize the copy for one signature at a time. There always were changes. Sometimes it was because an executive at the company decided the wording wasn't right and conveyed the wrong meaning or a number wasn't correct or, in some cases, some event occurred that needed to be mentioned as press time drew near. My responsibility was to make sure the copy reflected the final version, that it was factually accurate and that there were no errors.

During busy times, most plants run a three-shift day and print round the clock. If there are changes to the copy, it could add large chunks of prep time, sometimes up to eight to 12 hours.

Press time is booked well ahead of the printing date, often months in advance. Most of the reputable printing plants get booked solid. So if a company gets behind schedule due to a lot of changes that translate into multiple eight- to 12-hour delays, hefty overtime charges can go into effect.

The next step is to read and approve the proof sheets for a given signature. This is the final opportunity to check the copy to make sure each page is accurate in every way and that the color is right.

Once the proof sheets are approved, the presses start to roll. Due to the tight press schedule, the team would be required to convene anytime day or night when the proof sheets were ready for review, thus the reason for the crazy hours.

The annual report is a document required by the U.S. Securities and Exchange Commission to be filed by a public company. It's also the company's chance to provide shareholders, as well as potential shareholders, and analysts with an in-depth view of the organization.

It's a high-visibility, sensitive piece. Therefore, great care is taken to make sure it is 100% accurate and presents the right tone and face to the world.

There was one occasion where sensitivity was the basis for a costly decision. This particular company had signed off on the proof sheets for a 32-page signature, and the presses were running.

The paper stock that had been selected months earlier was a handsome light gray. Due to the texture, the ink on the proof sheets was dimmer than had been expected. There was concern that readers might think the company was not being transparent, trying to make the report difficult to read and understand (the Enron debacle of 2001 and subsequent bankruptcy were fresh in everyone's mind).

Much discussion ensued, and the decision was made to stop the presses, order new paper stock that would take 24-36 hours for delivery and start anew.

That was a big decision considering the overtime charges and extra days of hotel and meal expenses for the team, not to mention the waste in discarding the thousands of already printed pages. But that's how sensitive companies are about transparency – they want the shareholder to be fully informed.

These press checks took me to plants across America. A couple of my clients had a long-standing relationship with Anderson, a printing firm in California. Every year, the team would head to Los Angeles, check into a resort hotel on the beach in Santa Monica and prepare for the printing of the annual report.

This group considered the trip an excuse to dine at the finest restaurants and then party through the night, LA style. Each trip, the team had a standing reservation at Ivy At The Shore, and we were sure to see some movie stars (Mel Gibson was just as handsome in person as on the silver screen).

On this particular night, I went back to my hotel room after dinner to prepare for the morning's work. But the others were off to the Beverly Hills Hotel to close up the bar. Later, they returned to our hotel bar and took a bottle of champagne to the pool for a nightcap and swim. Having called it quits around 4 a.m., the wake-up call came way too early. They dragged themselves out of bed after a couple of hours of sleep and staggered to the printing firm barely able to function.

But they said all would be fine: "Joyce will take care of everything."

To both my chagrin and my relief, there have been several occasions where I caught an error that was serious enough to require stopping the presses: chagrin because I hadn't caught it earlier and relief because I had caught an error that no one else (often dozens of people) had noticed, albeit late in the process. Sometimes you see things when you're under that kind of pressure that you just don't notice otherwise.

Speaking of pressure, yes, there is pressure. Let me paint the picture: Since it's my responsibility to make sure every word is correct, I feel I need to read all the copy as close to press time as possible. There are thousands of items to check – from spellings to word divisions to grammar to fact checking. This should have been done earlier, but I always confirm everything again at press time.

And I check and double check that all changes were made properly and did not create new problems and that nothing has dropped out. There is a lot to verify, and it takes time.

Fortunately, my clients have been very understanding of the time requirement, but I was always aware that they were waiting for my sign-off so I tried to move along as quickly as possible so as not to incur overtime press charges.

On a couple of occasions, I had back-to-back press checks at the same printing firm for different companies. That was tough because I didn't have a chance to recoup or regroup between the two – and it was a long time to be away from home and Ray.

Another press check took me to Minneapolis, Minnesota, five months after I had broken my ankle on the boat. On the way home, I had to change planes in Chicago and walk the length of O'Hare Airport. My foot was so sore and swollen, it took days to recover.

It wasn't all work, though.

I had fun times on some of those trips. Sprinkled throughout the grueling schedule over the years were lots of opportunities for dinner at fine restaurants or treats from specialty shops.

And, after the printing was finished, I sometimes stayed an extra day and took in the local sights. On one trip to California, I spent a day at Disneyland. Of special note, on another occasion, I rented a car, drove from Los Angeles to San Pedro and took a high-speed ferry to Catalina Island "26 miles across the sea."

Today, the procedure is a little different. First of all, most people read the annual reports and financials online so the number of printed copies is greatly reduced. And many companies have eliminated those magnificent marketing sections and extraordinary photos. Instead, the emphasis is on the financials accompanied by a letter from the CEO and maybe some infographics.

Second, most everyone on the team works remotely. The drafts are sent electronically to each person. Because of that, security becomes critical, and we all get vetted and have sophisticated systems to prevent any problems. And we have access to tech support 24/7. The hours are still long and late, but, working from home, we can grab a few hours' sleep whenever we can. I just stock up the fridge with food for a week or two at a time and never leave the house. The designer generally is the only person needed on press.

Armed with earmuffs and magnifying glass, Joyce reviewing proof sheets on an annual report press check.

In a way, I miss the love-hate experience of getting on a plane and traveling to a printing plant, knowing that by the end of the week my days and nights will be turned upside down. Gone are the times we had to get up at 3 a.m. and drive half an hour or more in all kinds of weather to the plant to check proof sheets or attend to some problem. I now do that from the convenience of my home office – whether it's

3 p.m. or 3 a.m. These are all great memories for me, and I have been known to say, "Ah! There's nothing like the smell of the ink."

Wyeth: Blizzard/Stretch Limo Stories
For more than two decades, I went on the press check for the Wyeth annual report. Initially, we went to Cincinnati, then Rochester (New York) and then New Jersey.

On a trip to Rochester one year, a blizzard dumped 42 inches of snow on the region. At one point, the wind was blowing so hard the snow was coming down horizontally.

I had flown in from Florida and had purposely chosen not to bother lugging winter garb from Connecticut to Florida to Rochester and then back to Florida and Connecticut since the duration entailed only one week and it would be March – how bad could the weather be?

Well, I was caught off guard and probably was the only person in upstate New York without appropriate apparel. Since the city was shut down and the shops closed, I called Lost & Found at the hotel to see if I could borrow, for starters, a pair of gloves and a scarf. The attendant said it was against hotel policy to parcel out items, even temporarily, to patrons. I did survive the storm aftermath but went prepared for the worst possible weather every year thereafter.

When the press check location was changed to a plant in New Jersey, Wyeth graciously offered me car service to and from the plant. I was relieved because I had driven to press checks in Jersey for other clients and had gotten hopelessly lost.

So one snowy evening, a limo – a stretch limo, mind you – showed up at the house. First off, the long, black, shiny car had trouble turning around on the narrow streets of Rowayton. But the most memorable part of the trip was when we neared the hotel in Jersey and the driver got lost.

He circled round and round but could not find the hotel. After what seemed like hours, he pulled off the road and announced to me way in the back seat that he was dumbfounded (we had to shout to each other because, although the limo was very luxurious, it was about the length of a bus).

Suddenly, a snowplow passed by. The limo driver sprang into action and flagged down the operator and asked directions. It turned out that the hotel was not far away and that it actually was on his route. The operator told the limo guy to follow him. So we did.

It was quite the picture, with this large, shiny stretch limo closely following and nearly tethered to the dirty old snowplow.

I also learned from this experience that it was best to book a limo service based in New Jersey for the trip to the printing plant since the Connecticut drivers tended to get lost in the maze of roads for which New Jersey is famous. Additionally, the state highway system utilizes jughandles at many of the exits: Instead of bearing off from the right lane, right-turning traffic must use a ramp on the left side of the road (or vice versa for left-turning traffic). That means that some highway exits are on the left even though your destination is on the right. But you have to watch for the signs so you'll be in the proper lane to exit. I nicknamed them "the Jersey jughandles."

On another trip, it took the limo driver three times longer than normal to get from Jersey to Connecticut due to the snow and ice on the roads.

I was grateful that Wyeth offered car service for these press checks so I didn't have to drive. Rich Feldheim, president of the company's advertising agency, was the project manager. He said he wanted to keep me fresh so I could do my job and not have to deal with the stress of driving in that crazy, nerve-wracking traffic. That was good management, Rich.

Throughout my career, I brushed shoulders with a number of Fortune 500 chief executive officers and top management. In many cases, my contact person was a CEO's direct report, which means there is just one layer between the CEO and me.

Early on when I was doing a lot of work for General Electric, I was invited to the Christmas party every year. Chairman and CEO Jack

Welch always attended and would greet each person and thank him or her for their contribution to the company. I remember that Jack, with fists in air, would enthusiastically shout, "We're going to win!"

I also met IBM CEO Lou Gerstner at a conference I was manning in Nashville, Tennessee.

But my claim to fame is the work I have had for the last 14 years with the great Jamie Dimon, chairman and CEO of JPMorgan Chase. I work with his chief of staff, Judy Miller.

Jamie Dimon Story

For two decades, I have been on the JPMorgan Chase annual report team, providing editorial assistance to the firm. Jamie Dimon became chairman of the board and chief executive officer in 2006 and, according to certain authorities, is considered to be one of the most powerful businessmen in the world.

Being the pioneer that he is, Jamie decided early on to put a different spin on the shareholder letter in the annual report. He felt it important to provide an analysis of world events and explain how those happenings impacted the company.

From then on, Jamie would write a time-sensitive review of his perception of the major events of the year and detail how they affected economies throughout the world and on JPMorgan Chase in particular. He would reiterate the company's position on key issues, explaining where the firm had been and where it was going. It was his vision of the company's business model. The letter generally ran around 40 pages.

Every March, Jamie makes his shareholder letter a priority and personally writes it (which is most uncommon – generally a professional writer or management committee will compose the letter, and the CEO merely endorses it).

The shareholder letter became Jamie's signature piece. It was so well-received from the outset that a separate booklet containing just his letter is distributed around the world every spring.

It has been my honor to have been an integral part of the small team (four people) that takes Jamie's words and tweaks the copy to make it presentable to the global business community. It's a tough assignment. It's about a month-long project, and our team works round the clock the week leading up to press time.

One spring after the annual report had been published, Jamie's good friend Warren Buffett told Jamie that the letter that year was the best one yet.

Jamie decided to reward the core team by hosting a reception, which was held in his private dining room at world headquarters in New York City. I was one of 22 people invited, the only non-employee. I was thrilled to be included but was a little nervous. Ray put it in perspective and said, "You've already proved yourself. Just relax and enjoy."

And indeed I did.

The weather that day in May was misty, but I opted not to drag an umbrella with me on the train. And when I gazed out the floor-to-ceiling windows at the skyscrapers in every direction, the sun came out and shone brightly on the Big Apple.

I had achieved my goal – that vision I had had on the IU campus oh! so long ago.

Jamie spent an inordinate amount of one-on-one time with me. He is just as charismatic in person as in the news clips on TV. I also remember noting that his lips were so unusual – almost like they had been sculpted.

The event was a highlight of my career. Subsequently, Jamie and Judy often send an elegant floral arrangement to thank me for my work on the annual report. And I'm proud to call Jamie Dimon and Judy Miller my friends.

Working Together

Through it all, I was able to keep my customers happy and, at the same time, keep Ray happy by not being chained to my desk.

Ray was retired for two-thirds of our married life, and he had lots of things he wanted to do with his free time. He did not want me bound to my office or on-site at some company and unable to join him in his endeavors and adventures.

At the same time, he wanted to support me in my desire to run a successful business and fulfill my clients' requests and needs.

So it worked out well: My work could be done anywhere as long as I had overnight delivery service and a fax machine and later a laptop and smartphone. I came across a photo that was taken at our rental house in Florida one morning with three different overnight delivery vans parked out front at the same time.

Although it took some doing, I was also able to work on the boat from most any port. When Ray and I ran Intrepid down the Intracoastal Waterway to Florida and back, I still was able to meet my deadlines. And when we spent three months in Seattle taking care of Ray's daughter Diane after her bone marrow transplant, I just up and moved my office temporarily, as I had done all those winters we spent in Florida.

Ray and I joined forces for several years and had the pleasure of working together on managing the pressroom at IBM conferences across the United States. We stayed at the best resort hotels and worked hard – and we didn't have to be apart. It was an ideal arrangement.

One time at the Opryland Hotel in Nashville, Tennessee, we were manning a breakfast for reporters. Ray, always the early riser, went ahead to make sure all the details were in order.

I followed 30 minutes later and ended up getting lost trying to find the meeting room. Some hotels are like little cities, and one can't go directly from point A to point B (the Waldorf Astoria in New York City is like that with its Towers).

I finally showed up at the breakfast meeting, but it became a house rule to check out the territory ahead of time and figure out the lay of the land. Ray was known to say, "If you're not early, you're late."

At the end of that trip to Nashville, there was an ice storm that paralyzed the region. Ray and I were flying to Raleigh for meetings and sat on the runway for hours. In fact, the plane had to be deiced twice. When we arrived in Raleigh, not one restaurant was open due to the storm.

Wherever we went, we put in long hours but managed to see some of the local tourist attractions (like the Grand Ole Opry in Nashville – I was a country music fan – or live shows in Las Vegas) and taste the food at highly recommended restaurants.

If the city was located on a body of water, Ray always managed to arrange for a boat ride of some kind (tour boat, ferry, riverboat, sailboat, powerboat). Destinations included Atlanta, Las Vegas (every year), Miami, Nashville, Newport, New York, Orlando, Raleigh, San Diego, San Francisco, to name a few.

Along the way, I learned a little something about business protocol and always tried to say and do the right thing. But I never got embroiled in any serious ploys. Ray said I had the best of both worlds: involved in corporate business but free from the entanglement of the politics.

Ray and I also spent two years or so setting up customer meetings in Europe. Lyle McGuire was the manager in charge of these overseas assignments. Cities visited included Frankfurt, Brussels, Paris, Amsterdam, Vienna and Cannes. Ray and I relished flying business class and gladly scheduled a meeting on the first day in order to qualify for the upgrade.

Ray never skipped doing his exercises in the mornings no matter where he was: traveling around Europe or transiting the waters of Long Island Sound on the boat. In Frankfurt on that first day, I remember Ray saying, "Do you realize it's just 1 a.m. at home, and here I am doing my morning pushups?"

Wherever we went, Ray managed to get the office equipment set up, including computers, copy machines, fax machines, slide projectors, video equipment, microphones and the like. This was no easy feat since operating instructions for each were in that country's native language.

In Brussels, we stayed at the Hotel Le Dome. I had talked with a few of the other guests, and they were raving about the room key the hotel provided.

The key was attached to an oval-shaped key ring about 3" x 2" and made of heavy brass. There was talk of "forgetting" to turn the key ring in when they checked out of the hotel.

I wanted to take it home but didn't want to steal it. So I asked the manager if I could purchase one. He said, "Sure. We sell them for $40 each, and they're quite popular even though we know a lot of people conveniently forget to turn them in." I paid the money, and the clerk thanked me for my honesty. I've kept the house key on it for years. I had it engraved on the back side. It says "Brussels, June 1, 1995."

Oh, the price we pay for honesty, but that is a principle that has always been important to me.

These trips also taught us about country customs. In Brussels one time, we were attending a business luncheon. Wine was offered, but we both passed. Ray had stopped drinking alcohol in 1982, and I didn't drink while on the job and never during the day.

We learned later that turning down "a glass" had offended the hosts. That probably wouldn't be the case today. The hosts weren't too upset, though, because they presented to Ray and me a lovely silver platter as a thank you for arranging a successful customer meeting. I often said about these trips, "We worked hard, and we played hard. It was great fun!"

When the work schedule permitted, we would treat ourselves to a meal at the wonderful local restaurants in each city. In Paris, we had some downtime one day and had a delightful lunch in a charming café close to the Louvre.

Everywhere we went, I loaded my pockets with the tchotchkes, such as chocolates and matchbooks, that were on display in the cashier area and offered free of charge to patrons.

On this particular day, I was casing out the goodies while Ray was still at our table nearby. With a fistful of matchbooks (I thought) and a happy voice, I loudly called over to Ray, "You just can't get enough of these!"

"These," it turned out, were not matchbooks – they were condoms! The diners smiled from wall to wall.

Lyle McGuire, our manager and friend, was a world traveler and was proud to introduce us to the Eiffel Tower and other notable sights in the City of Light (some also call it the City of Love). In fact, Lyle and I went to the top of the Eiffel Tower and could spot Ray in his turquoise jacket far below (he wouldn't go to the top).

We had many good trips and times with Lyle over the years. And Lyle's wife Mary Pat became a friend as well.

Between work at home and abroad, I was living my dream.

At the end of one of these trips, Ray and I took a week and toured several European countries via rental car, which was an experience in and of itself.

One of the destinations was Alsace-Lorraine because that is where Ray's father Sylvain was born, and Ray had spent summers there as a child. (Ray was first-generation American as his mother Emma was born in Europe as well, just down the road in Basel, Switzerland).

Alsace-Lorraine is a territory that has been part of both Germany and France, depending on which country had won the most recent military conflict. It was reverted to French ownership in 1918 as part of the Treaty of Versailles and Germany's defeat in World War I.

Upon our arrival on the original Alsatian side of the Rhine Valley, Ray found that the people couldn't (as opposed to wouldn't) speak English. He was able to dig to the depths of his mind and pull up enough French to get us through the visit.

He also noticed that a lot of people there have blond hair and crystal blue eyes. Worldwide, only 8% to 10% of people have baby blues, but in France it's 22%, and in Germany it's 40%. All three of Ray's kids have blond hair, and Scott has those piercing eyes. They are striking and beautiful.

From Alsace, we drove to Zurich and toured the city for a few days and, of course, took a boat ride on Lake Zurich. We also visited some relatives in Basel, Switzerland.

Ray's father Sylvain's last name, of course, is Meurer. What is interesting is that Ray's mother's name before she married was Maurer – only one letter different. Ray was constantly being challenged when asked the security question, "What is your mother's maiden name?"

Throughout my life, I have read a number of biographies of the great entrepreneurs, self-made men who built this country, and I appreciate the fortitude they demonstrated in order to achieve their vision.

I thirsted to learn of their stories and read about the robber barons of a hundred years ago, as well as modern-day billionaires: Astor, Rockefeller, Vanderbilt, Gould, Getty, Ford, Kennedy, Watson, Field, Rothschild, Walton, Braun, Jobs, Zuckerberg, Dimon.

I wasn't partial to just men – I also loved reading about the life of females from varied walks of life who made a name for themselves. I read about the dedication and drive it took to make it to the top by notable successful women in business. And I read the biographies of Patsy Cline and Reba McEntire and Lauren Bacall and Lucille Ball and Rose Kennedy and Barbara Bush.

Ray and I continued to work together on projects for my clients until the bitter end, as well as on pro bono and volunteer work. Ray was head of public relations for our church. He would write the news releases, and I would edit them. He joined the Darien Men's Association (DMA) in 2012 and was in charge of communications. He wrote copy and took photos for the newsletter and eblasts, and I would do the editing. We were a good team.

We had been a good team since the very beginning.

After Ray passed away, I offered to continue editing the DMA newsletter and have attended some of the speakers' events and social activities. These include the annual picnic at Weed Beach and the Christmas party at The Country Club of Darien.

Ray and I had wonderful times working together and just being together. It was a charmed life.

Throughout my career, I have enjoyed helping friends and colleagues with their resume or other important papers or their kids' college application or essay. It has been one way I could "give back" for all the good fortune I have experienced.

I have great admiration for the business leaders of the country's corporations, and I believe that capitalism will sustain America. I am a patriot and feel privileged to enjoy all the freedoms that so many have perished trying to save.

Yes, in America, you can do anything, and you can be anything. It is the Land of Opportunity. You can achieve and live the American Dream.

I am proud to be an American and think the United States of America is the greatest country in the world. If you work hard and play by the rules, every person here has the opportunity to make their dreams come true.

Sports Fan

Ask any Hoosier what their favorite sport is, and, undoubtedly, the answer will be "BASKETBALL."

Growing up in Indiana means one is exposed to the sport from birth when infants are toted to games in their parents' arms. I have been an avid fan all my life.

I have a memory from my elementary school days – I probably was a sixth grader at the time. I had attended a high school basketball game, and the Grass Creek Panthers had lost in a close one. I had retrieved my coat from the cafeteria (which doubled as a cloakroom during games) and was waiting for my parents (being a teacher, Mother usually volunteered to sell tickets so she could say hello to everyone and spent a good part of the first half of the game in the ticket booth tending to latecomers).

As I stood with my back against the wall, tears were streaming down my face. Our team had lost by one point.

No matter whether one is young or old, the game is emotional. In high school, I had been a member of the Pep Club, and the lessons learned have stood me in good stead ever since. As a loyal fan, I can hold my own against anybody and cheer or boo as appropriate. My diary from 1962 when I was a freshman at Caston High School is peppered with notations about attending high school basketball games and watching college games on TV. On January 6, the diary says: "IU beat Michigan by five points."

We kids went to both the varsity and the junior varsity high school games. We went to intramural games of other sports. In short, there was some kind of game about every day in season either right after school or in the evening. (Caston did not have a football team so that sport was not top of mind although the Hizers watched college and pro games when they were aired on TV on weekends and holidays.)

The 1960s was the era when the basketball uniform consisted of short shorts. It wasn't until 1984 when Michael Jordan, while playing pro for the Chicago Bulls, changed all that and is credited with the long and baggy trend that continues today. The length of the inseam went from three inches to (eventually) 11 inches and the size of the leg opening from 12 inches to 15 inches. The Fab Five at the University of Michigan idolized Jordan and requested the new look, and every team across America followed suit.

Whether physically at a game or in the comfort of my living room, it is not uncommon for me to jump up and down and shout at the players and the refs, pointing out bad plays and missed calls. Lousy officiating is a fan's nightmare.

With Midwesterners, fan loyalty runs deep. For example, my niece Julia Hizer was on the girls' basketball team in 1993-1994 at Winamac High School. In the Indiana state tournament, underdog Winamac upset the host team Rochester 42-37, another county seat 20 miles away, and made it to the regionals. Julia's team lost to favored LaPorte 56-45 the next weekend in Valparaiso, 49 miles away.

The Winamac fans traveled in a caravan to and from the games being played in both locations. It was like a scene from the movie "Hoosiers." There were miles and miles of headlights moving forward together in the procession. Inclement weather couldn't keep them home. Afterward, win or lose, the entire team was invited back to the local bowling alley for pizza, compliments of the owner. That's the kind of spirit that exists all across the state and region.

This is not an exaggeration. Basketball is in your blood from an early age. And you never grow out of it. As an adult, basketball is part of your being. The saying goes: "You can take the Hoosier out of Indiana, but you can't take Indiana out of the Hoosier."

Reams have been written about the sport, and I won't attempt to get into quoting any of the thousands of colorful descriptions. But they're fun to read.

I came upon a poem that was published in the *Indianapolis Star* in

December 1994 that takes the words from " 'Twas the Night before Christmas" and turns it into a story about an upcoming IU game against the Kansas Jayhawks. The article is bylined by Bill Benner, a native of Indiana who has had a long career as a sportswriter. His brother, David, is in the same field, and they've both done very well and are highly respected.

I followed the Grass Creek Panthers all through grade school until the school consolidation in my freshman year of high school. It was just another small Indiana community caught up in the frenzy of basketball. But Phil Wills put Grass Creek on the map. The star player had a one-game high of 60 points and a record average of 42.2 points in his senior year in 1957. He went on to play for Purdue (and competed against Bob Knight on the Ohio State team). Wills was inducted into the Indiana Basketball Hall of Fame in 1999. I talked with him not too many years ago, and he regaled me with tales of his basketball triumphs.

After the consolidation, we became the Caston Comets. All the kids went to every Caston High School game, at home and away. I played the flute and piccolo in the Marching Band that performed at halftime at home games. A necktie was part of the uniform, and we all learned how to tie our own tie (a valuable skill for male or female).

Cedric Berdine was the music teacher and required that we learn each Big 10 school's fight song. I have been grateful for that assignment because, to this day, I am able to recognize the various school songs when I hear them being played at games on TV.

As mentioned earlier, I also played the baritone saxophone in a swing band, played the piano and organ, and sang in the school chorus, a sextet and a trio. In fact, later in life whenever asked to play the piano, my old standby was "Over the Rainbow," a song from "The Wizard of Oz" that had inspired me from a very young age to reach for the stars. I'm sorry to say that after high school, I did not keep up with playing any instruments or singing.

Grass Creek is situated 55 miles northeast of West Lafayette,

Indiana, where Purdue University is located. Renowned for its agricultural programs in particular, Purdue was the school of choice for the majority of people I knew while growing up. But Dad had gone to IU (140 miles south) so the three of us kids went there – we were an IU family. The rivalry between the two schools was and still is fierce. Surprisingly, three of Alan's kids ended up going to Purdue so there has been a lot of friendly ribbing through the years.

Some Football but Mainly More Basketball
While at Indiana University, I watched football and basketball games from the stands and later regretted not auditioning for the Marching Hundred (Dad had been a member, as well as my Uncle Warren Hines and his sons, my cousins Ed and David). Dad talked about taking trips to other campuses. I especially remember him mentioning visits to Harvard, the University of Texas and all the Big 10 schools.

Sports events at the bigger schools can be electrifying. For starters, there are acres and acres of parking lots, and it's a thrill just walking along with the hordes of people heading to their seat. Then the sheer size of the stadium or arena filled to capacity, with fans dressed in school colors, is a sight to be seen. You can't help but get caught up in the spirit of the game when you hear the roar of the crowd – it just lifts you up off your seat. And the halftime performance showcasing the marching band in full dress completes the exhilarating experience.

Needless to say, I was a die-hard sports fan long before I moved to the East and later met Ray. He was not much of a fan and could take it or leave it. But once we were together, he didn't have much choice, and he was a good sport about it.

Having gone to Big 10 football games during my college years, with the stadiums seating more than 100,000 spectators, I looked forward to attending games in the East. When I first moved here, I went to a Yale game. Aside from the awe of being on a renowned and revered Ivy League campus, being a spectator in the stadium didn't have quite the same aura of excitement.

Regarding basketball, Hoosier Hysteria has always been a big part of my life. I graduated from IU just a year before Bob Knight was hired as head basketball coach (he was 31 years old and had dark hair back then). I watched every IU game that was aired on TV and felt very much a part of the euphoria. I still have a tee shirt from the 1987 NCAA championship that was one of three national titles won by Knight. In fact, I have all kinds of IU memorabilia and often wear a cream and crimson sweatshirt or tee shirt when watching a game – even at home by myself.

Then there's UConn basketball. I was living in Connecticut when the UConn Huskies men's team under Jim Calhoun was in its heyday. IU played UConn a few times, and there were some tough contests. And, of course, there was the UConn women's team under Geno Auriemma, the most successful women's basketball program in the nation, winning 11 NCAA championships since 1995.

Following the Big East Conference during its height was exciting. From its inception in 1979 till 2013, the men's Big East Conference, in particular, was a force to be reckoned with, and the competition was fierce. It was right up there with the Big 10 (still my favorite), the Atlantic Coast Conference (ACC) and the Southeastern Conference (SEC). There was a lot of thrilling basketball to watch.

In 2013, a conference realignment took place, and the Big East as we knew it had a completely new face. UConn, for example, joined the American Athletic Conference for a few years and played schools primarily in the Texas/Southeast region. Louisville, Notre Dame, Pittsburgh and Syracuse left and joined the ACC. And there were some surprising new members: Creighton, in Omaha, Nebraska, for example, dropped out of the Missouri Valley Conference and joined the Big East. Today, 11 schools (there have been as many as 16) comprise the Big East Conference (UConn is back in), and five of the 11 are not located in the East (Butler, Creighton, DePaul, Marquette and Xavier).

Another conference realignment will be taking effect over the next few years, and the member schools in the major conferences will be scattered throughout the country: Southern Cal and UCLA will be joining the Big 10, for example.

It's crazy. Those kids and coaches have to travel long distances at least once a week for their games. And the name of the conference doesn't have much bearing on where its member schools are located.

Thanks to expanded sports networks on TV, games are aired every day today. It wasn't always that way. In 1979, ESPN was born, and, gradually over time, fans could watch sports events more often than just on weekends and holidays. With access to Big East, Big 10, ACC, SEC, Big 12 and other Division 1 conference games, there was good basketball – and other sports – all around, and I caught every game I could and still do.

For several years when I was teaching at Greenwich High School, my direct supervisor was Frank Keaney. He had foresight and innovative ideas that made him an effective educator, and he was one of my first mentors.

We had a lot in common also because he was a sports fan. His father had been an icon in the basketball world. Frank Keaney, Sr., was head basketball coach at the University of Rhode Island for 28 years and was the inventor of the fast break. He was inducted into the Basketball Hall of Fame in 1960. One summer when Ray and I were staying on our boat at Peter Hicks' dock on Point Judith Pond in Rhode Island, Peter and his wife Kathleen drove us around campus in nearby Kingston. It was a thrill to see the tributes to the great Frank Keaney: Keaney Gymnasium and Keaney Road.

The game of basketball has changed since I was a kid. There wasn't even a three-point shot back then. No matter how far down the court a basket was made, it was worth only two points. Today, the three-point shots made from way downtown are an integral part of the game, adding to the jumper and points in the paint. The three-pointer was introduced in 1967 and adopted by the pro league in 1979, the year Magic Johnson and Larry Bird were rookies in the NBA. The NCAA universally implemented the three-point shot in 1986.

Larry Bird is an Indiana basketball legend. He was born in French Lick and played for Indiana State University. He then made a name for himself with the Boston Celtics. Another product of Indiana is Brad Stevens, who has served as head coach of the Boston Celtics since 2013. After college, he worked in marketing for Eli Lilly in Indianapolis and volunteered on the coaching staff at Butler University. In 2002 after just one year, he was officially named assistant coach. In 2007, he was promoted to head coach and led the team to the NCAA national championship game in back-to-back seasons three years later.

One sports tradition that has changed fairly recently is the color of the uniform worn by the home team. "Home white" used to be the norm for a number of sports, particularly baseball, football and basketball.

The convention started in the early days of major league baseball, long before radio and television. Players would slide into the bases, resulting in dirt and stains on their clothes. The away team generally didn't have access to laundry facilities and could not wash the uniforms after every game. So the visiting players wore colored clothes that did not show the dirt as much. Other sports soon followed suit, and it was easy to identify the home versus away players at a glance.

Today, the home team can wear either the light or dark uniform. So with no universal home white (and now gray as well) rule in effect anymore, it sometimes takes a few seconds to determine which team is which, especially if both teams have the same color combinations. This is particularly evident when surfing multiple games on TV.

In the late '90s, Ray had retired and was working as a consultant at IBM and was assigned the responsibility of putting together a motivational program that was to be held in Indianapolis. Bob Knight was still the head coach at IU (but his hair had turned white by then), and it was the off-season. Ray thought, "Why not try to get Bob Knight as the speaker? He certainly is a motivator." Contact with Knight's people proved to be successful, and the "show" was scheduled.

Knight said, in preparation for a game, there is a big difference between "hoping" to win and "preparing" to win. And after a win, he said not to dwell on the success but move directly to the next challenge. He also believed that negative thinking produces positive results.

His appearance at Ray's function was a hit, and I was heartbroken that I didn't get to go along on the trip and meet the great Bobby Knight. (My sister-in-law, Gloria Hizer, however, did go to the meeting as she worked as a stringer for the *Pharos-Tribune*, the local newspaper in the Logansport (Indiana) area.)

Wanting to keep up with the ever-changing rules of basketball, I read books on the rules and strategies of the game. Being an avid reader who especially enjoys learning about the lives of the "greats," I read a few of Bob Knight's books. I also read *Bleeding Orange*, Syracuse coach Jim Boeheim's story, and sportscaster Jim Nantz's *Always By My Side*. The late Tim Russert, television journalist, was a lifelong Buffalo Bills fan and talked about going to games in his book, *Big Russ & Me*. In *Every Town Is a Sports Town*, George Bodenheimer tells of his rise to the top at ESPN. Even John Grisham, who writes legal thrillers, wrote about football in *Bleachers* and *Playing for Pizza*.

But the book about sports that particularly fascinates me is *ESPN: Those Guys Have All the Fun*. It's an 800-page narrative about the startup and growth of Entertainment and Sports Programming Network (known to all as ESPN) and how it became the media empire it is today. Of note, the network was established right here in Connecticut, and, today, headquarters remains in Bristol, just outside of Hartford. Aside from the above, I read books on other sports, such as *A Full Cup* about sailing and the quest to win the America's Cup and *Seabiscuit* about horse racing.

I follow college basketball nationwide and keep track of the team standings. I watch all the major conference tournaments, can name the best players on all the top teams and know the personal history of many of the coaches.

John Calipari has built a program at the University of Kentucky that's known as "one and done," whereas many of the players spend one year under Coach Cal and then go pro. Whether they stay one year or a few years, I enjoy seeing the kids who played college ball go on and play professionally. And sometimes they go on to coach.

Behind every coach, there's a story, and volumes could be written about the various personalities. One person I've followed is Steve Alford. He grew up in Franklin, Indiana, was named Indiana Mr. Basketball in high school and played for the Hoosiers under Bobby Knight. He went on to play pro for four seasons, mostly with the Dallas Mavericks. Then he launched into coaching and, to date, has served as head coach of six colleges.

It's also interesting to see the many father-son combinations. Some fathers get to coach their own son while in high school or college. Some examples are Bob Knight, Rick Pitino, Jim Boeheim and Steve Alford. After graduation, some of these sons become an assistant coach and even head coach as their career progresses. And some go on to become sports commentators.

It's fun to have watched the career path taken by so many bright young athletes. As I grow older, I realize I started tracking some of these contemporaries during their college years and have seen their journey unfold through retirement.

The atmosphere at college basketball games is so exciting – with the team mascots pulling their pranks and the cheerleaders trying to inject energy into the crowd. Asked who my favorite teams are, I say, "Except for IU, they change from season to season."

Since Coach Krzyzewski at Duke is a protégé of Bob Knight, I cheered for the Blue Devils for a long time but defected to the University of North Carolina due to my friendship with Mary Pat McGuire. Sadly, I also learned that Bob Knight and Coach K had a falling out. As the years go by, I tend to root for a team because of the coach, but, oftentimes, coaches move around (if you don't win, you don't stay) so my allegiance changes as my favorites move from school to school.

I also follow certain pro players and have an attachment to them as they are traded from team to team. And, from time to time, I tend to favor specific owners and other personnel.

Sometimes I don't like a team for some reason so I'll root for any opponent. If two teams are playing each other in a playoff series and I don't have a favorite, sometimes I root for the underdog in order to extend the number of games to be played. But I always root for a team. It makes watching the game more exciting.

On the college front, late February and the first two weeks of March are critical for the ranking and seeding of teams for the upcoming conference tournaments and, ultimately, the Big Dance. Every game is important in tournament play, and it's win or go home.

In 2009 in a quarterfinal game in the Big East tournament, Syracuse beat UConn in the sixth overtime. Syracuse had not been ahead once since the end of regulation. The game ended at 1:22 a.m. after nearly four hours of play.

Then there's the unforgettable UConn Run, where the Huskies under Jim Calhoun won five games in five days in the 2011 Big East tournament. They went on to win the NCAA tournament, winning 11 straight games. That surprised everyone.

March Madness is an exciting time of the year. Big school, small school, it's when miracles can happen – for the teams and for the fans. Bracketology has become a science. There are seedings and underdogs (David and Goliath-type matchups) and buzzer beaters. There's some very exciting basketball. It will get you hooked if you weren't before.

Prior to Selection Sunday every March when the men's NCAA tournament is about to begin, the guys from my church in Rowayton who wanted to participate in the Swanky's and/or the Darien Men's Association pool would cozy up to me during Fellowship Hour to pick my brain for which teams to select. I loved it! I felt very flattered. And I have a pretty good track record.

Gehr Brown would say, "I'll take any tips you can give me. I'm not necessarily trying to win first place – I just don't want to be embarrassed." Gehr is a collector of sports memorabilia and no stranger to the world of athletics so it was an honor to have him seek my advice.

Pete Scull, a former basketball player at Darien High School and then Colgate University, would say, "I'll give you a call at home, and we can go over the teams." That first year, Pete won second place in the DMA pool.

And the conversation in 2019 with Bill Close went something like this. Bill asked: "What teams do you think are the best picks for the tournament this year?" I named Virginia and a couple of other schools. Bill said, "Mmm, Virginia. I know someone who went to school there. I think I'll pick Virginia as the overall winner. Thanks."

An ESPN documentary, "Survive and Advance," is aired every year as the games begin, a must-see.

The Big Dance is my favorite part of the season. For three weeks, it's nonstop basketball. With so many games being played simultaneously on TV, I can switch around the channels during every ad and timeout and keep track of multiple games at the same time (in our cable package, there are 15 different channels that carry sports programming during the tournament and half as many the rest of the year). I've become a master at surfing channels, not just during the tournament but year round, to catch snippets of games.

In 1983, Jim Valvano led his North Carolina State Wolfpacks to nine straight do-or-die, nail-biting wins, including the crown jewel: the NCAA championship. Jimmy V developed cancer a few years later and fought a brave battle but succumbed in 1993. At his last public appearance when presented with the ESPY Arthur Ashe Courage Award, he implored those listening with words that have stood the test of time, saying, "Don't give up. Don't ever give up."

Back to the 2019 NCAA tournament and Bill Close's pick: Virginia made it all the way to the Final Four that year and played Texas Tech in the championship game. Both teams were making their first appearance in the final game. The score was tied with one second to go in regulation when Texas Tech tried for a buzzer beater – but the shot was blocked.

The game went to overtime, and Virginia clinched the title for the first time in school history. And Bill won first place in the DMA NCAA tournament pool.

The song "One Shining Moment" signifies the end of another NCAA tournament. And, of course, the NIT and the women's NCAA tournament games are aired so there are playoff games to watch about every night during most of March and into April.

After the season ended one year, my brother Alan lamented, "It's a long time till December [and the start of another season]."

Final Four Story
The last time the IU Hoosiers made it to the Final Four (2002), I organized a trip to the big event to watch my alma mater try to capture another national championship. I convinced Alan to join me, and we met in Atlanta.

A friend and neighbor from the Rowayton Beach Association, Frank Sinatra (no, not the fabled singer), had expressed interest in going to the championship games. I held off booking a flight until I could get confirmation from Frank as to whether or not he would be going. By delaying, it cost an additional $100 for the plane ticket. I was a little miffed and told Frank about it, saying "You owe me a dinner." He responded by saying, "Joyce, there isn't a person in the world I'd rather have dinner with."

That deflated my irritation on the spot, and I felt I had just learned a valuable lesson in how to soothe hurt feelings.

I stayed with Cynthia and friend Margaret Putnam in their charming but rustic barn on the 10-acre farm in Covington (45 minutes east southeast of Atlanta), and Alan and gang took rooms at a nearby motel. I had managed to get four tickets from a lottery winner in Minnesota, who had sold his tickets to a fan in Kansas, who had upgraded and sold his tickets to me. The lottery process is quite involved, and it was educational in and of itself to learn firsthand how tickets to these big games get parceled out.

Cynthia picked me up at the airport on Thursday, and Alan et al. showed up on Friday after catching a team practice at the Georgia Dome. It was Easter weekend so there were church services to attend, meals to prepare and lots of visiting to do.

On Saturday, Alan, niece Emily's husband Jim and friend Marc, and I were taken to the train station by Emily, her friend McKenzie and Emily's infant Molly McClure. First, we caught the tail end of a pep rally. Then we hit the streets of Atlanta that were jammed with fans killing time before the games that night. Alan was on a mission to upgrade our tickets as he didn't want to sit in the nosebleed section. So I went to work, negotiating with scalpers up and down the alleyways and, in the end, succeeded in getting better seats for Alan and me. Then we headed to the games.

It was electrifying with all the fans, the huge arena, and the myriad of renowned commentators and coaches all under one roof. IU won that night and earned the right to play in the championship game on Monday night. I had taken the $800 pair of binoculars Ray had bought for the boat so I could see the action better. Wanting to be generous because their seats were so far up, I let Jim and Marc take the binocs. Afterward, Ray was not happy when he learned that the boys nearly left the binocs in the bleachers after the games ended (from then on, I didn't let the binocs get out of my sight).

The next day was Easter Sunday. We enjoyed the church service, a hearty meal and time on the farm. That night, we went to a nearby monastery, and Alan asked God to give the Hoosiers whatever weapons they needed to win the final game. Monday dawned a beautiful April 1 in Georgia so the guys went to the pond to fish and soak up the sun. In the meantime, I stumbled upon a plan for what turned out to be my greatest April Fool's joke of all time.

In the middle of the previous night, there had been a ferocious thunderstorm. At noon, I convened the group and stated that there had been a news clip about how the roof on the Georgia Dome was leaking after the storm, and all parties were scrambling to fix the leaks and repair the flooring to be ready for the big game that night. Reporters had said the game might even have to be postponed a day.

Alan went berserk. Being a country lawyer, he said he had a court date for a client early Wednesday morning that he couldn't miss. So he was calculating all the ways he could attend the game a day later, drive through the night and still make court that next morning in Winamac, Indiana. Needless to say, everyone in the group was doing the same and making contingency plans.

I explained that the announcement would be made at 5 p.m. In the meantime, Jim and Marc went back to the pond and resumed their fishing. Not realizing the sun's intensity, they found themselves burned to a crisp and not feeling well as they headed to Cynthia's barn at the appointed hour.

Everyone was on the edge of their chair waiting for the update about the Georgia Dome and the decision about the game. The TV screen was snowy, which added to the drama. Cynthia did the best she could to improve the reception by working the rabbit ears, but the antenna didn't do a very good job.

After the news program came and went and there was no mention of the status of the Georgia Dome, it was mayhem as everyone was in a quandary as to whether or not to get ready to go into Atlanta that night. Finally, I announced with great aplomb "April Fool's!"

Not unexpectedly, I found my safety at stake, and I feared for my life!

Preparations were made to get ready for the game. By that time, Jim and Marc realized they had heat exhaustion and didn't feel like going. I grabbed their tickets and said I'd try to sell them. Emily dropped Alan and me off at the train station, and I ended up dumping the tickets for a song.

The game went on that night, with IU losing to Maryland (I've never rooted for Maryland since). On the way home, the fans were scrunched into the train cars like sardines. Alan said he was just a country boy and was ready to be back in Winamac.

It was a weekend we'll never forget.

Baseball and Sports Miscellany

Starting with being a fan of high school and college basketball, I expanded my sports horizon by following the pro teams so that stretched the basketball season. Then I picked up with football and baseball to fill out the rest of the year.

Regarding baseball, I have followed the sport to some degree since I was a kid. My diary from when I was a freshman in high school notes that on October 4, 1962, the Yankees beat the Giants in game 1 of the World Series. And on our senior trip in high school, we went to a major league baseball game in Chicago.

In 2001, Ray and I watched the Mariners play when we were in Seattle taking care of his daughter Diane after her bone marrow transplant. Tickets were often donated to the hospital and passed on to patients and their family. Tickets to that particular game were for a private suite complete with food and drink, and some of the players' wives stopped by to say hello.

Locally, Bobby Valentine, former manager of the Texas Rangers, the New York Mets and the Boston Red Sox, is a familiar name around town. He grew up and lives in nearby Stamford, Connecticut, and for decades has operated a local sports bar and restaurant bearing his name.

In late August of 2011, Hurricane Irene made landfall in North Carolina, but Rowayton felt the remnants, and several streets and homes were flooded. Brian Cashman, general manager of the New York Yankees, was living three houses up the street from us. Neighbors Chris and Linda Dunn helped him place sandbags around the house to prevent water damage. He later moved to another part of town.

And, interestingly, there is a bat manufacturer right here in Norwalk, Tucci Lumber, that makes bats for baseball players at all levels.

So major league baseball has been a favorite sport for a long time. My allegiance is to the Yankees. One of the traditions at the home games is to honor a veteran and play Irving Berlin's "God Bless America" during the seventh-inning stretch. Kate Smith's rendition was part of the ceremony for years. I root for the Mets, too, unless they are playing the Yankees (called the Subway Series). My neighbor Sylvia Stuart is a die-hard Mets fan, and I've accompanied her to Citi Field and, of course, cheered for the home team. She says, "There are times when it's hard to be a Mets fan."

Another neighbor, Bob "Doc" Dowling, lives just up the street and is an inspiration to us all. At the age of 98, he walks several times every day (rain or snow or shine), swims off the Boathouse beach daily from spring till fall and has just recently cut back on playing tennis.

Bob has been an athlete all his life, playing football and hockey, as well as boxing. In his elder years, he competed in track and field. In 1997, he won a silver medal in the National Senior Olympics in the 50-meter swim in the men's category ages 75-80. Every day as I sit at my desk working, I see Bob out and about getting his exercise, putting me to shame.

Another Olympian from Rowayton, Dick Packer was a member of the U.S. Men's Soccer Team in the 1956 Olympics. Dick had made his mark at Penn State University, leading his team to two national championships and scored a record 53 goals in 24 games and then went on to play professionally. Since 1978, he has been running a summer soccer camp in Rowayton for kids ages three to 14.

Regarding football, I follow the New York Giants primarily because neighbor Ann DiLeone's grandson, Mark Herzlich, played on the team for seven years. I had met Mark a couple of times so that made the game even more interesting. Mark was an all-American linebacker at Boston College and was named ACC Defensive Player of the Year in 2008. The next year he was diagnosed with Ewing's sarcoma, a rare cancer that manifests itself in the bones. In Mark's case, it was a tumor in the femur. They said he would never play football again.

Mark went on to beat all odds and returned to college and played on the team two more years. He was signed as an undrafted free agent by the Giants in 2011, and the team played in the Super Bowl his first season. The setting was Indianapolis, and the city's preparations for hosting this big event for the first time included expanding the convention center downtown and building a new airport.

Upon leaving the Giants and going to work for ESPN covering ACC football, Mark and his wife and son moved to Rowayton, and I saw them a lot when they came to visit Ann.

A year ago, Mark came to the house when Ray was sick and couldn't get around on his own. Mark, being the big, strapping guy that he is, just lifted Ray up from the wheelchair and placed him gently on the hospital bed.

Also relating to football and the Giants, they played in Super Bowl XXV in 1991 against the Buffalo Bills. Ray and I were in the Fort Lauderdale airport awaiting our connecting flight to New York City from Marsh Harbour in the Bahamas when the Bills team landed. I saw lots of familiar faces as all those big guys proudly paraded through the terminal. They weren't so happy, though, after the game. They lost to the Giants when they missed a last-second field goal attempt. That was the first of four consecutive losses in a Super Bowl for the Bills. To date, they have never pulled off the coveted win.

The Super Bowl ads are famous for their ingenuity and boldness, and everyone looks forward to each season's "new crop." At the end of 2013, E*TRADE retired its successful baby ad campaign that had debuted during the 2008 Super Bowl. It's where a toddler is dressed in adult attire (suit and tie) and speaks in a mature voice, giving advice about the stock market.

Living in the New York metro area means we fans are exposed to some pretty great teams. For example, the Yankees won four World Series championships in five years in the '90s. All the teams have their winning streaks, and it's exciting to be swept up in the momentum. And note that three of the nicknames rhyme: Jets (football), Mets (baseball) and Nets (basketball).

Not to be left out, a second New York basketball team is the Knicks. The name is a shortened version of knickerbocker, the style of pant leg (rolled up to just below the knee) worn in Manhattan in the early 1600s by the Dutch settlers.

Knickerbocker also was the name of a beer made by Ruppert Brewery at 92nd Street and Second Avenue in New York and was the official beer of the New York Giants. Brewer Jacob Ruppert, Jr., was owner of the New York Yankees for nearly 25 years during the heyday of Babe Ruth and Lou Gehrig. The regional brewery was sold to Rheingold Brewery in 1965, which ceased operations in 1976.

As with any sports fan, I became a critic of the sportscasters. Nearly all commentators have either played the sport or coached and have an inside knowledge of the game.

Regarding basketball, I have high regard for Jay Bilas who is well-spoken and even-tempered, and his reporting is fair and balanced. I appreciate Brent Musburger's style. Brent is the one who is credited with coining the term March Madness. I think Bob Knight is good because he explains the mechanics of the game so well.

I don't care for Dick Vitale's overenthusiasm and usage of words like "Oh, Baby!" and "awesome," but he does "grow on you." And I do admire all he's done to promote the Jimmy V Foundation in an attempt to find cures for cancer. Dick is the one who said ESPN sounded like a disease when, in 1979, he first heard the name of the small media operation based in Bristol, Connecticut.

I respect Jim Calhoun as a coach and person but feel his Bostonian accent makes it hard to follow the game.

When it comes to baseball and the Yankees, I appreciate John Sterling's and Michael Kay's commentating. And for the Mets, announcers Gary Cohen, Ron Darling (who lives in Rowayton) and Keith Hernandez make a great team.

For football, I enjoy listening to the resonant voice of Cris Collinsworth. And, of course, I regard Jim Nantz as one of the "greats," commentating on football, basketball and golf.

To me, the common theme exhibited by the most successful commentators (along with speaking proper English) is a voice that is well-modulated and rich in timbre.

As an aside, I support the Yankees' Appearance policy, which stipulates that no coach, executive or player can display facial hair except for a moustache and that scalp hair cannot extend below the collar. This policy was instituted in 1973 by George Steinbrenner when he observed his players' long hair while the national anthem was being played. It is believed that "The Boss's" desire for neatness stems from the time he spent at Culver Military Academy (yes, my old stomping ground) as a teenager.

I never tire of watching a game – most any sport (well, maybe not boxing, wrestling and poker), college or pro. Immersing myself in a game is a great way to unwind after a long workday. I also like to watch the "30 for 30" documentary series on ESPN about the life story of different athletes and sports personalities or an account of an event or place surrounding sports. And I enjoy listening to Michael Kay's interviews on "CenterStage." In general, I watch "SportsCenter" to catch up on the sports news, and due to my business background, I find "SportsMoney" interesting.

Both of Ray's sons played hockey, and, for many years, Ray and I went with them to the New York Rangers games at Madison Square Garden. Today, I watch the Rangers on TV and cheer when Rowayton's Chris Kreider scores game-winning goals.

After Ray passed away and especially during this pandemic, watching games (even the many replays) has served as my life support, along with talking on the phone, exchanging email and texts, and browsing the Internet. Watching sports has helped carry me through those long and lonely evenings and weekends.

Sidd Finch Story

Being sports fans, Ray and I enjoyed talking with friends and neighbors about sporting events. Dave and Myra Wilson live nearby, and they would often chat with us on the street or in the yard. Myra worked at *Sports Illustrated* and always had some interesting story to tell.

But the Finch spiel is one of the magazine's most famous stories ever: "The Curious Case of Sidd Finch," published April 1, 1985. The subhead read: "He's a pitcher, part yogi and part recluse. Impressively liberated from our opulent lifestyle, Sidd's deciding about yoga – and his future in baseball." The article was written by George Plimpton and edited by Myra Gelband (Wilson).

It's the story describing an incredible rookie baseball player who had been training at the Mets camp in St. Petersburg, Florida, that spring who reportedly could pitch a fastball at 168 miles per hour with pinpoint accuracy. The standing record was 103 miles per hour. Batters said it was not humanly possible to hit his pitches.

Finch's performance had the baseball world ablaze, and he had been making headlines every day. But he wasn't sure if he wanted to pursue a career with the Mets or follow his dream of a life in the music world as a French horn player. He was to announce his decision on April 1 of that year.

After the April 1 issue hit the streets, the publication received 2,000 letters from readers about the article. On April 8, a press conference was held announcing Finch had suddenly lost the ability to throw his record fastball and would not be pursuing a career with the Mets.

On April 15, *Sports Illustrated* admitted the story was a hoax. Since the publication is known for its truth-telling, sports fans were disbelieving. The magazine's response was, "Read the subhead. The first letter of each word, taken together, spells Happy April Fool's Day."

That prank certainly tops my Final Four April Fool's joke related above about the 2002 Final Four championship game.

It just goes to show that there are myriads of ways sports can provide relaxation. It's a popular field, and millions of people turn to games as their favorite entertainment.

Ray and I discovered the TV show "Jeopardy!" with Alex Trebek as host late in our years together and had fun trying to solve the clues. Every so often, one of the categories would be a subject surrounding sports, and we did pretty well with our questions.

Derek Jeter Story

Having added baseball to my list of pastimes, my favorite home team is the New York Yankees, as mentioned above (a close second is the Mets). For years, I have followed the games, managers, coaches, players, standings and stats.

The 2014 season was about to end. Derek Jeter would be retiring after the last game. The Yankees had not made the playoffs so the game being played on September 25 against the Baltimore Orioles would be Jeter's last in Yankee Stadium.

I was glued to the TV in the living room as the bottom of the ninth inning wore on, and the score was tied. Jeter was at bat with two out and a runner on second. He slammed the ball between first and second base, and the runner found home plate.

Jeter had done it again – his RBI won the game! It was a fairy-tale ending.

I sprang out of the chair to cheer with the crowds – and immediately fell to the floor.

It turned out that my foot was asleep and could bear no weight. I ended up wearing a boot and walking with a cane for a couple of weeks but said watching that thriller had been worth it.

At church the next Sunday, a fellow parishioner asked what had happened to my foot. I explained, and George Albano, a sportswriter for the local newspaper, *The Hour*, asked if he could interview me for a story in his column. I said, "Of course. It's actually a fun story!"

Every once in a while, George mentions how much he enjoyed writing the Jeter article.

Team Nicknames and Mascots

Let's talk about team nicknames for a minute. There are hundreds of names used for teams spanning from elementary school to the pros. It's fun to take a look at these and see the variety and ingenuity.

The name of the team quite often represents a predator that is supposed to strike fear in the hearts of the opponents.

At the very least, the name may stand for strength and fortitude. This can also be accomplished by branding a force or movement that can't be stopped, like Big Red (Cornell), the Blue Wave (Darien High School), the Red Storm (St. John's) or the Wave (Pepperdine).

The names can be grouped into a dozen or so categories, but animals dominate the list (about 70% based on a study conducted in 2019). The cougars/tigers/wildcats category is the most widely adopted. Other species known for their brawn are next in line (bears, jaguars, lions, panthers, rams, wolves).

Birds are especially popular (blue jays, cardinals, eagles, falcons, hawks, owls, ravens). Other animal groups are dogs (bulldogs, greyhounds, huskies, terriers), flying squirrels, frogs, horses (broncos, colts, mustangs), insects (bees (hornets, stingers, yellow jackets), spiders), marine life (dolphins, sharks, skipjacks, whales), snakes (rattlers), turtles.

Another favored grouping is the human (or living things) category (Aztecs, brewers, cowboys, Hoosiers, patriots, renegades, tar heels), including non-human living objects such as tree names (buckeyes, sycamores) or fruit-bearing plants (berries – the Logansport High School Berries named after the loganberry).

Then there are names derived from geography (hilltoppers, lakers, mountaineers); history (buccaneers, gladiators, knights, pirates, spartans, titans, trojans, warriors; military (cavaliers, chargers, musketeers, raiders); occupation (boilermakers, senators, steelers); religion (avenging angels, blue angels, crusaders, friars, monks, saints); school traditions (Georgetown Hoyas, Tennessee Volunteers, Virginia Tech Hokies); outer space (astros, comets); weather (hurricanes, thunder, tornadoes, Newington High School's Nor'easters, Norwich High School's Purple Tornado, Vancouver's Whitecaps).

Names of mythical creatures and evil spirits include demons, devils, dragons, giants, phantoms, phoenixes and thunderbirds.

Lots of school names are linked in some way to the school or city's origin – such as the Philadelphia 76ers, San Francisco 49ers, Texas A&M Aggies, Utah Utes, Vanderbilt Commodores, Wichita

State Shockers – or even a color (Alabama Crimson Tide, Cincinnati Reds, Syracuse Orange).

Note that a number of the pro teams have maintained their original nickname even if the location changes. For example, the Los Angeles Lakers originally were based in Minnesota, "Land of 10,000 Lakes." The Memphis Grizzlies earlier had been based in Vancouver, where the grizzly bear is indigenous to British Columbia in Canada. And the Utah Jazz originated in New Orleans.

Working in tandem with the team's nickname is the school mascot, which typically is a symbolic figure to bring the team good luck.

The word itself is derived from the French word "mascotte," meaning lucky charm.

An example is Notre Dame. Its nickname is the Fighting Irish, and its mascot is the leprechaun, a little bearded man dressed in green who partakes in mischief and has a pot of gold at the end of the rainbow.

These mascots can be live animals, costumed people or giant size inflatable characters. For our discussion, we will consider the second category – real people who get dressed in the school's colors and an outfit befitting the nickname and liven up the stadium or arena.

Mascots are instructed to maintain constant motion and amuse and interact with fans, including children. A big part of the job is to be funny and spontaneous.

Most perform all kinds of antics and have a catchy name. Here are just a few: Aristocat, Benny Beaver, Bucky the Bronco, Cosmo the Cougar, Captain Buc, Ernie the Eagle, Felix the Cat, General Grizzly, Harry the Husky, Kasey the Kangaroo, Keggy the Keg, Lil' Red, Otto the Orange, Purdue Pete, Reggie Redbird, Sam the Minuteman.

Some schools have co-mascots who work as a team: Albert and Alberta Gator, Jawz, Jinx and Jazzy, Jay and Baby Jay, Mr. Met and Mrs. Met (both of whom I've seen in action).

Sports organizations came up with the idea of a mascot as a way to provide extra entertainment for spectators. Mascots have proved to be a most successful marketing tool, providing real value to the sports program. A mascot gives the team an identity and adds personality. If branded successfully, every time a fan thinks of the team, an image of the character will come to mind.

This establishes a connection. This connection creates excitement and enthusiasm, thus selling more tickets because everyone wants to go to the games (or watch them on TV, thus improving viewer ratings). That increases merchandise sales, which, in turn, adds to the aura and fun – and the bottom line.

It's all one big package.

People interested in becoming a mascot need, for starters, to enjoy entertaining a crowd and prepare by taking gymnastics and dance lessons to become agile and physically fit. Not all jobs are full time or permanent. Some colleges award scholarships that help with tuition. Some schools offer remuneration. The annual salary at the college level is around $30,000 and at the pro level about $60,000 (although a few of the pro teams pay 10 times that amount). Mascots frequently get an invitation to appear at various and sundry public functions and private parties and get paid by the hour.

It can be a lot of fun performing tricks at the games and getting bravos from the cheering masses. But if the team is losing, fans may take their frustrations out on the mascot with boos and even worse. Also, it can get mighty warm with the costume and headdress on if the weather is hot.

Thank goodness the pros outnumber the cons because the game would not be the same without these lively, energetic, colorful characters delighting the crowd.

Life in Rowayton

Rowayton, Connecticut, is a delightful place to live. It's one of a kind – there is no other town in the world named Rowayton.

It is situated on the shore of Long Island Sound and is adjacent to the archipelago that encompasses the 25+ Norwalk Islands.

Rowayton was discovered by the Dutch fur trader, privateer and navigator Adriaen Block in 1614 (the same captain for whom Block Island off the coast of Connecticut and Rhode Island is named and the first European to navigate the East River in Manhattan).

The small coastal village, spanning less than two square miles, lies 40 miles east of New York City. It has a rich oystering and lobstering history and, for many decades, was a popular homestead for fishermen and sea captains.

View of Five Mile River from Pinkney Park in Rowayton.

Several streets south of the shopping area feature signage that reads "Oysterman's Row." This area of town is where locals who worked in the oyster industry lived during the 1800s and early 1900s. For example, Craw Avenue is named for William Craw (1837-1897), a sea captain and co-owner of Craw & L'Hommedieu Oyster Company. The district is listed in the National Register of Historic Places.

Rowayton also borders Five Mile River dividing Darien (that's pronounced "Dairy-Anne") and Rowayton, a section of Norwalk with a population of around 4,000 residents.

The village features boating and beaches and all the fun activities associated with life on the seashore. One can see water views in every direction all over town. The small downtown area is home to eateries, a trendy market, a post office, a hardware store, two banks, two churches, a variety of small shops and a lovely park on the river.

All along Five Mile River, boatyards dot the waterfront. Approximately 350 boats of all kinds are tied to a fore and aft mooring or secured in a slip. It's a boating mecca. Except in the dead of winter, kayakers and paddleboarders parade up and down the channel.

Rowayton has become a destination.

Boating is a way of life in Rowayton. It seems about every other person in town owns, or used to own, a boat (or two). Some are small runabouts. Some are large powerboats. In between, there are vessels of every length, make and model. Boats are used for the full gamut of activities – from gunkholing to fishing to racing to long-distance cruising. Rowayton is a yachtsman's paradise.

Most of the yacht clubs have a racing program. On most any day all season long, there is a race somewhere nearby. People of varying ages throughout the area are seasoned racers. But competitions are not just local. For decades, Rowayton has been well-represented in major races and regattas such as the Bermuda Race, the Vineyard Race, the Trans-Atlantic Race, Block Island Race Week and dozens of others.

Sailors take their racing seriously. Ed Raymond was an ardent sailor, renowned for winning races up and down the East Coast starting in the 1930s. His dedication was so strong that he often had to sacrifice personal commitments. For example, he missed his daughter Bobbie's high school graduation one June day because he was away competing in the Bermuda Race. When it came time for Bobbie to set a wedding date, she chose January because it was more likely that her dad would be in town that time of year and could walk her down the aisle to marry Tom Murray. (In fact, I've heard people say they tell family and friends not to get married, have a baby or die during the boating season.)

Several of the Raymond family members were accomplished sailors. Aside from Bobbie's father, her brother, son and nephew also competed in the Bermuda Race. And son Tim, at age 19, was aboard the boat that won the Trans-Atlantic Race in 1993. There are family stories like this all over town – whereby sailing is a way of life.

With events at the yacht clubs up and down I-95 and all around the Sound, Ray and I came to know many people over the years who competed in races far and near and who have had all kinds of interesting and wonderful boating experiences.

It's fascinating to hear their tales.

Scott and Kitty Kuhner, for example, sailed around the world – twice, once when they were in their 20s and again 16 years later with their two sons, aged 11 and nine, as crew. Each trip took four years. Their longest passage without stopping for the day or night was 3,052 miles in 22 days. They determined that from Connecticut, Bali was exactly halfway around the world.

Scott and Kitty wrote a book about each circumnavigation: The *Voyage of Bebinka* and *The Great Escape*. Both books are available in paperback. In 2003, they sailed the Atlantic Circle to Portugal (via the Azores) and back (via the Caribbean). Since then, their sailing trips have been closer to home: They have spent their winters in the Bahamas and the summers in Maine.

For years, Ray and I belonged to the Corinthians, a group of boaters who rendezvous at various yacht clubs for races and cruises during the summer and for presentations and gams during the rest of the year. (A gam is a nautical term to describe one whaling ship paying a social visit to another at sea.) A very competitive species, the Corinthians are a fearless lot, and listening to their adventures can make the hair on the back of your neck stand on end.

In 1978, Ray and I bought a house built in 1924 in the Rowayton Beach Association across the street from Five Mile River. We lived our entire married life in this house in the charming seaside village of Rowayton. A longtime friend recently said I was the only person on her contacts list whose mailing address hadn't changed at least once over the last 40 years.

After retiring from IBM, Ray served as harbor superintendent of Five Mile River for a record 13 years and was responsible for the safe navigation of the waterway. In this role, he served at the pleasure of the Five Mile River Commission. Because the river borders both Norwalk and Darien, two commissioners from each town are appointed by the governor. For most of his tenure, Ray reported to Matthew Marion, chairman, and John de Regt representing Norwalk and Wim Jessup and Dirk Leasure representing Darien. David Snyder served as assistant harbor superintendent. Tammy Papp, a vice president at The Boatworks, served as Ray's administrative assistant.

Ray was charged with carrying out his responsibilities according to the town ordinances pertaining to Five Mile River. He became intimately familiar with these statutes, and people were amazed at how he could instantly cite the regulation applicable to the situation at hand. At dinner, Ray would share the happenings of the day with me, and, over the years, my horizon expanded well beyond the perspective of recreational boating. I benefited from the residuals – learning more than I ever dreamed existed about ground tackle requirements and inspections, mooring permits, dredging regulations and a whole host of other maritime activities.

Throughout the summer, Ray would patrol the river and look for signs of trouble, and I would tag along just for the fun of it. The last 10 years or so, kayaks and paddleboards have become extremely popular because they are relatively inexpensive to purchase yet provide a fun-filled experience on the water. Therefore, they attract lots of beginners – who can pose a danger to the powerboats and sailboats maneuvering in the restricted space.

Ray created a special channel for these small craft away from the federal channel. He installed several yellowish-colored buoys for guiding the operators and instructed them to "follow the yellow brick road."

At Ray's retirement ceremony at City Hall in October of 2016, Mayor Harry W. Rilling presented a proclamation, and Connecticut State Senator Bob Duff presented an official citation from the State of Connecticut General Assembly.

It is my pleasure to have been a part of all those wonderful memories surrounding Ray's service as harbor superintendent.

In January of 2008, we won the raffle in Rowayton Library's fundraising drive. The prize was a skillfully handmade quilt stitched by the Goodwives Quilters of Darien. Appropriately, that year's theme was Five Mile River. An image of Green's Ledge Lighthouse is sewn on the bottom right side (known in the advertising world as the anchor position (meaning choice location)).

Being so close to New York City makes upscale Rowayton an attractive place to call home. Many prominent people are drawn to the area, and it is not uncommon to see them around carrying on with everyday life – from movie stars to TV personalities to professional athletes to business tycoons. For example, one Sunday afternoon, I saw Scott Pelley, a television journalist and anchor routinely seen on CBS, wearing an old sweatshirt and khakis, loading groceries into his car at one of the local supermarkets.

In the early 1960s, Billy Rose owned Tavern Island, located across the harbor east southeast of Rowayton Yacht Club. An American legend, the songwriter and stage producer made quite a name for himself in the entertainment world and on Broadway in particular. The lavish parties he hosted for his show business friends are notorious, and guests ranged from Marilyn Monroe to Barbra Streisand. Rose was married five times to four different women. His first marriage was to singer and comedienne Fanny Brice, who had her big break in the popular Ziegfeld Follies in 1910.

More recently, other actors who have called Rowayton home include Horace McMahon, Betsy Palmer and neighbor Treat Williams.

Joyce and Ray on Five Mile River in Rowayton one December.

Dennis Conner lived part time in Thomas Place during the '80s. He skippered and won four America's Cup events. His tactician, Peter Isler, also was a Rowaytonite. Both live in California now.

Bruce Kirby, designer of the Laser dinghy, the Sonar keelboat and two America's Cup 12-meter yachts, among others, made Rowayton his home for many decades. He sailed in the Olympics representing Canada three times.

The crusty Andy Rooney lived over by the train station. He was known for his appearances on CBS' "60 Minutes" from 1978 till 2011. Ray and I would see him around town and had occasion to enjoy his company at dinner parties at Frank Fay's home on Sunwich Road in the RBA. I remember commenting after one such evening, "Andy is quite the storyteller."

The village library sometimes holds panel discussions featuring local authors. At one of these functions, Andy stood and said, "I'm up last as usual," referring to his slot that ended the TV program with some pithy remarks and pearls of wisdom.

Andy was a mentor to Frank Fay, who spent his entire life in Rowayton and became a well-respected reporter for the local newspaper, *The Hour*. He was known for his historical accounts about town 25 and 50 years ago entitled "The Way We Were." Frank could have gone to any one of the New York dailies but chose to stay close to home.

Elsewhere in this book, particularly in the preceding sports section, several other well-known Rowaytonites are mentioned.

The Rowayton Civic Association has been active throughout the time we lived in our little town. It sponsors events year round, including a Comedy Night, a Trash Bash, a Father's Day Fun Run, 4th of July Fireworks, the River Ramble, Ladrigan Swim Races, an Oktoberfest, a Santa Toy Drive and a live Nativity Pageant, among others.

The Rowayton Community Center is a historic building that houses the library and meeting rooms and is a center of activity. It also is the setting where the first business computer prototype was developed by the Remington Rand Corporation. The unveiling took place in 1951 at a gathering of government and military officials right here at the Rowayton facility.

Frank Raymond authored *Rowayton on the Half Shell*, a book depicting more than 300 years of the village's beginnings and growth. It is well worth the read. The Raymond family ancestry in Rowayton can be traced back to the 1660s.

The Rowayton Historic Society comprises an active group of residents who are devoted to maintaining Rowayton's rich history. Special programs feature speakers and demonstrations, and in December, a holiday bazaar and train show delight the young and the old. And the Frank E. Raymond Maritime Museum and Boathouse (named after Frank Raymond as mentioned above) is in the works. It will include exhibitions of Rowayton's history pertaining to the oystering and related shellfish businesses and the seafaring families who owned and operated them along with boats, models, ship-making tools and a host of other pertinent topics.

Getting to Rowayton is fairly easy unless traffic is heavy. I-95 gets congested often, and it can take an extraordinary amount of time to go a short distance. When the interstate gets backed up, traffic spills onto the main artery, the Boston Post Road (in Fairfield and New Haven counties). The Post Road runs between New York City and Boston and was used by the colonists for mail delivery (thus the name "Post").

Throughout Westchester and Fairfield counties, separate towns blend into each other, making it more or less one continuous suburb from Manhattan eastward to beyond New Haven, Connecticut (about 80 miles).

Roton Point

Roton Point in Rowayton sits high on a hill and has spectacular views of Long Island Sound. On the most sultry of days, there is always a breeze under the grove of tall oak trees.

For about 150 years, Roton Point is where families have gone to relax, have a picnic and enjoy the sun-kissed beach.

A map of the area, dated 1872, shows three buildings used for entertainment on the property. Prior to that, it was used exclusively for swimming and picnicking.

Due to the improvement of mass transportation over the next few years, large numbers of visitors seeking a getaway were making the trip from Manhattan to Roton Point on excursion steamers.

Throughout the 1880s, facilities were added to the park, including a hotel featuring a two-lane bowling alley, midway games and concessions, particularly the popular glass-blowing booth. Roton Point Park was emerging into a full-fledged amusement park on the beach.

In 1891, the property was sold to investors who put in motion plans for further expanding the enterprise. Within a year, the park consisted of a number of buildings, including the hotel, dance pavilion, bathhouse, carousel, an open-air photography gallery and horse sheds. And a 100-foot pier was constructed to accommodate the steamships bearing passengers eager for a day at the park.

The advent of trolley cars is what sparked the growth of Roton

Point Park. The original trolleys were horse-drawn. Then on May 25, 1894, the first electric trolley car made a run from South Norwalk to Roton Point. It was a 20-minute ride and cost 5 cents. From then on, multitudes of visitors came by land to visit Roton Point Park.

And by sea, the excursion steamboats out of New York City brought thousands of passengers for a day trip to the beach and park. It was about a two-hour trip each way that entailed a boat ride on beautiful Long Island Sound while listening and dancing to a live band. Parkgoers would land around noon and spend the afternoon swimming and partaking in the delights of the amusement park. After dinner, they would return to New York, disembarking around sunset.

The Belle Island was a 2,000-passenger steamer designed and built in 1925 by the park's management exclusively for travel between Manhattan and Roton Point. It was used extensively for many years. In 1942, it was purchased by the U.S. government and became part of the war effort.

Research shows that on one particular day in the 1920s, nine boats arrived at the Roton Point Park pier, each carrying approximately 2,000 passengers. The dock could berth only four steamers at a time. So after dropping off the passengers, five boats had to lie to for several hours in the open waters of the harbor between Green's Ledge Lighthouse and Sheffield Island ("lie to" on a boat means the captain tends to the helm and maintains the vessel's position without the benefit of anchoring).

It also seems to be a fact that the multitudes of people (in the above case being between 15,000 and 20,000) descending on tiny Rowayton did not disturb the peacefulness in the surrounding areas of the village.

At the beginning, there was a carousel, a roller coaster and a variety of other rides. An assortment of booths dotted the grounds. Typically, the prizes were stuffed dolls or salt water taffy. Around 400 bathhouses were built for dressing after swimming. Concession stands and restaurants offered food treats. Local fare, such as fresh roasted clams, was prepared on-site.

In 1914, merry-go-round salesman Neville Bayley arrived on the scene. His experience, energy and vision molded the property into the successful entity it became, drawing thousands and thousands of people. Roton Point Park grew to be a notable destination for sun and fun.

As time went on, more rides, games and booths were added (the roller coaster was upgraded several times). A gazebo was built that still stands today (it's been renovated, as have all the structures). And the entertainment was expanded. For example, spectators were thoroughly entertained by balloonists: daredevils dressed in colorful tights who performed acrobatic stunts from a basket high in the sky. At the end, they would open the parachute and drop to the ground (or sometimes, by mistake, into the water or, worse, the mudflats).

As the park grew, a major attraction was the dance pavilion. Sunday nights were booked with big bands, drawing throngs of fans who came to listen to the live music and to dance. The hall was situated on stilts in the water above an outcropping of rocks and was open on all four sides to let the breeze in off Long Island Sound.

Many of the well-known big bands and popular performers of the day made an appearance in Rowayton. Just a few of them include Bunny Berrigan, Cab Calloway, the Dorsey Brothers, Duke Ellington, Benny Goodman, Billie Holiday, Guy Lombardo, Rudy Vallee, Fred Waring. Even the Ziegfeld Follies came to town.

Fireworks are an age-old favorite. Roton Point Park featured fireworks as part of the entertainment on Friday nights. And on the 4th of July, there was a dazzling display drawing large crowds.

Changes and improvements were continually being made in an attempt to keep people interested in coming to the park. At some point, the original carousel was moved to another part of the property, and a vaudeville theater took its place, which eventually became a roller skating rink. A two-story building was erected, containing a central hall, a dining room, a bar and bowling alleys. A shooting gallery was added. There were dog shows and juggling acts and fortune tellers.

There were even beauty pageants. In fact, a 15-year-old from West Haven won the Miss Connecticut title in 1933 and went on that September to be named Miss America in Atlantic City, New Jersey (the only time Connecticut or any New England state has produced a winner).

As well, Roton Point was a place for churches and organizations to hold their outings and for audiences to listen to concerts. Dance competitions (especially during the Depression years) and endurance contests were held at the Point.

People came in droves.

The hurricane of 1938 wreaked havoc on the grounds and severely damaged many of the buildings, rides, structures and pier. Compounding those dire circumstances, World War II started a few short years later. The steamships were used in the war effort – and the amusement park was stilled, closing its doors for good in 1941.

After the war, Roton Point reverted to a family picnic ground and gathering venue and remains that way today as a private association. You may recall reading that Ray and I held our wedding reception there.

As a private club, its sailing program has attained a highly respected reputation. In fact, from 1977 to 1985, a 25-foot International C-class catamaran named Patient Lady won the Little America's Cup four times and put Roton Point Club on the racing map. Catamarans are known for their speed. With just a little wind, they move along at 12-15 knots. In the right wind, they can attain even greater speeds. From aboard our boat, Ray and I watched the catamarans practice on many afternoons during those years.

These days, during the summertime, I go to Roton Point on Thursdays at noon to enjoy the company of my Bible Buddies from church.

-30- Story

In the media world, in which both Ray and I were involved, "30" means the end of the copy – or end of story.

When we bought our home in Rowayton in the Beach Association, the address was #30. We laughed and glibly commented that maybe this would be our last house.

After keeping an eye out for a home at other locations, in Rowayton and elsewhere, through the years, we ended up staying in our original house. So the "30" was a harbinger of where we would call home for the duration of our marriage.

Also, I met Ray when I was age 30. On the program for Ray's memorial service, I added -30- at the bottom to signify the end.

And look for the -30- on the last page of this memoir.

Around the 'Hood
The Rowayton Beach Association is a section of Rowayton that boasts its own beach and craggy rock formation that juts out into Long Island Sound. The view of the water from the beach is spectacular with Green's Ledge Lighthouse, Sheffield Island and – seven miles due south – Long Island in sight. Adirondack chairs are situated along the length of the seawall, and picnic tables and umbrellas fill out the space. Grills are available for barbequing. A sizable grassy area is home to net games and foot races.

The Boathouse on Five Mile River is a rustic but charming one-story gray building, the venue of the annual meeting of RBA residents each September. There is a yearly spring and fall cocktail party at the Boathouse for members, and residents are welcome to rent the facility for private functions except during the wintertime (no heat). It has its own beach and provides access to boats large and small on the river.

People congregate in these common areas, and neighbor meets and greets neighbor.

For these reasons, members of the Beach Association get to know each other, on and off the beach, and they look out for each other. In years past, the association was especially social with lots of house parties throughout the year. That doesn't happen as much today.

A walk to the beach is a daily routine for many residents. Green's Ledge Lighthouse is named for a pirate who sailed with the infamous

Captain Kidd. Legend has it that Green was captured and executed, and his body was fastened to the ledge with chains as a lesson to others to deter them from entering into illicit and nefarious activities. Later, the lighthouse was built to help guide vessels navigating the entrance to Wilson Cove and Norwalk Harbor.

Rowayton Beach Association beach looking east over Long Island Sound.

The rock formation at "Our Beach," as it came to be called by RBA residents, is most distinctive and represents character and perseverance. People of all ages climb the rocks and appreciate nature at its best.

A plaque in remembrance of Eric Lund rests in the midst of the rocks. Eric grew up in the RBA and was a soccer star at Brien McMahon High School. Shortly after enrolling at the University of Connecticut in 1967, he was diagnosed with acute lymphoblastic leukemia. He fought the disease by continuing to play on the soccer team and working out between treatments, trying to keep his body strong. During his time at UConn, he was the All-New England pick in 1970 and captain the next year.

He lost the battle in 1972, and his mother Doris Lund wrote an inspirational story about his determination and fighting spirit in her book titled *Eric*. It also was made into a movie, starring John Savage and Patricia Neal. Ray and I knew both Eric's mother Doris and father Sidney, who served as RBA president for a number of years.

The streets are flat in the Beach Association and have become a popular route for joggers and walkers. On any day of the year, a steady stream of people of all sizes, shapes and ages would pass by our house. Ray always commented on their different gaits. I said I recognized who the person was by the dog on the leash.

Joyce and Ray at Rowayton Beach Association beach.

When we bought our house, there was a vacant lot across the street, and we had a view of the river. Our front porch faced the water, and we called it the River Room. We had a back room with a wet bar, and we hung charts of Long Island Sound, Block Island Sound and the waters around Shelter Island on the walls and called it the Chart Room.

We appointed the house with furniture purchased from department stores like Bloomingdale's and Macy's to consignment shops and tag sales, as well as custom-ordered upholstered loveseats and chairs from Henredon and other well-known manufacturers.

All this took time, and at the beginning, the furniture was sparse. We spent the first night in the house eating dinner on the kitchen floor – just like in the storybooks.

View of Five Mile River from our living room.

We strove to retain the beachy feel, supplemented with a Country French look. The house was airy with lots of windows (no curtains in order to maintain the outdoor feeling) and wainscoting in the dining room and Chart Room to preserve a New England look. Just below the mantle, tiles with sailing scenes were built into the fireplace, and people commented on how appropriate they were.

We were always on the lookout for household items with a nautical theme. Over the years, we collected trappings that portrayed that maritime look and feel, including a handmade model of two of our boats, framed pictures, miniature lighthouses, a two-foot sailboat for the front bay window, throw pillows, various replicas of a blue heron and numerous knickknacks, to name but a few.

Everyone said the house had a real seaside feel and was "so Rowayton."

Most years, the Rowayton Civic Association sponsors fireworks on the 4th of July. The fireworks are launched from a barge just off the beaches, and people come from far and near to see the show. Since parking is limited to off-street locations, those of us with extra parking spaces on our property in the RBA discover we have more friends than we realized.

Our periodontist and friend Gerry Strassberger used to park in our driveway during the fireworks. He once joked that if we ever sold the house, he'd like parking privileges put in the contract.

Five Mile River from Rowayton Beach Association Boathouse beach across the street from our home.

Many people choose to watch the fireworks from the water and come by boat. It's quite a spectacle to see the hundreds of lights bobbing in the local waters, onlookers tooting their horn when the fireworks are especially good. And, of course, some residents and boaters add to the festivities with their own pyrotechnics.

Every year, the RBA hosts a Halloween party, and the Boathouse is transformed into the ultimate haunted house. For many years, Tammis Lazarus and Christine Kiggins were in charge. Someone – Tammis and then Julie Begos and now Heidi Keelips – would make a huge batch of chili. (Julie said it took all week to prepare. She made it a family affair, with her "little ones" helping out in the kitchen.) The entire neighborhood is invited to the party, and volunteers take shifts serving chili, hot dogs and dessert.

With tummies full, the "kiddleberries" hit the streets around 5 p.m. Our home is kitty-corner to the Boathouse, and by evening's end, on average, 200 trick-or-treaters in full costume will have elbowed their way to the top step at the front door.

Frank Sinatra (not *the* Frank Sinatra but a not-too-distant relative) lived in the RBA for 25 years. He was the party organizer. Frank was the one, along with John St. John and Bart Kathner, who, every spring, grilled hot dogs and burgers for the volunteers after cleanup day at the beach and Boathouse.

In the summertime, Frank would host a neighborhood dinner party and transform his backyard into an outdoor café complete with a standup bar. Music would be provided by a band at Wee Burn Country Club just down the beach a few hundred feet. Frank also hosted an annual lobster bake at the beach that included the whole megillah (clams and mussels for hors d'oeuvres, baked potato, corn on the cob, lobster, dessert). The only complaint was that the cocktail hour turned into hours, and the main course wouldn't be served until after dark. But people came back year after year.

Frank was in the cosmetics business, and I introduced Cynthia to him when she had some opportunities in China surrounding her organic soap business. Since Frank made an annual trip to the Far East, he had contacts there. Frank and Cynthia worked on several projects. She was the neophyte and he the seasoned negotiator. He was a class act businesswise and otherwise.

By the way, Frank was christened his first name because it is tradition going back to his ancestors in Sicily for the first grandson to be named for the grandfather. In Frank's case, special permission had to be granted to use the shortened version of Francesco. When Frank's turn came and his first grandson was born, tradition was broken. Frank didn't want to burden another generation of Franks with having to explain the connection to ol' Blue Eyes whenever meeting someone new (I always was sorry he didn't carry the Frank Sinatra name on).

Like so many others in the RBA, Frank and Rita (Leone), his significant other, moved south, seeking a warmer clime. A lot of people came and went over the years, but many stayed for decades, as did the Meurers.

Mary Wilson was a neighbor when we first moved into our home in 1978. Mary was up there in age – in her late 80s or early 90s – and had the usual senior ailments so we kept an eye on her. I took care of Mary's garbage can for a long time. We also drove her to the elementary school to vote on community issues – until we realized she always voted the opposite way. That was the end of the car service.

The neighbors in the RBA watch out for each other and keep tabs on one another. On one occasion, Ray and I had returned from a business trip in Europe. The limo had dropped us off in front of the house, and our luggage was still in the street when Sally Cross, a neighbor from down the road, happened to bike by. She said, "Well, hello! I've just returned from Jersey. Where did you come from today?" We told her we had flown in from Zurich. Soon everyone around us knew we were back and made it a point to welcome us home.

Charley and Joanne Schreiber bought their home in the RBA in 1960. It was a small, two-story red beach house situated on the north side of the Boathouse. They called it their "slice of paradise." After Charley passed away, Joanne stayed on and passionately loved living directly on Five Mile River and being a Rowayton resident for a total of 53 years. She became a good friend, and we had many conversations while watching the boats go by on the river. She moved to Norwalk and has a condo overlooking the Norwalk River. Although no longer in the RBA, she is close enough to come round a couple of times a week to keep up with the happenings in the old neighborhood.

Diane and Perry Caminis lived (and still do) in the RBA when we bought our house. We were destined to become friends not only because we were neighbors but also because they both worked for IBM in the same building as Ray and, later on, me. We commuted together on many occasions to White Plains, New York. And I still remember one Halloween when their daughter Argo (short for Argyro) came trick-or-treating and knocked on our front door dressed as an apple. She went on to earn her M.D. degree from Yale and a master's in public health from Harvard and has a private psychiatric practice in the Boston area.

I always tried to be good to our neighbors. The fact that I was ensconced in my office so much of the time limited my availability to walk the streets and stumble upon opportunities to help people in the neighborhood.

One time, though, I noticed the lady across the street, Margot Draycott – who walked with a cane – was having difficulty carrying bags of groceries from her car to the house. So I vacated my office and dashed over to help. Upon heading back home, I looked up and saw the most beautiful full rainbow in the east. The colors were extraordinarily vibrant, and it filled the sky. I remember thinking that if I hadn't assisted with the groceries and was still in my office facing west, I would have missed a spectacular sight. So many times when you give, you get more back.

Pam Davis and Gary Schpero have lived next door for years, and we've waited out many storms side by side (and, needless to say, a hurricane or two). Ray and I watched their son Will grow up and become an upstanding young adult. He earned his undergraduate and master's degrees from Dartmouth and a doctorate from Yale. He is a health economist and is involved in research in the healthcare field. He also is a professor at the university level in New York City. Pam was happy when Will proposed (on the pier steps at Farm Creek in Rowayton) to his sweetheart Kristine ("that's Kristine with a K" as Gary would say). I remember Pam saying, "We like her very much. And they'll be good together – she makes him laugh."

Talking about the Beach Association would not be complete if Ann DiLeone were not included in the conversation. She moved in across the street from us in 1995 and has been the model for what being neighborly is all about. She has always offered a smile and a kind word and often a token gift (a flower or tomato from her garden) to make one's day a little cheerier.

During Ray's illness and afterward, Ann was a steadfast friend, calling me nearly every day to see how I was doing. Having lost two husbands, Ann understood how hard those days can be.

She said many times that grieving is a process and that "life is not a dress rehearsal." When our twin granddaughters would come to stay with us during the Salty Dog summer program at Rowayton Yacht Club, Ann always invited the girls to swim in her pool – her only rule was that an adult had to accompany them. Both girls loved the distinctively shaped pool, and Amanda went on to become a champion swimmer at St. Lawrence University and broke several school records, specifically in the butterfly and freestyle relay competitions.

Ann and her late husband Roland enjoyed many happy years together in that house across the street, and Ray and Roland were buddies. Roland was a master at fixing and building anything. His garage was a small warehouse filled with every tool imaginable. In fact, he made the handsome wooden Boathouse signboard that still hangs above the entryway.

There are many neighbors and townspeople who have played a role in my life. And there are dozens of others who have graced our roads and beaches in the RBA but no longer reside here. I'll not go into any more detail – suffice it to say it has been a pleasure to have known so many delightful fellow Rowaytonites.

Getting Acquainted with the Kids
Ray had three children from his first marriage: Diane, Michael and Scott. When Ray and I were married, the kids ranged in age from 14 to 20.

As is common, it took a little time for them to get to know and accept me. It was not my intention to try to become a mother to them – I just wanted each one to know I accepted them for who they were. There were a few trying times, but we became friends and are close. They have become responsible adults and were especially caring and helpful when Ray was sick.

Each has been attentive and continues to be part of my life since Ray passed away. Diane surprises me with homemade goodies, from muffins and cookies to side dishes and with flowers from her garden. Michael comes loaded with groceries and baked goods and, sometimes, barbequed ribs and helps with fixing or replacing household appliances.

Scott brings lunch and can be counted on to help with handyman chores, run errands and tote me around to family get-togethers. All these gestures are greatly appreciated.

During the early '80s, both Diane and Michael lived with us for a short period of time, and Scott was in high school and spent some weekends here at the house and on the boat. One summer when he was in college, we went on a cruise on our boat, and Scott stayed at the house. When we left, Ray said, "No parties in the house."

Upon our return, we learned that Scott had hosted quite the party on our front lawn, and everyone in the neighborhood was talking about the event and the great music. When confronted about it, Scott said, "The party was not held inside the house."

Kids will be kids.

Babysitting the Twins
Ray's three children each had two children. Both Ray and his father before him were called "dad" and "grandpa." Earlier generations of Meurers had used the names "pop" and "grandpop."

Ray's kids and their families live within an hour of Rowayton, and Ray and I would see them on holidays and throughout the year.

Michael and Elizabeth had twin daughters, and we spent a lot of time babysitting. Amanda and Rachel were born in July of 1999. The next month, Elizabeth's father became gravely ill, and she and Michael needed to make a quick trip to Michigan. So Ray and I offered to babysit for the week.

Little did we realize what a challenge that would become. The girls were three weeks old and had to be fed every four hours, which translated into every two hours for two babies. Ray and I split up the schedule through the daytime, and at night, I took the 10 p.m., midnight and 2 a.m. feedings. Ray would pick up at 4 a.m.

As time passed, the days became a blur, and Ray commented that it got to the point where we stayed in our jammies till noon. We were exhausted. Amanda was a good eater and was always hungry, but

Rachel wasn't much interested and took forever to finish the bottle of formula. A big cheer went out when Michael and Elizabeth returned.

Time Marches On

The years sped by. Ray and I enjoyed a full social life, personally and professionally.

We made monthly trips to Lakewood, New Jersey, to visit Ray's father Syl and his second wife Frances. After Syl stopped driving, someone in the family would pick them up and transport them to wherever a holiday gathering or special event was to be held, in either Rowayton or Long Island.

Ray's sister Alice had married John (Jack) Garabedian in 1948 and lived in Great Neck and then Carle Place on Long Island. As their family size grew, Ray spent lots of time with them. Jack's family operated a taxi business, and Ray helped out on the weekends. After Ray was married and living on Long Island as well, he and his first wife Jane frequently visited with Alice and Jack and their three kids (Bruce, Gregg and Lynn). After Ray and Jane had their own children (Diane, Michael and Scott), there were frequent family get-togethers.

Alice's kids are all grown up now, of course, and we keep in touch with "the cousins" as they are called. I go into greater detail about the relatives later in a chapter devoted to the Meurer ancestry.

Through the years, my sister Cynthia and I have remained close, visiting each other often. So it was a treat when she studied for a year in 2006 at The General Theological Seminary in New York City, and we could spend most weekends together either in Rowayton or in the city.

Ray's work in advertising and later media relations provided social activities as colleagues all over the tri-state (Connecticut, New York, New Jersey) area often entertained in their home. IBM rewarded employees with luncheons and dinners for performance and work milestones. The Quarter Century Club was a gala event that always promised great entertainment. For example, one year they brought in the Beach Boys for a concert.

Joyce (left) and Cynthia at her graduation from
The General Theological Seminary in New York City.

Being in advertising, Ray was invited to all kinds of affairs, and it was my pleasure to accompany him. In New York, the Madison Avenue ad agencies hosted events all over the city, including Broadway plays, dinners at trendy restaurants (we were treated to the finest food from soup to nuts) and boat trips to watch the fireworks.

One of the annual highlights for the advertising folks was dinner and a boat ride around Manhattan aboard Malcom Forbes' 151-foot yacht, the Highlander (it housed a helicopter named the Capitalist Tool for easy access to land). In fact, we were aboard not long after a major New York City event when President Reagan and Frank Sinatra had spent time on the megayacht and both had used a particular head (word meaning "bathroom" on a boat). I was proud to have visited the same lavatory. It was decorated in green marble and gold and was exquisite.

IBM maintained a dress code in those years. It consisted of the men wearing a dark suit, white (generally) shirt and a tie. My mother loved to buy Ray dress shirts for Christmas, birthday and just about any occasion, and he had a wardrobe full (at least 40-50 at any given time) of white-on-white shirts that were very classy. I spent many hours keeping those shirts laundered and ironed by hand. Routinely, I would spend all evening ironing and listening to my country music. Two of my favorite singers were Patsy Cline and Reba McEntire.

Having lived in the East now for so many years, I had explored much of New York City. Numerous movies were filmed in the Big Apple, and it was fun to see on the silver screen scenes and places where I had been.

For media relations, Ray handled assignments surrounding IBM products and the company's sponsorship of many events and did his share of traveling around the country. He especially enjoyed the sports marketing work covering the PGA (golf) tours and the ATP (tennis) tournaments. But his favorite was the BOC single-handed around-the-world sailboat races. Twice, Ray managed the press relations for the major sailing event based in Newport, Rhode Island, and I delighted in meeting the skippers and touring their boat. (To attain the fastest speed, most were stripped bare except for sophisticated navigational systems.)

It wasn't necessary to go into New York City to find culture. Locally, there are countless performances to attend. The Rowayton Civic Association sponsors Sunday afternoon concerts all summer long in Pinkney Park or at Bayley Beach, and spectators come by land and by sea. Since 1995, Shakespeare on the Sound has been presented each June, and attendees picnic on a blanket in the park before the show. The Darien Library often presents a recital during the holiday season, sponsoring entertainment such as Yale's renowned a cappella singers, the Whiffenpoofs. A symphony orchestra resides in both Norwalk and Greenwich. A full menu of quality performances of concerts and plays is offered regularly throughout Fairfield County towns. Art centers and libraries abound, and events are staged year round. There's so much to see and do right at our fingertips.

Life was good and very social. In Rowayton, we belonged (and I still do) to two yacht clubs that filled the calendar with boating-related functions 12 months of the year. I came upon a pocket calendar from one year in the '80s with a social affair noted on 14 consecutive nights. (Unfortunately, during Ray's last year, that schedule was replaced with consecutive days of medical appointments.)

Even the weddings in the East were far different from the typical wedding in the Midwest. They ranged from simple to tastefully elegant to lavish with lots of pizzazz. And the reception could be quite creative.

We attended one wedding where the attire was black and white (tuxedos and cocktail dresses). Each male attendee was given a key at the door. Later, the emcee was explaining that until the bride met the love of her life, she had been known to give the key to her apartment to a special beau or two along the way. The master of ceremonies then asked that anyone still possessing a key to return it. Of course, every guy in the room came forward!

Oh, there were lots of fun times.

And let us not forget the dinner party era. Everyone entertained, including us, and there was a repast at someone's home about every other weekend. We had many celebrations at Claudia and Harry Tzucanow's home. Claudia always liked to make it a theme evening – from the food and decorations to our attire.

One holiday, we were invited to David and Cinda Cartee's for a New Year's Eve black tie affair. They transformed their basement into a New York City café for the evening, and the champagne flowed until the wee hours of the morning.

We hosted dinner for four to 10 people on a regular basis and had a full array of accouterments to make it a fashionable presentation, including candles burning all around the dining room. Unless the group was large, I would assemble the plates in the kitchen and serve dinner restaurant style. Mimicking the most elegant eateries, I even steamed small fingertip towels and, just before dessert, presented one to each guest on a small china plate. It was fun. We had an open house one New Year's Day and sent printed invitations (on light green paper stock) to 125 people.

By that time, I had refined my tastes and delighted in eating steak rare, fish almost undercooked and pasta al dente (and scrambled eggs wet). We served lobster with drawn butter and made meals with fresh garlic. Ray was the master chef, and I made a few specialty dishes such as stuffed shells with my homemade tomato sauce. And everyone loved Ray's fettuccine alfredo. Of course, whatever was being served was placed on a warm china plate, heated in our plate warmer.

The Rowayton Market for many years was owned and operated by an Italian named Rocco. He had the finest cuts of meat you could ever find. At holiday time, he would keep track of the orders for turkeys and hams and roasts by taping a large white sheet of paper about 20 feet long and 10 feet high to the wall listing the orders. They were categorized by weight so Rocco could keep it all straight. It was a sight to see. And his wife and daughters would cook and bake round the clock making the most sumptuous Italian specialties and sides and desserts.

Rocco sold the market to Vinny Taliercio, who had been affiliated with Flynn's Food Store in Darien. Vinny and his wife Arlene ran Rowayton Market until they retired in 1997, moving to Tampa, Florida, in 2000.

It seems that people from the Northeast like their food a little less spicy than those of us from other parts of the country. That was the way it was with Ray and me, and we were always accommodating each other. When I first moved to Connecticut, I served my specialty chili loaded with hot pepper flakes to some friends one evening. I noticed they were eating only the celery and warm bread served on the side. When asked why, they said the chili was just too hot for them.

Whether we were eating in or dining out, we made a toast to each other before every meal: "Cheers! To our love. I love you." All our married life, we made it a point to say "I love you" several times a day. We never took our special relationship for granted.

For more years than I can remember, we kept a well-known saying on our refrigerator door, and I would see it several times every day and try to live my life accordingly. William W. Purkey's motivational and inspirational words encourage everyone to dance and love and sing and live life to the fullest every single day.

And we appreciated Norman Vincent Peale, clergyman and author, who was known for popularizing the concept of positive thinking. His words help people understand life and feel better about themselves.

The United Church of Rowayton became an important part of our lives. Starting in 2000 following Ray's first cancer scare, we attended worship service every Sunday and participated in many of the activities and programs. Over the next 20 years, Ray served as a deacon, chair of the deacons and lay leader. We both helped out with public relations, and, at different times, both belonged to the Bible Study group.

John Livingston, having answered the call in 1986, has been the pastor since we became active members. He had been at two other churches on Long Island for a couple of years; otherwise, John has served his entire ministry in Rowayton.

Before he became a man of the cloth, John had aspired to become an actor and performer. With those talents, he is a master at delivering his messages from the pulpit. And he is well-known for his sage advice. At Christmastime, he would tell parishioners to keep in mind that not everyone gets along with every single person at every gathering so "don't beat yourself up if you have an unpleasant experience." And Ray would follow it up with "there's no such thing as one big, happy family" (per Pastor John).

John has been instrumental in overseeing the church's musical program and outstanding performances during his tenure. Under the direction of Marsha Hall, a gifted local musician and music teacher, the church routinely presents special programs, and the weekly church service includes exceptional renditions by the choir, bell choir, soloists, and all kinds of combinations of voices and instruments.

For years, John and his wife Judi put on a Christmas program for the Lunch Bunch senior group and periodically would stage, for the whole community, a musical presentation, often a replication of a Broadway show.

Over the years, a meaningful relationship was formed with Pastor John and many members of the church. When Ray developed his last cancer, those wonderful people gave willingly of their love and support.

The church building itself, built in 1962, must be mentioned because it is so unusual. It's a modernistic design with a swooping roof that reminds one of a sail. Inside, the high ceilings appropriately allow for a sense of openness and freedom. It's a beautiful structure.

I mentioned the Swanky's NCAA pool earlier in the sports chapter. Let me take a minute to tell you about the Swanky's group. It's a great story.

Around 10 years ago, one of our church members, Jim Mulhearn, developed ALS. A few of the guys (mostly retired) from church decided to take Jim to lunch one day to get his mind off medical issues and give him a mental boost.

They chose to meet on a Thursday at Swanky Franks, a roadside diner here in Norwalk that was known for its greasy hot dogs and butter-slathered grilled cheese sandwiches along with French fries and onion rings – food that most of the wives frowned upon and normally wouldn't allow.

That luncheon started a tradition, and most every Thursday, the group met at Swanky's in an effort to support Jim. It appealed to everyone. It was an opportunity to get out of the house for a couple of hours and hang out with the guys. There was no agenda – they talked about everyday topics, especially sports, and maybe told a joke or two and had some laughs.

The group got bigger and outgrew the diner. They tried a couple of other eateries but eventually were invited to bring a sandwich and gather in the Meeting House at our church.

Another person, Scott Anderson, was diagnosed with ALS, and he joined the group. Scott was the one who ran the NCAA pool. Ray won first place one time and treated the gang to lobster rolls.

Taylor Strubinger started sending out a weekly reminder about the Thursday gathering. Then Ray took over the task. He took it seriously and spent a lot of time in an attempt to make it clever. He combed the Internet for humorous characters or jokes or some theme appropriate for the time of year that made everybody smile when they opened their email.

All along, they continued to be called the Swanky's group.

Jim passed away in 2015 and then Scott, as well as some of the others, but the group continued to meet on Thursdays at the church except in the summer when they convened at Roton Point.

One summer day, Ray and I were under way on our boat around noontime on a Thursday, heading to Ziegler's Cove. We ran close to shore as we passed Roton Point and waved a big hello to the Swanky's guys sitting at the picnic table up on the hill.

In unison, they stood up, turned around, dropped trou and mooned us!

Remember, this prank was carried out by church-going retirees in broad daylight in a public place.

In 2017, Swanky Franks closed its doors after serving the best greasy hot dogs in town for 60 years.

The purpose of the Swanky's group remains the same today: a little getaway during the week with "the guys" – good people who always make you feel welcome.

I had always wanted a house directly on the water, but that wasn't to be – life got in the way. We looked for years but always felt the price was just out of reach, and we didn't want to leave Rowayton even if prices might be lower elsewhere.

In hindsight, we probably could have swung it if we'd gone out on a limb at the time because one's income generally increases as one becomes more seasoned. Also, inflation usually occurs over one's lifetime, and the high prices of a decade or two before become more manageable. For example, we looked at a house on South Beach Drive in 1989 that was on the market for just under $500,000. It would have been a real stretch then, but, today, the market price for that same house is upward of $4 million.

I've said many times that I would encourage young people to "go for it." However, real estate taxes in Connecticut, and in Norwalk in particular, for waterfront property have increased disproportionately in the last 40 years. Some of the homeowners in the area are paying in excess of $75,000 a year in real estate taxes for direct waterfront property.

Around 1990 when Ray was nearing retirement at IBM, he came home one day and announced that we needed to start looking at various places and figure out where we wanted to move. He said everybody in his department was planning to relocate (the Carolinas, Florida) for the next phase of life in order to avoid the high taxes and cost of living that were prevalent in Connecticut and neighboring states – and would only get worse.

We spent a few years scouring communities from Maine to Florida but always came to the conclusion that pretty little Rowayton topped the list as the place where we wanted to live. And Ray believed Long Island Sound offers the best boating on the East Coast, with protected waters and charming harbors on both sides of the Sound.

I was ecstatic. Indiana born but a Connecticut lifer, I had not seen one other place during our search where I would have wanted to put down roots.

Over time, many residents did move away, seeking warmer climes or lower taxes, and others passed away. And some people moved to a complex or facility to get away from the continuous maintenance required in owning a home. As people move about, it's easy to drift apart and lose contact unless you make a concerted effort to keep the relationship going.

Change happens whether we like it or not. However, I didn't expect the extent of change that would occur. When you're young and then middle aged, you see, one by one, people move away or pass away or get sick and have to deal with illness: grandparents, parents, aunts, uncles, cousins, friends, neighbors, even just acquaintances, and, at some point, you and/or your spouse. It happens gradually, but, all of a sudden, you realize the enormity of the impact in its totality.

So many people: They were always there – until they weren't.

Today, the new people in the RBA generally are young and have small children. Thus, the dynamics of the community have changed for those of us elders who have chosen to stay. We're considered the old-timers, and life is different from when we were younger. We don't necessarily fit in with the millennials' social life or lifestyle, and it's not as social as it once was for us. I'm not complaining, just stating facts – "that was then, and this is now," as Ray would say.

Life in Rowayton and the RBA has been filled with good people and pleasant memories.

I want to take a minute to talk about aging. As I get older, there are some days when I "feel my age." I'm not as energetic as in yesteryear, and sometimes I feel a little stiff. Then there are lots of days when I have my old stamina back, and I can work till 3 a.m. and be just fine the next day. And I can tackle an agenda like there's no tomorrow.

As we morph into an older state, I am reminded that it's not unlike breaking out of the earlier phases of life. The process of kids becoming teenagers and then teenagers becoming responsible young adults, etc., is a part of life. It's gradual, and we literally take one step forward and two steps back. It's not as if we turn the page and instantly and permanently become a member of an older population group like when we have a birthday.

If we're lucky enough to live a long life, we must appreciate every day and every phase of our journey, and we must accept change.

Indiana

With the exception of Cynthia, my family lived in Indiana, and, with or without Ray, I would visit once or twice a year. Ray loved driving on those country roads. "You don't see a car in any direction!" Because of that background, I never have liked driving the interstates in the East.

On trips to Hoosierland, I always made it a point to contact my friend Loisann Hartzler Crimmins, and the two of us would spend hours catching up. In high school, we had become best friends forever and have maintained a close relationship throughout life, sharing happy times and heartaches. I have said from time to time, "I've been all over the world, and yet my best friend lives on a farm '10 miles from nowhere,' " as Loisann's husband Herd has been known to say.

Herd Crimmins is fourth-generation farmer. He, along with Loisann, owns or cash rents several hundred acres of farmland and grows corn, soybeans, wheat and hay. He raises enough Black Angus cattle to feed the family for a year and sells freezer beef to locals, the balance going to market.

Additionally, Herd has been a distributor of feed grain and gets involved with numerous farm projects, such as buying silos for storage so he has control over the timing of the sale of his crops (and, thus, the price). His inventory of equipment includes tractors, planters, semis, sprayer and combine to plant and harvest crops, each of which is costly to purchase and maintain. His day starts at 6 a.m. and ends at dark, which in the summertime is around 10 p.m., seven days a week.

Herd and his family run one of the largest pig facilities in that part of the state. Every six months, 8,000 piglets are delivered, and he raises them till they are ready for market at the meat packing plant in Logansport, Tyson's. Between each cycle, a complete washing and disinfecting take place, and he prepares for a new batch. It's quite an impressive operation, and he's an enterprising entrepreneur. The license plate on his pickup truck reads "EAT PORK."

And Loisann is the quintessential "first lady." She's up at dawn. She cooks meals for the farm hands and always-hungry grandsons who routinely work the land. Much of the year, they descend on her large kitchen counter to eat, but she delivers lunch/dinner to them in the fields during the planting and harvesting seasons (lunch is a big meal for the laborers, who work up a hearty appetite by noon).

She keeps the house as clean as a whistle. She hosts separate Thanksgiving and Christmas gatherings for both sides of the family (and decorates about five trees).

Outside, she grows fresh flowers and herbs, and she plants a vegetable garden and cans the excess for the winter. She mows the grass in the yard (in the Midwest, there's peer pressure to keep not just the lawn but also the grounds mowed – and the grassy areas alongside the country roads bordering one's fields now that the state and county have drastically cut mowing services).

She keeps the house running and shops for food (remember, it's 10 miles to the nearest grocery store). She attends practically every grandchild's ball games. She even manages the books for the farm. That's just the tip of the iceberg.

And she does it all with grace and a smile on her face.

It is no easy task being a farmer's wife. Here's a shout-out to all past, present and future ladies who fill that role. Of course, Mr. Farmer has a full plate, too. It's a team effort, and everybody pulls their weight.

Life on a farm calls for hard work and maybe some good fortune, too, since weather is critical and can make or break the outcome. Too much or too little rain or temperatures that are too hot or too cold, for example, not only make it difficult to work the fields but can ruin a harvest.

Everyone hopes for a bumper crop from time to time, which can carry one through some tough patches and lean years.

Farmers make decisions every day, and the wrong choice can be costly. I remember one visit when the hay was ready to be baled. Herd had to call ahead to the baler and earmark the dates a week in advance. That's fine. It's just that if it should rain in between now and then, he would have to postpone until the hay was dry but still pay several hundred dollars since he had reserved the time. On that particular visit, Herd told me he had gotten lucky again.

The Caston girls, those high school friends from the Class of '65, still get together periodically, and I join them whenever I am "Back Home Again in Indiana."

After my father passed away from a heart ailment in the early '70s, Mother remarried and moved to Logansport. She and her husband Glen Reid would drive from Indiana to Connecticut every October for a taste of New England in the fall.

Their car would be loaded for bear. One time they brought trays of myrtle from their lawn that Glen planted all over our property. It took hold and thrived for years. And every time they came east, they brought a 20- or 30-pound Emge ham, renowned in Indiana for superior quality and flavor.

The week here was jammed with dinners out, a visit to every knitting shop in the area and, of course, outings to the myriad of department stores located in every direction.

Mother and I would shop till we dropped. That was about the only time I hit the malls and boutiques – ordinarily, I didn't like to shop, even with the huge selection of every kind of retail establishment imaginable at my fingertips. Some people would have felt as if they'd "died and gone to heaven" to have access to that kind of shopping and would have taken full advantage of it. Certainly a lot of Midwesterners would as they, in many cases, have to drive a couple of hours to get to a mall (of course, online purchasing has changed all that). I always said Ray was lucky that I wasn't a zealous shopper.

During the early part of our marriage, Ray and I would fly to Indiana for Christmas. The family would gather at Mother and Glen's house in the afternoon and visit while the food was being prepared. At that time, my nephew Kirk Dooley was the only child in the family. One year, after what seemed like hours, dinner was finally served. After that, the cleanup began, clearing the table and washing the dishes.

When he could stand it no longer, Kirk blurted out, "I need presents!"

That saying became a standard joke when some situation called for extreme patience. The other part of the story is that the first gift we handed Kirk that day turned out to be a pair of socks. He didn't think much of that and preferred the toys that followed.

Kirk went on to serve in the U.S. Marine Corps for nearly 25 years and had an illustrious career mainly in Intelligence and Special Operations, rising to the rank of major.

After that, he went on to work in top management in the exciting world of car racing. He moved his family (wife Tiffany and sons Jack and Colt) to Indianapolis, the Racing Capital of the World, upon landing a job with the Indianapolis Motor Speedway, where he was in charge of orchestrating operations for the Indy 500. Although he has moved on, Kirk continues to be involved with the Indy 500 race day each year. He now is a key player at the Skip Barber Racing School and also has started a venture of his own.

The Indianapolis 500-Mile Race is one of the oldest and most prestigious racing events in the world. It's important to the economy of the state as well, drawing around 300,000 spectators every Memorial Day weekend. Each year's winner drinks milk after the race, a ritual started by Louis Meyer, who drank buttermilk to refresh himself on a hot day in 1936 after his third win. An executive in the dairy industry spotted the picture that was in all the newsreels and saw an opportunity to inspire and promote the consumption of milk – and tradition was born.

Prior to the race each year, drivers are asked to select their milk preference. After the race, the "milk people" present the winner with his or her choice. The most popular type is whole milk (chosen by more than 75% of drivers).

As mentioned earlier, my cousin Ed Hines' daughter, Sarah Mullins, is heavily involved with the Indy 500 as her company, Accent Indy, is in the destination management business in Indianapolis.

My stepfather was a sentimental guy who couldn't understand why both his stepdaughters had left Indiana, leaving the son (Alan) nearby. Glen much preferred female company and reluctantly drove me to the airport when it was time to return to Connecticut. While visiting, I would appease him by saying there was love all around whether Cynthia and I were in Logansport or elsewhere. And Glen would say, "I wish you could bottle it up and put a lid on it."

So for Christmas one year, I decided to do just that. I went to the Darien Library and found 365 phrases and quotes that mentioned love. Using my electric typewriter, I copied them onto a sheet of paper and then cut them into strips, one for each day of the year. I then stuffed them into a clear glass bottle with a big red bow, closed the lid and presented "A Bottle of Love" to Glen.

The quotes were by well-known people like Saint Teresa of Calcutta (Mother Teresa) and Norman Vincent Peale, as well as unfamiliar authors and poets. All the sayings were about love – how being kind and loving to others makes for a happier person and a better world in general.

Christmastime was special in the Meurer household, too. I loved wrapping presents and decorating them with the handsome paper received from my client Champion International and bows and ribbons I picked up on sale all year long. And I wrapped everything – even the most insignificant stocking stuffer, such as a Sharpie marker.

For years, a hundred or so packages would adorn the space on the floor under the tree and adjacent area. And the tree itself, put up over Thanksgiving weekend and taken down sometimes as late as mid-March, was loaded with a thousand colored lights and beautiful ornaments, each of which had a special meaning (including about a dozen lighted lighthouses). Neighbor after neighbor, particularly Kathleen Hagerty, would comment on how much they enjoyed seeing the welcoming beacon on their way home from work or shopping. The entire downstairs was festive looking, and I had Christmas music playing from Thanksgiving Day on.

Every season, Ray and I wrote a Christmas letter telling about the year's highlights, which everyone referred to as our "annual report." Until recent years, it was stuffed inside the Christmas card along with a photo or two. Now the letter gets sent electronically via email with a photo or two embedded amidst the copy.

In the past, most everyone sent Christmas cards, and it was a chore people took seriously – they didn't necessarily like doing it but felt obligated. I would see colleagues scribbling furiously during their lunch break, trying to get their cards out on time.

All year long, for the fun of it, Ray and I would take photographs of everything and everyone and would send the film to a processor via the U.S. postal service. It took about two weeks to get the prints back. We always ordered two sets and would give the extras away in person throughout the year but always saved one or two of each person to put in their Christmas card. So that added to the time necessary for sending 200 cards – it took days to complete the task.

Just selecting the right card for each person was a big deal. I bought cards after Christmas when they went on sale and always had a plentiful and varied supply. Come December, I would update the mailing list and run out a set of address labels. Then I would sit in my office chair with a dozen boxes of cards spread out in a semi-circle. I would take a label and look for a card that was appropriate for that particular person. Then I would place the address label on the envelope.

And think of all the other steps required: standing in line at the post office to buy the stamps, writing the letter and preparing the layout, making copies, signing the card, folding the letter, affixing the stamp and return address label on the envelope, sealing the envelope and mailing it.

In comparison, email seems like a breeze, especially if you have a distribution list.

Box Full of Kisses Story

For many years, one of my clients was Champion International, a pulp and paper company. Every holiday season, Champion sent its vendors an assortment of elegant wrapping paper. A colleague and friend who worked there, Eileen M, introduced me to the idea of "decorating" gifts instead of just wrapping them. I took the concept to heart and, for years, had fun creating spectacular packages.

One December, I heard a Christmas story that touched my heart. I wrote it down so I could pass it along. I selected some gorgeous wrapping paper and an exquisite bow and presented the stunning package to my mother.

Written on the ribbon was the notation "Box Full of Kisses." It was a tender moment, and Mother kept the gift on a table in her living room until she vacated the house years later.

I adapted the story (below) for two of the grandchildren when they were young.

There once was a boy named Tyler and a girl named Carly. Christmas was approaching, and they wanted to give a special gift to their mom.

So when they were alone one afternoon, they searched the closet where the boxes and wrapping paper were kept and started to wrap the prettiest gift you can imagine. They selected a sturdy box. Then they chose the most colorful paper they could find. They picked out a beautiful bow. They found scissors and tape and had a wonderful time wrapping their surprise.

They did make a bit of a mess but were pleased with their handiwork and couldn't wait to give the present to their mom on Christmas Day.

When she came home from shopping late that afternoon and saw the mess they'd left, she was upset. She said, "It looks like a war zone in here! And you used the best bow and wrapping paper in the house! How could you do that? I was saving those for a really special gift for your dad."

Days passed, and all of a sudden it was Christmas morning. After Tyler and Carly had opened several of their presents, they remembered the gift they had for their mom. They ran to the secret hiding place and proudly presented it to her – they were so excited!

Diane, their mom, remembered the hard time she had given them about the wrapping paper and felt bad. She would have to forgive them because – after all – they were learning the joy of giving rather than just receiving. So with a smile on her face, she opened the box.

AND IT WAS EMPTY!

Now she was mad. She looked at them and said, "The box is empty! How could you have done this?"

And they said, "But Mom, it's not empty! It's a box full of kisses."

Our Christmas letter in 2001 announced that Ray's son Scott had proposed to Heather Bonosky on the romantic Caribbean island of Saint Lucia and that she'd said YES! Beforehand, Scott asked us to postpone mailing the Christmas cards until he actually popped the question – just in case. We got the call that it was a "go" in time to get our cards out before Christmas Day.

Their nuptials were held the next September here in the RBA. Ray and I hosted the rehearsal dinner at the Boathouse, and it was lovely – a mixture of white linens and lace in a rustic setting with a view of the river and a steady procession of boats.

The wedding and reception took place the next day at our RBA beach and patio overlooking Long Island Sound in all its splendor. It was a perfect summer afternoon and evening even though the priest was late because of traffic on I-95. At the appropriate time, our friend Alex Mackintosh shot goose-busters (fireworks with a loud bang) from his bright red powerboat just offshore to commemorate the occasion. Scott thought that was pretty cool.

Scott and Heather took their honeymoon in New Zealand with a stopover in Fiji on the way home. Ray had graciously volunteered to pick them up at the airport upon their return. Their flight was scheduled to arrive in the early morning so Ray had to get up at 3:30 a.m. to get to JFK on time.

Ray waited and waited at the curb and was forced to take a few spins around the terminal because you can't stay parked for long. To add insult to injury, he needed to use the bathroom but had no place to leave the car so he had to endure.

After a long wait, he finally called Scott's new in-laws, Rich and

Chris Bonosky, on the cell phone and was informed he was a day early! Due to crossing the international date line, we had miscalculated the newlyweds' day of arrival. So Ray had to get up in the middle of the night and make the trip to JFK two mornings in a row before "mission accomplished." Scott and Heather live in nearby Fairfield and have two daughters: Zoë and Charlotte.

While I was diving head first into life in the East, I had some resistance from back home. Mother was pleased that I was so happy here but missed those frequent get-togethers one has when you live fairly close to one another. And as noted above, my stepfather was always sorry to see me get on the plane.

And my Uncle Warren Hines never gave up hope that I might return to the Hoosier state. But he had felt that way all his life – he wanted those dear to him to stay nearby. When he was nine years old, his big sister, my mother Miriam, was heading off to college. He didn't want her to go away and used chains from the porch swing to tie her to the cherry tree in their front lawn.

Ray and I both dabbled in the stock market. Back in June of 1978 after having just met, we were sitting on South Beach on Bell Island, and Ray said, " 'Buy low, sell high' so said Bernie Baruch, Wall Street magnate back at the turn of the century." But Ray didn't always follow that advice. He made excellent picks but would panic the minute the price of a stock dropped and would "sell it for a song."

I had selected some winners prior to meeting Ray so I took a bigger role in the stock picking, and we collaborated about when to sell. I did all right. Ray always said I had a touch of "Charlie's luck."

Charlie Hines, my maternal grandfather, did well in the stock and bond markets. He was a self-made man. He had dropped out of school in a small rural town in southern Indiana at a young age to help support his family (he was one of nine children). He ordered self-help books and learned accounting on his own and landed a decent-paying job.

Granddad Hines eventually opened his own insurance agency

in Worthington, Indiana, and was highly respected throughout the region. He lived to be 99½ years old. He worked until he was well into his 90s (or at least went into the office every day and visited with people – it's wonderful to have a place you need to be when you get up there in age).

Along the way, Granddad Hines started investing and, it turned out, had a sixth sense for choosing winners. The joke was that he instructed his broker to buy specific stocks and bonds, not the other way around.

In order to become well-informed about the stock market and make smart buying and selling decisions, Ray subscribed to various newsletters, and we started watching PBS' "Wall Street Week with Louis Rukeyser" on Friday nights. It was the first TV program offering financial advice and became the longest-running show (32 years) on the air after CBS' "60 Minutes." Rukeyser's stock picking experts were called elves.

During the '80s when Ray and I were watching the program, the cast, in black tie attire, would celebrate the new year on the Friday night preceding New Year's Day. We even interrupted the New Year's Eve party we were hosting one time in order to catch the Rukey program. And one Halloween, my costume was a Rukeyser elf sporting a red cape, scarf and cap complete with red shoes with upturned pointy toes that Ray had concocted using masking tape.

Ray eventually changed his mind about handling our own investment decisions, and we turned our stock picking over to a financial investment firm. We decided that the professionals who monitor the market day in and day out could do a better job than us amateurs who try to "beat the market" on a part-time basis.

That is an example of where Ray realized it's okay to change your mind if, after appropriate evaluation, circumstances warrant it. "Upon further consideration" became the justification because we change – and things change – as the years pass by.

Starting in the early '90s, I learned from Ray's stepmother Frances how to cover hangers. This became a passion. I bought a box of 1,000 wire hangers from a local dry cleaner and a glue gun. Mother was happy to donate bags of skeins of leftover yarn in every color imaginable, and I was in business. I made hundreds of hangers in every color combination possible. It was a great hobby for me, and everyone loves them because clothes do not slip off, and the hangers don't rust (on the boat).

Friends from different stages of my journey have popped in and out of my life. Lynne Gerber, one of my college roommates at IU, lived in various parts of the Midwest after graduation. She was at the church when Ray and I were married, wearing a Diane von Furstenberg wrap dress with yellow and white flowers, and graciously handled the guest book at the reception at Roton Point.

Lynne is a runner, and one day in 1981, she and her fiancé made a stop at the courthouse in Chicago and got married in their running clothes. Lynne also is a hiker and climbed Mount Kilimanjaro, Mount Kenya and Mount Meru, three of the highest peaks in Africa, at the age of 63. She was so intrigued with the area that she returned and lived there for 18 months.

A few years later, Lynne solo hiked the southerly half of the Appalachian Trail and then Crater Lake in Oregon and Lake Superior Hiking Trail in Minnesota. She ran in the New York City Marathon four times starting in 2014 (from ages 67 to 71).

Recently, Lynne moved to Brooklyn to be near her daughter Signe and had lots of time on her hands. Having been limited to short, infrequent visits since college, she and I looked forward to the countless afternoons and evenings we would have in the spring and summer of 2020 to spend time together and catch up. But the pandemic changed all that. Here we are just an hour apart with no time restrictions but can't meet in person because of the quarantine. That's called bad timing and missed opportunity. When this pandemic is behind us, Lynne and I will make up for lost time.

Joanne Taran-McGuire was one of my secretaries at Berkeley. After

I left my position there, Joanne moved on, too, and relocated to Scottsdale, Arizona, for a few years. Then she moved back to Dutchess County in New York state. We reconnected last year, and Joanne has been an important support for me during my bereavement.

I must take a moment to mention political views. Both Ray and I have been conservatives since the beginning. Over the years, we've watched and listened to all the conservative talk shows and spent hours discussing the state of affairs – in our great country and around the world.

It is my fervent hope that the differences of opinion between conservatives and liberals will not rip our relationships apart and that we can live together in harmony and appreciate and enjoy this wonderful world in which we live. In other words, let's not let politics get in the way of friendships.

Kidney Cancer

Life was good and full of promise from the get-go. Ray and I had a lot of ups and not too many downs. One of the unfortunate episodes, though, was when Ray was diagnosed with renal cell carcinoma in 1998.

We had run the boat north from Florida on the Intracoastal Waterway in the spring and were aboard our newly acquired 42' Grand Banks in Oxford, Maryland. We had planned a fall cruise on the Chesapeake Bay and had commissioned the boat with food and drink for a month. Prior to departure on Saturday morning, September 12, Ray discovered blood in his urine. We went immediately to the hospital in nearby Easton where the doctors said there could be a hundred different reasons for this. So we drove home to Connecticut the next day, Sunday.

After a flurry of medical appointments and tests the next three days, it was determined that Ray had a cancerous tumor about the size of a grapefruit in his left kidney. All indications led to the assumption that the cancer had not metastasized. He was scheduled for surgery with Dr. Maloney at Norwalk Hospital the following Wednesday,

September 23. We were driving to the hospital that morning and were sitting at an intersection waiting for the light to turn green. Ray looked around at the cars idling beside us and said: "It's just a normal Wednesday morning, and people are on their way to work or to shop or to do all the routine things we do. But you never know if one of those persons is on the way to the hospital with cancer. You just don't realize the worries people around you might be having or the tough time they might be going through."

We all need to be more observant.

To diminish the possibility of letting any cancerous cells remain in the body and metastasize, the plan was to remove the entire left kidney instead of extracting just the tumor. The surgery to extricate the kidney was successful, and Ray spent the next three months recuperating.

In order to access the kidney, a rib had to be removed. The procedure was highly invasive: His incision started at the belly button and extended to the middle of the back. Healing from the surgery was almost worse than worrying about the cancer. But Ray was a good patient and did everything the doctors suggested.

Through it all, I was thrown into the kitchen and tried to make taste treats for Ray – he wanted a full meal akin to Thanksgiving dinner every night. That was a real challenge.

By the end of the year, Ray asked the medical staff if he was strong enough to take a road trip to Florida. The doctors gave him the go-ahead, and we found a waterfront rental in St. James City for two months and chartered a runabout. My annual report season was just starting, but I said I would move heaven and earth to make the arrangement work. I said I would do anything if it was to Ray's benefit. So we loaded the trunk with the computer and printer and all the ancillary office supplies and headed south.

We had a delightful stay in the Sunshine State while Ray continued to heal. The kidney cancer event had been a wake-up call, and we wanted to make the most of every single day we had together. Life was to be cherished, and we never lost sight of that thought.

Here's a story that demonstrates that point. I had a press check in Rochester, New York, during our time in Florida that winter. The day I was to leave, there was a blizzard up north. I was unsuccessful in making contact with the project manager so I went ahead and boarded a plane from Fort Myers. Within minutes of being airborne, all northbound flights were diverted, and I waited out the storm in Orlando. I was sorely disappointed that I had been needlessly denied a day with my love and would never be able to get that time back.

While in Florida that winter, we drove to Marco Island to visit Bill and Lisa Hammond and fell in love with the upscale canal community on the cusp of the Everglades. We spent the next 10 winters there renting the lovely home owned by Mary and Luis Navarro. It is situated directly on a canal with a beautiful vista of the Florida waters and mangroves. My office was by the pool under the lanai looking out on it all.

We bought a runabout and spent every free moment when I wasn't working speeding off to one of the islands to bask on the white sandy beaches. We primarily went to Coconut Island, Sand Dollar Beach and Coon Key. And we frequented Tigertail Beach to watch the sunset sink into the Gulf of Mexico. It took about 90 seconds from the time the bottom of the sun touched the surface of the water till it disappeared completely.

And just minutes from the house, we could make a daily run through Whiskey Creek, where Ray would run full bore in and around the bends in the mangroves, thrilling everyone on board.

As an aside, it was determined that the blood in the urine that initially alerted suspicion must have occurred because something happened to disturb the tumor. Ray was asked if he could remember anything in particular. As it turned out, he did.

Remember we were on the boat when this happened. Our double bunk was located on the starboard side of the aft cabin up against the bulkhead. Ray always took the outside so he could easily slip out of bed at night to check the anchor or mooring lines. Ray also generally went to bed ahead of me. So for me to get into bed, I had to hoist myself over his body and slip into the other side of the bunk.

That night, as usual, Ray retired first. When I went to bed, somehow the covers were wrapped all around his body, and I struggled to untangle and pull some of the bedding over me.

In so doing, I yanked the twisted sheet and blanket and inadvertently jabbed my elbow into Ray's abdomen. He awoke, nearly doubled over in pain. I felt terrible.

We both went to sleep, and the bleeding started just hours later.

The doctors said it was a blessing. Evidently that jarring agitated the tumor. If it had gone undetected longer, the cancer probably would have metastasized and gotten out of control.

Thereafter, Ray would tell people that I had beaten him up – and saved his life.

Seattle Story

Ray and I spent three months in Seattle, Washington, during the spring of 2001. Ray's daughter Diane had been diagnosed the year before with chronic myelogenous leukemia (CML). She underwent a bone marrow transplant at the age of 43. Below is an account of that experience. After the transplant, Diane had about five years of on-again/off-again medical episodes, but she did recover and has lived a fairly normal life ever since.

After Diane's diagnosis, the entire family used the ensuing months to learn everything we could about the cancer. Ray, always the researcher, delved into the cause of the disease, treatments and outcomes, including reputable medical institutions specializing in CML.

It was determined that the most effective treatment for Diane's diagnosis would be a bone marrow transplant. An experimental drug called Gleevec had recently been approved by the Food and Drug Administration and was showing great promise as an alternative to a transplant, but the medication was too new to forecast the probability of success beyond five years. Subsequently, Gleevec was found to be extremely effective long term. Thanks to continual research and discoveries in modern medicine, for those eligible, taking a pill once or twice a day is so much easier than undergoing a transplant and the long aftermath.

The search for a bone marrow donor started. Ray and Diane's husband Glenn Hewes and both brothers, Michael and Scott, were tested to see if a relative might be a match. They weren't. So the doctors turned to the bone marrow donor registry, which includes potential donors from around the world. People usually register to be a donor because a family member or friend has a blood cancer and needs a transplant. If the person is not a match, he or she is given the opportunity to remain in the database to potentially become a donor to someone else.

Selecting a donor is a complex matter, and extreme care is taken in determining whether a person qualifies. In 2000, each test cost several thousand dollars, which insurance does not cover. After screening numerous candidates, a strong match was made with a woman named Roswitha Heller in Germany who was around Diane's age and, believe it or not, had the same birthday. Roswitha agreed to be a donor to Diane, and arrangements were set in place.

Diane was not surprised that a donor was found in Germany because the Meurers came from that part of the world (as you will read about later on).

A major decision surrounding a bone marrow transplant was where to have the procedure performed. A number of medical institutions were considered, and an exploratory trip was taken to those on the short list. The Fred Hutchinson Cancer Research Center in Seattle was selected because thousands of transplants had been performed there, and it served as the training facility for doctors across the country.

All the plans were in place for the transplant to be conducted in March of 2001. We were informed that each patient must have a caregiver who is available 24/7, and Ray offered to serve in that capacity.

It was decided that Diane's husband Glenn would stay at home in Danbury, Connecticut, continuing to work and watch the children, Tyler and Carly, aged eight and four, respectively. Glenn would fly out to see Diane every few weeks.

Diane was to have two weeks of pre-op tests and procedures and would be in the hospital after the transplant for approximately one month followed by two months of follow-on care in Seattle.

Ray managed to find an apartment to rent in the delightful section of town called Madison Park that overlooks Lake Washington in one direction and Mount Rainier in another. It was within the required 30-minute drive from the medical clinic. Diane flew to Seattle-Tacoma International Airport (commonly known as SeaTac) with a friend and started the prep work (during which time Seattle experienced a fairly severe earthquake).

What basically happens with a transplant is that the patient undergoes a full week of intense chemotherapy and radiation. This kills the cancerous cells in the body. Unfortunately, healthy cells can be damaged as well. Once the patient's body has been flushed out, then the donor's marrow is infused so new healthy cells can start to grow. In the meantime, the patient has no immunity.

While Diane was undergoing the chemo and radiation treatments in Seattle, Roswitha was being prepped for her procedure in a hospital near Munich in Germany. The process entails injecting around 125 needles into the donor's hip bones and ejecting the marrow. Recovery generally takes the good part of a week. Donors are to be commended for being willing to go through this, particularly if they don't even know the patient.

The marrow has a shelf life of just a few days so it is imperative that it gets transported to the patient without delay. Ray and I and the entire family were concerned about the long flight from Munich to Seattle. If there was a problem and the marrow didn't arrive in time or at all, Diane would not survive. There was no backup marrow.

All went according to schedule, and the marrow was delivered right on time. It was infused into Diane's body, and, thus, the long recovery began.

Ray had flown to Seattle to assume the role of caregiver, and I arrived two weeks later. I was able to keep up with my work remotely for the duration of the stay in Seattle.

As is not unusual, Diane had good days and bad days. Transplant rejection is always a concern, and she was given immunosuppressants to counter this possibility. There were some scares, but she pulled through and was released from the hospital on the 32nd day after the transplant.

Getting the apartment ready for Diane's arrival required sterilizing the entire place. Having no immunity meant she would be susceptible to catching germs and would have no protection from illness, which could be fatal. We learned later that of the patients who did not survive, the vast majority were those whose living conditions did not include a stringent cleaning routine.

Keeping the living quarters sanitized took a chunk of time every day. For starters, it involved continually wiping down all common surfaces, scrubbing every pot and pan before use, washing every food item and wiping down the packaging after every grocery run, scouring the walls with disinfectant once a week, changing the sheets every three days, laundering the blankets weekly, changing clothes twice a day, cleaning the bathrooms daily and washing hands often. (This sounds a little like life today during the pandemic, doesn't it?)

Diane lost her sense of taste, and food didn't appeal to her, but Ray (and sometimes yours truly) made the meals prescribed even though Diane would barely take a bite. The fridge temperature had to be kept at 30 degrees or below, and leftover food had to be refrigerated immediately after being served. Diane was always cold – shivering cold. Fortunately, the apartment was U-shaped, and her bedroom was on one end and had its own thermostat. Even though she kept the setting at 90 degrees, it didn't affect the rest of the space.

The days were busy. The first order of business was to get a blood draw every morning. Diane had had a port installed to avoid having to prick the skin every time. From there, the weekdays were filled with appointments at the clinic with every kind of doctor imaginable. There were informative meetings for caregivers as well.

After a full day, Ray and Diane normally arrived back at the apartment just in time to start dinner preparations. One of my responsibilities was overseeing Diane's medications, of which there were a couple of dozen. Based on daily medical reports and test results, the meds were continuously changing. Ray wrote in a journal each evening about the events of the day and sent an email to family and friends every night.

The Hutch, as it was commonly called, was fantastic. The doctors and nurses were dedicated professionals whose caring was evident every moment. They were on a three-week rotation so the team members changed frequently. The reasoning for that was so the patient wouldn't become too attached to any one medical person or persons. Diane especially remembers and was fond of Dr. H, a renowned researcher who now heads Global Oncology at the Hutch.

As time went by, Diane started feeling a little better and was able to take advantage of seeing some of Seattle's local sites on the weekends. Skagit Valley, an hour's drive north, is famous for its Tulip Festival that lasts the entire month of April. The flowers are planted in strips of varying colors and span as far as the eye can see. They are magnificent when in bloom and are touted to match the flower fields in the Netherlands, the Tulip Capital of the World.

On the first Saturday in May, Ray, Diane and I watched the Seattle Boat Parade on Lake Union, marking the official start of the boating season. And the next day, we toured Mount Rainier National Park. In mid-May, Ray's son Scott flew out for a week and took care of Diane so Ray and I could take a break.

We drove to Vancouver, British Columbia, and toured the beautiful city set against a backdrop of majestic mountains, took a ferry to the capital city of Victoria and drove the length of Vancouver Island, and then ended up on San Juan Island and marveled at the panoramic vistas. We also caught an orca festival at the popular Roche Harbor Marina. The Strait of Juan de Fuca offers protected waters, and Ray said it was too bad this boating paradise was so far from home.

With islands dotting the landscape throughout the Pacific Northwest, the common mode of transportation is by ferry. For those with deeper pockets, seaplane generally is the preferred choice for commuting or getting around. Everywhere one goes, ferry boats can be seen crisscrossing the waterfront and seaplanes filling the skies and landing on the surface. On the ground, interstates as well as local roads are jammed and slow-going.

Back in Seattle after the getaway, Ray, Diane and I trekked off to Olympic National Park and were caught in a surprise snowstorm in early June. We went sailing with Ray's high school friend Tom Nylund on Puget Sound and had the privilege of watching a Mariners baseball game from a private suite.

The three of us enjoyed the local coffee shops, of which there was one on about every block as Seattle is home to Starbuck's and Seattle's Best and a few other brands and is considered one of the best "coffee towns" in the world. We shopped at the flagship Nordstrom department store, and there were lots of bargains at the Seattle-based Eddie Bauer retail outlets.

Across Lake Washington, the town of Kirkland boasts the founding of Costco in the early '80s. And Bill and Melinda Gates' 66,000-square-foot mansion faces west and overlooks the lake from Medina.

On weekdays, Ray and Diane occasionally would venture to a movie theater and catch a matinee. Diane still had to avoid crowds because of an insufficient immune system so the best time to go was in the afternoon when the theaters were relatively empty.

Along the way, I discovered a local wine named Columbia Crest. When I arrived back in Connecticut, Mickey Interlandi, owner of my favorite liquor store, White Bridge Wines & Spirits in Darien, was able to special order the brand. It became my go-to choice of wine from then on. Mickey established his business in 1980 and goes out of his way to accommodate customers.

After three long months, Diane was cleared to go home in mid-June. Arrangements were made through the Corporate Angel Network for Diane and Ray to fly on a corporate jet. This was greatly appreciated: She would avoid being exposed to germs in a busy airport or crowded commercial plane. Forever after, Ray was spoiled. Every time he boarded a plane, he lamented that it wasn't a private jet.

Diane continued to get stronger, but it was a slow process. Because of an insufficient ability to fight off bacteria, she was told to stay out of the garden and away from flowers and steer clear of pets for a couple of years.

She experienced lots of setbacks but gradually improved. Her body still rejected the foreign marrow from time to time, and she had to have frequent blood transfusions. In fact, she spent about a week a month in the hospital for one reason or another for the first five years after the transplant. The extensive chemo and radiation aged her body, and she had procedures that normally an older person would undergo, such as two hip replacements, cataract surgery and shoulder fusions, among others.

Over the next few years, Diane and Ray made two trips back to the Hutch for a follow-on checkup and care instructions. She was told she was cancer free and that the transplant had been a complete success – *no small miracle.*

If both parties agree, the donor and the patient can make contact after one year. Diane's donor Roswitha and her husband Klause traveled from Germany to America to meet Diane. They had an immediate bond and have stayed friends ever since, and, of course, they always remember each other's birthday. Roswitha and her husband have made subsequent trips to the United States and spent time with Diane.

After about five years, Diane was able to lead a normal life without too many visits to doctors and the hospital. The Hutch is still in the picture and will be for the rest of her life. She is surveyed once a year about her health and well-being and has 24/7 access to professionals who can answer questions.

She is happy to be alive and is grateful for the family and friends who helped her get through the ordeal. With her husband Glenn beside her, Diane was able to watch the children, Tyler and Carly, grow to adulthood (Tyler is engaged to Olivia Mullen and will be married in September).

Diane has spent all the years since showing her love of life and gratitude by giving of herself in dozens of ways and is a generous and loyal friend to many.

9/11 Story

It was mid-June 2001. After spending the spring in Seattle caring for Diane, Ray and I were glad to be back in Rowayton. Diane stayed with us for several days while her husband Glenn sanitized their home and made ready for her return.

That's when Ray and I got the call notifying us that the boat we were having custom built would be ready for pickup soon. Two weeks later, we packed the car and headed to Stonington, Maine. It took about a month to complete the finishing touches, and we then ran Blue Heron from Maine to Rowayton in record time. The rest of the summer was spent becoming familiar with the new boat in local waters and taking a cruise to Block Island.

In September, we made ready for a second trip to Seattle. Nine months earlier, Ray had been diagnosed with prostate cancer. After having had kidney cancer three years before, Ray and I were not as upset since the prognosis for a full recovery was close to 100%. Of the options available, Ray had decided to have a seed implant.

After in-depth research, he had elected to have the procedure done at the Seattle Prostate Institute. A large percentage of the doctors across America performing implants had been trained there, and it was considered one of the best facilities in the country.

Ray had had an appointment there in the spring when we were in Seattle taking care of Diane and felt certain he would be well-cared for. Surgery was scheduled for September 11, 2001, with a Dr. Grimm (we laughed about his name being so pessimistic, but it was not a harbinger of bad things to come – Ray had a complete recovery).

On Monday, September 10, Ray and I took a late flight from JFK to Seattle. There was a fierce thunderstorm in New York that night, and we sat on the runway for hours before taking off. Needless to say, we didn't get to our hotel till late – 5 a.m. Eastern time.

With just a few hours' sleep, we dragged ourselves out of bed on September 11 and dashed to the hospital. A medic was going over pre-op procedures and happened to ask how long we would be in town. Ray said we had a flight back to New York on Thursday. The medic looked at us and said, "I don't think the planes will be flying by then. Oh! Haven't you heard?"

That was how and when we found out that New York and Washington, D.C., had been attacked by terrorists, along with commandeering a plane over Pennsylvania: forever after called 9/11.

As predicted, planes were grounded for several days. All travel except by car came to a standstill. The country was paralyzed. Ray and I were staying at the Sorrento, a charming hotel with old-world service from a bygone day. The staff members couldn't do enough for the guests. Since few new patrons were arriving at the Sorrento, our accommodations were upgraded to a corner suite at no extra charge.

Like everyone, we were glued to the TV. We watched in horror as the planes torpedoed into the Twin Towers, causing them to catch on fire and then collapse. We saw the Pentagon attacked and then the crashing of the plane in Shanksville, Pennsylvania. The footage was more gruesome than in a movie, and, eventually, the worst scenes were taken off the air. Everyone was trying to understand what was happening.

To fill the hours, we took the short bus ride to downtown Seattle and enjoyed the city's shops and restaurants. We passed by a church, and people were in line a block long waiting to enter. Elsewhere, we saw dozens of people ready to donate blood.

The first flight we could get to JFK was on the following Sunday morning, and we grabbed those seats and booked the early morning departure. The staff at the Sorrento even opened up the breakfast area an hour sooner than usual to accommodate our travel schedule.

As a result of the terrorist attacks, security checks were instituted at airports – on the grounds, as well as inside the buildings – across the country. The lines were long, and these checkpoints took time. Our car was stopped and searched by an armed guard as we approached the perimeter of SeaTac. It was still dark, and the miles of red taillights leading to the terminal made a lasting impression of just how serious this situation was. It was very sobering.

Once inside the airport, the security lines were a block long. But with Ray being in a wheelchair due to his surgery that week, we were able to go to the front of the line.

This security protocol was all so new. Everyone was used to arriving at an airport, checking in at the ticket counter, and going directly to the gate and boarding the plane. If we were running late, there was the possibility of making a mad dash through the airport and still managing to make the flight (if your feet were fast enough and fate was with you). Those days ended with 9/11.

The flight itself was uneventful. Since much of the air space above New York City was off limits, the flight pattern took us to Boston and then down the coast to New York. On the ride home in the car, we could see smoke from the Twin Towers still smoldering as we crossed the Whitestone Bridge. Everyone was fearful and didn't know what was ahead in this new world of terrorism.

Being a bedroom community to New York City, Rowayton's residents had lots of personal experiences surrounding 9/11. As the days wore on, story after story unfolded. Being boaters, one account, in particular, stood out. A couple, John and Pam W, lived on South Beach Drive on Bell Island (yes, that same beach where Ray and I met) and kept their sailboat moored in the cove off the beach. When John didn't come home from work in New York on 9/11 or the next day or the next, Pam was fearful that he might be a victim of the terrorists.

Wrought with worry and despair after 10 days and still no word, she met with the Rev. John Livingston from our church, and, together, they prayed. Even if the family's worst fear was true and her husband had not survived, they needed to know. They prayed for God to send a sign – any kind of sign – that John was in a good and safe place.

Three days later, the area braved a severe storm. All the boats moored off South Beach remained intact except for John and Pam's boat, which was washed ashore. The boat had nary a scratch and stood strong and erect with her keel buried securely in the sand pointing directly out to sea.

God does answer our prayers.

The subsequent months wore on as we all settled in, trying to make sense of 9/11. Ray volunteered on Saturdays to mentor the son of one of the victims in an effort to provide him with some fatherly guidance.

It was good to be home in Rowayton after spending most of the preceding seven months away – three months in Seattle taking care of Diane, a month in Maine, a cruise on the boat and a second trip to Seattle in September.

"It Never Rains in Rowayton"
Ray coined this term. He would call me at home in Rowayton every afternoon from his office at IBM in White Plains, New York, just to touch base.

Many times he would comment, "It's raining buckets outside," and I would respond, "It's not raining here."

Ray would answer with, "It never rains in Rowayton."

And that became a motto because our life in Rowayton was happy and carefree, and the sun shone on us.

It is only fitting that the phrase be used as the title of this memoir.

We would often say, "Life is good," never forgetting to be thankful for the happy times. In fact, it is easy to take the good times for granted until they aren't so good. Then we look back and pine for them. Pastor John says, "If times are bad, don't worry. They won't last forever."

When something especially good happened, Ray would say, "Stick with me, kid." Ray was the "sunshine of my life," just like Stevie Wonder used to sing. And the song "You Are My Sunshine" always made me think of Ray. Mother used to play that tune on the piano or organ at our singalongs when I was growing up.

In addition to belonging to Wilson Cove Yacht Club, we bought a membership in Rowayton Yacht Club in 1999 and kept our boat on a mooring there for a few years. We enjoyed getting to know a whole new set of boaters. On Friday evenings during the season, members congregate for happy hour on the porch overlooking the harbor. A highlight is the five minutes or so of seeing the sparkling reflection of the setting sun in the west on the boats moored to the east of the clubhouse out toward Tavern Island. It is almost magical seeing the boats twinkling in the distance.

A familiar face at these get-togethers, Jim Frayer is one of the founders of Rowayton Yacht Club and its first commodore. Jim also teaches a course that qualifies participants for a Connecticut Safe Boating certificate. Now retired, he serves as facilitator of a discussion group on world affairs at our village library and writes articles for publications on subjects of interest around Rowayton. Some of the topics include services available at local yacht clubs, plight of the disabled power plant on Manresa Island, and restoration of Hoyt Island as a bird sanctuary and wildlife preserve.

Although Ray and I joked about it never raining in Rowayton, our little town does have its share of inclement weather. In fact, I used to have a bright yellow dress that I wore to work on rainy days. Everyone would comment how cheery it looked on such a dreary day.

I love a rainy day (whether on land or on sea, winter or summer). The water takes on many different moods and can be calming or unsettling and everything in between.

Even though most hurricanes veer off, every summer/fall brings the worry of a direct hit. Homeowners and storekeepers become well-versed in hurricane preparation and take the watches and warnings seriously. On the water, there are designated "hurricane holes" scattered up and down the coast offering a harbor of refuge to boaters seeking shelter from a severe storm.

Even if a storm misses and moves out to sea, it generally affects the surrounding bodies of water for days. This often means turbulent seas, sea swells, high winds and rip currents, and boaters typically steer clear from venturing out until the storm and its after-effects have passed.

This thinking is uppermost in every skipper's mind when cruising. Sometimes yachtsmen postpone their departure, and sometimes they scoot home early to avoid being caught in foul weather. We certainly did. In fact, I learned not to tell people our departure and arrival dates because they were weather-dependent and more often than not slipped.

The wind direction aids in predicting the weather along the shore in Connecticut. A prevailing southwest wind brings in warm air masses and fair weather and, in the summertime, humidity. A northwest wind blows cool air down from Canada and clears out humid air masses. An easterly breeze cools the atmosphere with winds coming in off the Atlantic. And a southeasterly generally means rain within 24-48 hours.

Identifying the different cloud formations also is helpful in predicting the weather, and boaters, in particular, become adept at this. For example, white puffy cumulus clouds mean fair and stable weather, whereas a mackerel sky (looks like fish scales) means a change in the weather, usually rain (or snow in the wintertime). Watching an anvil thundercloud form can be transfixing – and scary, especially if one is in open water and can't outrun the oncoming storm. And when the sky is full of big mamas – those broiling, pouch-like dark gray rolling clouds – head for a safe harbor.

There is a saying that boaters take to heart: "Red sky at night, sailors' delight. Red sky at morning, sailors take warning." This weather prediction has remained true through the ages – all the way back to the Bible and a Shakespeare proverb.

Ray, especially, was fascinated with the basics of the universe – how it all works together day after day, year after year, century after century: the sun and the moon rising and setting, the tides ebbing and flowing, the stars forming clusters and constellations, the earth rotating on its axis, all in symmetry.

The air temperature on land in the four shore counties of Connecticut is affected by the water temperature of Long Island Sound. For instance, in the spring and early summer, the air is not as warm along the Connecticut coast versus inland because the water is still cool from the winter lows of around 35 degrees. For example, in May, the water temperature mid-Sound is in the 50s. Even on hot days in the early summer, the prevailing southwest breeze is cooled as it is carried across the Sound from Jersey and Long Island.

Likewise, once the temperature of the water in the Sound rises to its summer highs of close to 80 degrees (and warmer in the harbors), particularly in the western section, the shoreline no longer gets relief from the heat and humidity. And the harbors on Long Island during the hottest part of the summer are warmer than Connecticut's because the offshore breeze is hot from blowing over the landmass.

By the way, one definition of a Sound (as in Long Island Sound) is that it's a narrow sea or ocean channel between two bodies of land or islands. Conversely, a bay, bight and fjord are adjacent to just one landmass. A Sound is usually deeper than a bight and wider than a fjord. Globally, there are 140 bodies of water named Sound; the definition is applied loosely. The United States heads the list with 42, Canada is next with 30 and New Zealand follows with 16.

Saltwater freezes at 28 degrees Fahrenheit. In the wintertime, water in Long Island Sound rarely freezes, although I've heard the stories about ice forming from Green's Ledge Lighthouse to the beaches to the north (RBA, Wee Burn, Bayley, Roton Point, Pine Point, South Beach/Crescent), a distance of one mile. And when Ray and I were staying at the Bluff Avenue house in 2013 after Superstorm Sandy, we can verify that it was solid ice from Rowayton Yacht Club to Tavern Island. Mike H, former caretaker at Tavern, said he had actually walked the distance (on ice). And Five Mile River often freezes all the way across, especially farther up from the mouth by Pinkney Park.

Rowayton is at sea level. Flooding is not unusual when a storm dumps several inches of rain, particularly if there has been an east wind for a couple of days. Keep in mind this is saltwater, which leaves a residue of salt, and that causes corrosion.

Residents become accustomed to having to move their cars to high ground when flooding is predicted. It's just part of the territory and a small price to pay for living in this seaside village. In fact, I had been introduced to the kind of damage flooding can cause when I lost my GTO in a winter snowstorm not too many years after moving to Bell Island in the '70s.

I was in Vermont skiing for 10 days during winter break and had parked my car on the green at the bottom of Yarmouth Road. When the floods came, none of the neighbors had a key so after the water receded, the car sat for five full days.

Had I been able to get it to a car wash immediately, it might have been salvageable. My dad still conveniently arranged to be at the State Exchange Bank in Culver, Indiana, for lunch occasionally, and he filled out the paperwork for my auto loan. I soon was the proud owner of a tan Chevrolet Monte Carlo that I bought in Greenwich. It had its own set of bells and whistles, but the design was a little tamer than the Hizer's Oldsmobiles of the '60s.

When there is high water in Rowayton, it generally fills the streets and even covers lawns in the low-lying areas – nothing too serious. A few times every year, we all get stranded for a few hours.

Occasionally, however, a storm causes major damage. If low pressure forms and stalls in a location that creates an east wind for an extended period of time, the water in Long Island Sound cannot recede. After a couple of cycles of high tides, the water level rises because the incoming tide has nowhere to go but up. As well as water washing in from the Sound and Five Mile River, it comes up through the storm drains in the RBA. And all over town, there are dips in the roads that fill with standing water so it is easy to mistakenly drive through puddles and coat the bottom of your car with saltwater. When that happens, head for the nearest car wash.

I remember the Blizzard of '78. I was renting a house on Yarmouth Road on Bell Island. Two feet of snow fell, and then the tide came in a couple of times and flooded the low areas. I looked down the street from the wraparound porch and saw that the snow was up to the doorknobs of the parked cars.

The snow wasn't really that deep – it was floating on top of the high tide!

On average, Rowayton gets 50 inches of rainfall a year. In 2018, that amount was nearly double, and it didn't take much precipitation for the drainpipes to get backed up because the water table was saturated. On this particular day in October, the rains came down, and the water filled the roads.

Across the street from our house, Margot Draycott's daughter and her husband were waiting to be picked up to go to the airport for their return trip to France, but the car service couldn't get through. The driver told them to meet him toward the bottom of Craw Avenue, a block away. So Meredith and Sébastien carried their luggage over their heads through knee-deep water till they reached high ground. Ray took a photo and sent it to them, and they said their departure from Rowayton that day was one of the most memorable of all their trips.

Ray and I had heard the war stories about hurricanes over the years, the one most talked about being the Hurricane of '38. But we lived through a few, too, in our years in Rowayton. In 1985 during Hurricane Gloria, we holed up at a friend's house on high ground in town. When the winds temporarily calmed during the eye of the storm, we dashed over to Wilson Cove Yacht Club to check on our boat Intrepid. It was fine.

After hours of ravaging winds and rain, we couldn't believe the blue, cloudless sky and burning sun that greeted us. But we still had the other half of the storm to get through so we returned to our friend's house to wait it out.

I remember Hurricane Gloria particularly because I was getting ready to print the first edition of my Long Island Sound Tide Calendar. It was the last week of September, and I was making trips back and forth to the printer (Marv Pozefsky, owner of Standard Print in Derby, Connecticut, just north of Bridgeport). Production was in the final stages, and I was hoping the storm wouldn't hold up the print schedule. It didn't.

Another time one October, my mother and stepfather Glen were visiting from Indiana when someone in the neighborhood came knocking on the door, shouting, "Better move your cars to high ground." Glen, being a landlubber, immediately responded, "Let's just pack the car and head home to Indiana!"

They didn't leave – and we did survive yet another storm.

The nor'easter in December of 1992 caused major flooding. A low stalled over the Delmarva Peninsula and created a strong east wind for three days, causing the water level of Long Island Sound to rise to an extreme level.

The streets filled with several feet of water. At one point, a volunteer from the local fire department rowed down Rowayton Avenue in a wooden skiff to deliver a prescription to one of the residents.

At the Meurer house, the water rose to the top of the outside steps just below the front door. Inside, a few inches of water accumulated in the back room, and minor flooding occurred on the first floor. It took a few months to restore the house and exterior areas, and flood insurance covered a lot of the expense.

The storm was somewhat traumatic at the time, but it was nothing compared with Sandy 20 years later.

Superstorm Sandy

On Monday, October 29, 2012, Superstorm Sandy hit the New York metro coastal zone with full force. The storm clouds had been building for days, and everyone was alert to the potential threat. The usual storm preparations were made, and everyone braced for what they hoped would be another miss.

But this one would be far worse than any storm we had lived through. Every element in the equation was in place, and it was the perfect storm. Ray and I prepared a little more than usual but did not go the extra step and, for example, move furniture to the second floor. On Sunday afternoon, we packed up and checked into a hotel in Stamford, staying four nights.

The storm was fierce. The high tides came again and again, and the water kept rising. There was no such thing as low tide because the winds kept the water from ebbing.

The rain was horizontal, and the winds approached 90 miles per hour. It was bad. But it would have been even worse if the storm hadn't veered inland just as it approached Connecticut on yet another rising tide. Ray had said during the height of the storm, "I've got a bad feeling about this one."

On Tuesday, we drove to Rowayton to assess the damage. The streets were still flooded, and we couldn't get into the Beach Association until the water receded in the mid-afternoon. So the first place we visited was Wilson Cove Yacht Club: Blue Heron, our boat, was fine. The water in the basin had risen to ground level but was not higher than the pilings, and the boats did not break loose. The ramps were inverted, but all the vessels had survived.

That was not the case down the road at Rowayton Yacht Club. There, the boats stored on land had floated across the street and docked themselves haphazardly on residents' lawns.

Back in the Beach Association, Ray and I finally were able to get to the house. Eighteen inches of water had filled the back room, and there had been about 12 inches in the rest of the first floor. Everything the water touched was ruined, leaving a thick layer of mud. The power had been turned off for the entire area and would stay off for six days.

Ann Martin DiLeone, our neighbor across the street, invited us to stay with her starting Thursday since she had a working fireplace that provided warmth on those cool November nights. Along with another neighbor, Joanne Schreiber, we spent the days working through the debris and mopping up the mud and the evenings commiserating about the dark unknown. On one occasion, we were cooking dinner on a camp stove in Ann's kitchen, and the propane caught on fire. The fire extinguisher did its job, but it took three hours the next morning to clean up the mess (no hot water).

After nearly a week, the power was restored. Ann had retired for the night, and Ray and I were in the living room when Ray whooped, "The streetlight just came on!" We raced outside and joined a dozen or so neighbors who were "dancing in the street" in jubilation.

It was learned that the local sewage plant had broken open during the storm so the water that flooded the streets and homes was contaminated. This translated into having to throw away anything that had come in contact with the water.

We salvaged some household items but had to discard, for example, all the upholstered furniture. Needless to say, every appliance was ruined. For all practical purposes, we lost just about everything on the first floor. Many of the items could be replaced, but some couldn't be. Most of the photographs, for example, were gone, including our wedding pictures. It took months to clean up and sort out.

Meanwhile, we had to find a place to live while the restoration took place. Neighbor Sylvia Stuart invited us to stay at her home for a period of time, and Kip and Eve Ford on Bell Island offered their home while on vacation. Then a couple who had a home on Bluff Avenue graciously offered their house overlooking the Norwalk Islands since they were living in the Carolinas for the winter.

So the long haul began. Through a friend at church, Frank Mullaney, we were lucky to find a contractor to handle the project since every tradesman in the region was booked solid. Lining up subcontractors was a juggling match because they were so backed up. And inventory was sparse. For instance, one morning the contractor called and said a subcontractor would be installing the kitchen door that afternoon. So we dashed to The Home Depot and selected a door that we could pick up at noon. An hour later, the salesperson called and said it wasn't in stock after all. So we had to go back and settle on a door that we could pick up immediately.

The restoration was a bit complicated because the house was old (built in 1924). The back room wasn't salvageable, and the entire kitchen had to be rebuilt. It meant countless trips to select every item needed – from wood for new cabinets to marble for countertops to appliances and light fixtures. Ray said the refurbishment was especially unsettling and exhausting because it was so unexpected. We didn't have the luxury of leisurely checking out samples and discussing alternate plans with a designer (for example, there was a three-week wait to get an appointment with a kitchen planner).

Finally in February, we moved back home. And that night, the weather stations warned people to use caution because of the impending winter storm that could dump a foot of snow and cause flooding to low-lying areas.

Our hearts sank.

The havoc and disruption in our lives caused by Sandy were fresh in our minds. The next day, Ray made the decision to elevate the house. He said he couldn't live with the chance of flooding every time there was a storm.

We thought about tearing the house down and building anew, but we didn't want to be dislocated any longer than necessary. And, again, finding available workmen for that size project would have been nearly impossible. So we opted to elevate – as did dozens of fellow Rowaytonites.

Practically every home in the Rowayton Beach Association and lots of houses all around town had damage and were being either restored or elevated. Within months, there were 50-some houses under construction just in the immediate neighborhood. The roads were filled with tradesmen of every kind, and the noise was endless. The streets themselves, as well as the lawns, were covered with thick, sticky mud that took months for the rain to wash away. As a result, there was a pungent odor in the air (it was foul – not like the sweet smell of the earth after a rain shower).

Pretty little Rowayton looked like a war zone, especially at first when everyone was told to stack all the damaged furniture and appliances on the front lawn until trucks could haul the wreckage away. Joanne Schreiber, a neighbor who lived across the street in the little red house by the Boathouse, decided not to renovate. She put her ravaged house on the market and bought a third-floor condo – where it never floods – overlooking the Norwalk River. "Sandy was just one too many storms," she said. Joanne did salvage the flagpole that was made from the mast of their catboat, named Catherine, and donated it to the neighbor on the south side of the Boathouse. The oar at the top acts as the perfect wind indicator.

Elevating our house took a year. A general contractor and architect were engaged in March of 2013, and the initial planning started. To comply with the town building code, we needed to elevate four feet. There were countless details to attend to, and it was a full-time job making all the arrangements. We found a house to rent close to the train station and moved there over Labor Day weekend. Step by step, the house was raised and the power lines reconnected. We moved back home the weekend before Thanksgiving.

But it took many more months to finish the job. The washer and dryer, for example, were hooked up in mid-January after we returned from a short trip to Newport, Rhode Island. We were staying in a hotel overlooking the harbor and watched boats coming and going even in the blizzard that blanketed the port town with inches and inches of swirling snow. It was good to get away for a few days.

For weeks we had had to do our laundry at friends' houses or the public laundromats. So it was a treat to have the use of our own appliances again. It's so easy to take things like that for granted. The ice maker in the fridge was finally hooked up in February.

The weather that winter was one of the coldest on record, and we kept the house relatively warm by covering the door openings with heavy blankets and running electric heaters until the garage and new back room were enclosed (our electric and heating bills were enormous). Little by little, tasks were completed.

Ray was thrilled to finally have a garage with a storage room above it. For example, ever since 1978, our Christmas decorations, having grown to nearly 20 boxes, were kept in the attic. To get to the attic, Ray had to bring in an extension ladder and place it on the staircase landing in the living room. He would then climb the ladder and lift the hatch door, two stories up.

Carefully, he would inch his body up to the attic floor and then spring himself the rest of the way up. Years before, he had come up with the idea of tying string with an extra long tail around each box so he could lower it to where I could retrieve it.

It was an arduous undertaking we both dreaded, and we limited the number of trips up to the attic to about three a year (in the 35 years we had lived in the house prior to Sandy, I had never physically been in the attic – and still haven't). With our new storage area above the garage, those unpleasant trips are no longer necessary.

Homeowners insurance generally does not cover damage caused by natural disasters. And elevating a house is considered an improvement so those expenses are not reimbursable. We had some relief from FEMA (Federal Emergency Management Agency), but replacement values are based on a proportion of the purchase price and age of the item so we bore most of the costs.

FEMA eventually established a fund for victims, and we spent months filling out mounds of forms and copying receipts. We were denied any aid. About two years later, additional federal funds were earmarked for Sandy victims, and we were told we were eligible to receive a partial reimbursement. The program was set up whereby the recipient takes out a loan, which is forgiven five years later. However, during those five years, the loan is considered a mortgage, and all mortgage holders are required to carry flood insurance.

We had paid off our mortgage with Ray's retirement package in 1992 but continued to carry flood insurance until the house was elevated. Since we were four feet higher, we assumed we would not have to worry about future flood damage so we dropped the flood insurance.

The caveat with the relief program, though, was that flood insurance would have to be carried for the life of the property (which translates into infinity), not just for the duration of the so-called loan. We didn't want to be saddled with the mandate to carry the very expensive and always increasing flood insurance while we owned the house or would have to pass the requirement along to all future owners – so we turned down the funding.

All in all, it took 22 months to recover from the storm and resume somewhat of a normal life. To this day, there still are a few boxes I haven't unpacked.

For the next several years, Superstorm Sandy was considered the line of demarcation: life before Sandy and life after Sandy. That, however, would change. The new dividing line would become: life with Ray and life without Ray.

In addition to dealing with the house, a lot was going on around that time. Ray's sister Alice Garabedian died in January of 2014, Ray had cataract surgery in March, and Ann Mackintosh, a dear friend, passed away in April at the age of 102. And later that month, Ray's older son Michael had a stroke and underwent brain surgery. He survived, but it was touch and go for a long time. And on Halloween night, my mother passed away at the age of 98.

The Meurer Heritage

As with most families, the Meurer lineage is peppered with accounts of courage and fortitude along with tales of embarrassing moments and secrets in the closet.

This chronicle is based on research and stories about the Meurer genealogy written specifically for family members. Those of you who are not relatives are invited to read about an immigrant family that came to America and lived out their lives in the Land of Opportunity.

Over the years, several people in the family have dabbled at putting the Meurer ancestry on paper, but the efforts have been piecemeal. So I thought I'd try to make some sense of the paperwork and legends that have been passed down and put everything together in a chronology.

Ray's father Sylvain (known to all as Syl) constructed a family tree in 1974 and left for posterity a lot of important papers, all neatly organized in a box, that includes birth certificates, marriage licenses, death certificates, citizenship papers, passports, etc., going back to the second generation.

Syl also left a shoebox full of photos arranged in chronological order representing important events starting with his retirement and move to Lakewood, New Jersey. From it, I was able to construct a log of his travels during that period of his life. In the 10 years after his first wife's death, Syl traveled to Europe seven times, to Hawaii three times and to Asia once along with visits to regional tourist attractions up and down the East Coast.

Alfred and Aline – the First Generation
Spanning six generations, the earliest records go back to Ray's great grandfather Alfred Meurer, born around 1850 in Dinglingen, District of Lahr Baden-Württemberg in Germany near the Rhine River, 25 miles southeast of Strasbourg in the region of Alsace-Lorraine.

At about age 20, Alfred was living in Paris and worked as a gilder, applying gold leaf to picture frames and mirrors. He married Aline Lukas, a Frenchwoman who came from a family of meatpackers and butchers (some of whom were named Roth) in Orléans, a French city about 75 miles southwest of Paris.

The Franco-Prussian War of 1870 was in full force, and, because he was German, Alfred's status was greatly improved after he married this native Frenchwoman.

After the war, they moved to Dinglingen and had five daughters and, finally, a son, Frédéric Auguste (Americanized as Frederick and shortened to Fred).

Alfred did very well. He owned and operated a prosperous furniture factory and provided his family with a comfortable lifestyle.

However, he couldn't resist his dalliances.

One day, he absconded with all the cash and any assets at hand and ran off to Brazil with a chambermaid, settling in Manaus, the capital city. Subsequently, he was bitten by a mosquito and contracted a disease that took his life. Alfred's effects were returned to his kinfolk in Alsace-Lorraine by the German consulate in Manaus.

No attempt has been made to track down any Meurers in Brazil, but there probably are relatives there.

Alfred's wife Aline became destitute and, along with a couple of the daughters, went to live in the Lutheran convent in Colmar, France, about 40 miles from Dinglingen. Aline died circa 1928, and her only son's wife Anna traveled from New York City to Alsace for the funeral, representing her husband Fred's arm of the family.

Several decades later, Ray's father Syl tracked down the early family members in Colmar.

On the next trip Syl and his wife Emma took abroad, they traveled to Colmar to visit his long-lost relatives, but the Meurer descendants refused to meet. Evidently, they didn't want a reminder of anyone linked to Alfred because of the heartache and hardship he had brought to the family 75 or so years earlier.

Ill feelings sometimes die hard and are never forgotten or forgiven.

Fred and Anna – the Second Generation
Alfred and Aline's only son, Frederick (called Fred), was born in 1876 in Dinglingen, District of Lahr Baden-Württemberg in Germany, the same town where Alfred had been born.

By his late teens, Fred was working as an apprentice to a cabinetmaker. In 1900 at the age of 24, Fred married Anna Maurer, a Catholic. She had been born on July 4 in 1879 on a farm in Walbach, Haut-Rhin, Alsace, in the Vosges Mountains just outside of Colmar, France.

Anna was the daughter of Thomas Maurer and Anne Marie Better. In 2007, Ray's cousin Dick and his wife Ruth went to Walbach and were able to locate Anna's birth certificate in the record books at the mairie (city hall).

Fred and Anna settled in Mulhouse, France, in Alsace, located near the German and Swiss borders. Six months later, their first son, Sylvain Thomas Meurer, was born in December of 1900. Two more sons followed: Frederick (Fritz) Carl (inadvertently changed to Charles by Immigration in New York – a not uncommon occurrence) Meurer born in 1902 and Erwin (Erv) Meurer born in 1903.

Fred emigrated to New York City from France shortly after the turn of the 20th century, probably around 1904 after his third son was born the year before. The story goes that Fred walked all the way across France to get to the French port.

As he was leaving for America, he promised Anna he would send funds for the family's passage as soon as he could find a job and save some money.

Having apprenticed as a cabinetmaker in the old country, he found a job as a carpenter in his new country. Being a jolly sort of person, he got along well with his co-workers, and everybody liked him.

Anna, not having heard from Fred for nearly three years, bundled up her boys, took the train to a port of call in France and crossed the

Atlantic (can you imagine a young woman with three little tots doing that on her own?).

There was a lot of confusion in steerage, and upon arrival in New York, Anna found she had lost Fred's address so she and the boys were put in detention.

Lutheran Social Services of New York stepped in and placed an ad in the local papers. Her husband's boss saw the notice and said, "Fred, your wife and boys are in town."

They were reunited and started their life as a family in America in 1907.

Fred and Anna settled in Jersey City, New Jersey. Fred's job as a carpenter enabled him to provide for the family. Money was tight, but it was a good life, and he and Anna tried to instill a deep-seated work ethic, importance of family and strong values in the children. Fred was a prankster, and there was never a dull moment. He especially liked to play tricks with his cat.

The three Meurer boys must have been a handful – or maybe it's just that "boys will be boys." One story goes like this: Fred enjoyed his schnapps. He would sometimes notice that, although it looked normal, his drink didn't taste very strong. It turns out that the boys had added water to the clear-colored alcoholic beverage. Once the secret was out, Fred blamed Anna, but the boys were the culprits.

Becoming a U.S. citizen was a goal of many immigrants. Fred completed the naturalization process and was granted U.S. citizenship in 1919. Anna's citizenship certificate is dated 1930. Syl's certificate of citizenship is dated 1952. It is presumed his two brothers were awarded theirs as well.

Syl, Fritz and Erv – the Third Generation

Time went by, and the boys grew up. All three of the Meurer sons graduated from Dickinson High School in Jersey City.

Jersey City's population at the time was about 300,000. It borders Hoboken, the hometown of singer Frank Sinatra, to the north.

Its neighbor to the south is Liberty State Park, home to the Statue of Liberty. Lower Manhattan is directly across the Hudson River.

Generally speaking, the average young person at that time attended high school (although not everyone did – some kids dropped out of school and started working at a very young age) and then found a job. Going to college was not top of mind or even feasible for many.

As luck would have it, Syl, the oldest son, was presented with the opportunity to go to Carnegie Tech in Pittsburgh, Pennsylvania. In order to qualify, he had to pass a trigonometry test. Not expecting to go to college, he had not taken the course in high school. He borrowed books from the public library (there was no summer school back then) and studied on his own all summer long and passed with flying colors.

As it turned out, the two younger brothers also went to college in Pittsburgh, and all three graduated with a degree in engineering: Syl, Carnegie Institute of Technology, electrical engineering; Fritz, University of Pittsburgh, chemical engineering; and Erv, University of Pittsburgh, electrical engineering.

The arrangement was that Fred and Anna would help pay the expenses for each son's college education. In addition, the brother, upon graduation, would help with the expenses for the next brother's college education. When that brother graduated, he would help with the expenses for the next brother.

To earn extra money, the brother in school would find part-time work. For instance, Syl worked in the steel mills shoveling coal.

Syl took his studies seriously, and he took full advantage of all Carnegie Tech had to offer. He became a member of the Delta Phi Delta fraternity. He joined the American Institute of Electrical Engineers, a club on campus for future engineers, and listened to guest lecturers talk about advancements in the field.

He was a member of the YMCA and made good use of the weekly swimming privileges. And being a patriot, he served in the newly established ROTC on-campus program.

On the lighter side, he joined the Musical Clubs and was praised for his performances. The notation in the yearbook his senior year reads, "Syl tickles a wicked mandolin."

Carnegie Tech's yearbook was called *The Thistle*. The national flower of Scotland, the thistle was chosen to honor the heritage of Andrew Carnegie, philanthropist and founder of the institution, who had made his fortune in the steel industry.

In 1967, Carnegie Institute of Technology and Mellon Institute merged to form Carnegie Mellon University.

I recently came across Syl's 1923 yearbook (which is in mint condition after a hundred years) by accident – it had been sitting on a bookshelf for several years, and I hadn't noticed it.

Of course, it represents the typical yearbook of its day. I had grown up looking through my parents' college yearbooks: Mother's *Sycamore* from Indiana State University and Dad's *Arbutus* from Indiana University.

The Thistle was the yearbook published by the junior class for the senior class at Carnegie Tech starting in 1906. Publication of *The Thistle* ceased just this year, in 2020 (that's 115 years of these "works of art"). The 1923 edition is a compilation of 400 pages of individual and group photos and descriptions of the students, faculty and administration, the athletic teams, the activities, the organizations, the clubs and the traditions. In a number of the group shots, the men are wearing not only a suit and tie but also a hat, and the young ladies are bundled up in a fur coat.

The cover is of a heavy-duty brown stock with embossed wording and the image of a thistle on the front cover. The owner's name is printed in gold (S.T. Meurer). The text is printed on a handsome paper stock, and the black-and-white photos are as crisp today as the day they were taken. The last page is reserved for signatures, and about 20 of Syl's colleagues signed his book, probably with a fountain pen. The ink, too, has not faded with time (unlike the pens of today).

The book contains well-written accounts of events along with sketches, drawings and cartoons.

Many of the descriptions are clever references to happenings in the early 1920s. Some are inside jokes, revealing a sense of humor akin to college kids.

Here's one from Boss Hall*, a men's dormitory:

An Ode to Boss Hall

Oh, Boss Hall! Boss Hall!
King Dorm of them all!
Of all the places where men abide
You are the worst we have ever tried.

*The name Boss Hall was changed to Boss House sometime after 1965. One of the oldest dorms on campus, it is still being used as a residence hall, reserved for freshmen.

Every group attempted to entice fellow students to join the organization, whether it was a frat house or residence hall (as above) or theater club. The competitiveness comes through loud and clear.

Sometimes the message was more of a personal nature. Here's one notation from Woodlawn Dormitory – Group 1 that housed female students:

"Shoot a nickel in the telephone box and drop us a call. We have excellent service on all four lines. It's your loss only if you allow yourselves to remain ignorant of our charms, good nature and pep.
Every day in every way we're growing better [sic] and better educated."

It's rather surprising to look through the yearbook and see pages and pages of females at a time when it was not customary for girls to go to a four-year college. According to one report, 7% of the bachelor's degrees awarded in 1920 went to women.

There's a 20-page section of ads at the end of the yearbook, and several talk about the trends of the future. For example, one ad by a bank encourages people to use checks as a form of payment, a fairly new concept in 1923.

The ad reads: "Pay by Check. It is businesslike, convenient, safe. It provides a receipt that is proof conclusive for money paid out. Open a checking account with us. It need not be large to be welcome."

And there's an ad by a clinkerless power producer for a furnace that "burns crushed coal in suspension with absolute control of fuel and air." And, the ad further promises, "Not a pound of iron [is] exposed to destructive furnace heat."

Note that just a couple of ads include a phone number. Research shows that in 1920, only 35% of households in the United States had a telephone.

After graduation in 1923 with a B.S. degree, Syl moved back home to Jersey City. He was offered and accepted a job at Consolidated Edison (Con Ed) at 4 Irving Place in New York and commuted into New York City.

He paid rent to his parents. This was a way he could thank them for making it possible for him to go to college and for helping with his expenses. As the older brother now employed in a respectable job and earning a decent salary, he helped with Fritz' college expenses.

Let's take a minute to talk about the Palisades, the striking rock formations and geological phenomena bordering the Hudson River that were part of the everyday scenery in Jersey City.

The Palisades are a line of steep cliffs that extend about 20 miles. They sit on a ridgeline that stretches from Hoboken, New Jersey, north to Haverstraw, New York, along the western shore of the lower Hudson River. At Hoboken/Jersey City, they tower about 300 feet in the air. Farther north, they rise majestically to 540 feet.

To the indigenous Lenape tribe thousands of years ago, these outcroppings were "Wee-Awk-En" or "rocks that look like rows of trees" because of their vertical, striated appearance. The name stuck, and Weehawken Township in New Jersey, directly across from Midtown Manhattan, has enjoyed a rich history. In 1524, Italian explorer Giovanni da Verrazzano sailed past the ridge and thought it looked like a "fence of stakes" or a barricade.

On July 11, 1804, a ledge on the Palisades in Weehawken was the setting for the famous duel between Alexander Hamilton and Aaron Burr, who had become bitter enemies over political and personal matters. In case you've forgotten, Burr fatally shot Hamilton.

Hamilton had served as aide-de-camp to General George Washington during the Revolutionary War and became the nation's first secretary of the treasury under President Washington. Burr served as President Thomas Jefferson's vice president.

In the presidential election of 1800, Jefferson and Burr were tied with 73 electoral votes each. The House of Representatives broke the tie and voted in Thomas Jefferson as our country's third president.

About 20 years after the duel, property owner John B. Coles, successful flour merchant and senator from New York, made plans to turn some of the land along the Hudson River into a public park in memory of Hamilton. But Coles died shortly thereafter, and the project languished.

About 25 years later, in 1848, Hamilton's heirs contested the municipality's ownership of the land, but the 5.5-acre property was officially conveyed to the township. Hamilton Park was opened and, with its stunning views of the Manhattan skyline, has been a favorite place to visit by locals and tourists alike.

Ray and I used to stop at one of the lookouts on the Palisades Parkway on our way home from visiting his dad in Lakewood, New Jersey. It was almost like being on a plane and looking down on the city. The views are magnificent, with panoramic vistas spanning every direction but west. With the Hudson River in the foreground, we could see the expanse of Manhattan in all its glory.

Farther east, Long Island Sound came into view. We could even see "the stacks" at Northport, Long Island, near the harbors where we frequently anchored for the night on the boat.

"The stacks," as the locals call them, are part of the Northport Power Station infrastructure, the largest power-generation facility on Long Island. The four distinctive red and white columns extend more than 600 feet into the air and can be seen from ground level as far as 40 miles away. In fact, on a clear day, Ray and I could spot the smokestacks as distant as Falkner Island near New Haven, Connecticut, when returning from a summer cruise on the boat. With the aid of binoculars, it was always fun to see the four sticks become visible through the mist or haze as we chugged our way west toward home port.

On an everyday basis, the stacks are a part of the scenery from our beaches in Rowayton.

Back to the Meurer family story: Around 1925 or so, Fred and Anna decided to build a house in Hasbrouck Heights. Syl and both brothers pitched in whenever they could.

Hasbrouck Heights is about 15 miles north of Jersey City. The parcel of land was situated high up on a rise facing neighboring Teterboro Airport to the northeast and the Manhattan skyline across the Hudson River eight miles to the east.

Fritz, the second son, joined the ROTC at Pitt and, upon graduation from the university in 1925, was commissioned into the U.S. Army Coast Artillery Corps. He served in the Reserve for 17 years while working his day job in the city.

After America entered World War II, he was called to active duty and served from 1942-1944. He was stationed in California for Basic Training. His parents, ever the travelers, journeyed to the West Coast to visit him before he was deployed to Hawaii. His first year was spent on the island of Kauai. Then he became a convoy officer and was in charge of transporting recruits to their deployments, mainly to England and to Algeria and Morocco in North Africa.

Fritz spent much of his career working for American Can Company in New York. Before that, he had several jobs (for the railroad, the telephone company, DuPont and a stint of unemployment during the Depression years). Fritz and his wife Eilene lived in Demarest, New Jersey, and had two children, Richard (Dick) and Anne. Fritz and Eilene traveled the world over. In fact, they were on a trip to North Africa when their daughter was involved in a fatal accident. Locating them took some doing back in those days.

Erv, the youngest son, left for school in 1924 and remained in the Pittsburgh area after college. He worked for the telephone company and was the envy of all because he didn't have to pay for long-distance phone calls. Erv and his wife Teresa raised two sons and a daughter, Robert, Charles and Irene.

Syl continued to live at home and work at Con Ed and commute into the city. After three+ years of paying rent, he felt his obligation to his parents had been satisfied, and he left to marry Emma Maurer and set up his own household.

Emma

Emma Maurer was born in Basel, Switzerland, in 1899.

Her mother was Marie Dietzi, born in 1877 in Obernai, Bas-Rhin, a picturesque Alsatian city 20 miles southwest of Strasbourg, France.

It is not known who Emma's biological father was. One story is that Marie was raped by a German uhlan (a warrior on horseback or cavalryman) during one of the infiltrations in France. At any rate, Xavier Maurer, born in 1873 in Walbach, Haut-Rhin, married Marie either before or soon after Emma was born, and Emma was given the Maurer surname. Emma lived with her parents Marie and Xavier in Saint-Louis, France, a suburb of Basel, Switzerland (it's a 10-minute walk from Saint-Louis to the Swiss border).

In fact, the Basel Tramway Network maintains stations in France and Germany, as well as in Switzerland, and is the only tri-national transit system in the world. And only two cities offer mass transit service to passengers in one other country: Geneva, Switzerland, makes stops in France; and Strasbourg, France, makes stops in Germany.

Emma's father Xavier had a sister six years younger named Anna, who was married to Fred Meurer. They had emigrated to the United States in the early aughts ('00s) and were living in the New York City metro area.

By her late teens, Emma was working as a chambermaid on an estate in Dijon, France, about 150 miles west of Basel.

A few years later, in 1923, the family in Dijon made the decision to move to America. They asked Emma to go with them and work as their au pair, and she agreed to do so. (On a trip to Ellis Island a few years ago, Ray, Diane and I were able to locate Emma's name on the ship's manifest. The record included how much cash she was carrying.)

As payment for her passage to America, Emma was to work for the family six months for free at their new home in Scarsdale, New York, which she did. At the end of that period, she asked about being paid going forward, and the family told her she had to work another six months for free.

Alone and with nowhere else to turn, she contacted Anna Meurer, Emma's father's sister (her aunt), who took Emma into her home in Jersey City. Anna's youngest son Erv drove to Scarsdale and transported Emma to her new home.

In a letter to Emma for her 70th birthday celebration, Erv mentioned making the trip and meeting her for the first time. He said he didn't know how he had found the house where she was staying in Scarsdale (there was no GPS back then, of course), but he had. He said she was "beautiful and was wearing a gray business-type suit."

Syl was finished with college and back home by then, working in New York City. Living under the same roof and seeing each other daily, he and Emma fell in love. Syl's mother Anna was furious and threw Emma out of the house and forbade Syl to see her ever again.

Although Anna had come to Emma's rescue during the Scarsdale crisis, Anna had long held a grudge against Emma. Anna strongly believed Emma's mother Marie Dietzi, unmarried and pregnant in war-torn Alsace-Lorraine, had taken advantage of Anna's brother Xavier

Maurer and tricked him into marrying her.

On top of that, Anna felt Syl, a college graduate – a highly respected feat in those days accomplished by only about 5% of the population – could have married so much better than a lowly, temperamental chambermaid (although Emma had been an au pair and then a governess).

Having been evicted by Anna in Jersey City, Emma found a job as a governess for a family in New York City. She and Syl continued seeing each other against Anna's wishes and were married in June of 1927. Anna refused any contact with Syl and Emma and banned the newlyweds from her house.

After Alice Marian Meurer was born a year later, Emma urged Syl to tell his parents about the baby. He did so and tried to make amends time and time again, but Anna never forgave him for marrying Emma. Syl was saddened by this for the rest of his life. Anna and Fred hosted frequent family gatherings, but Anna remained aloof to Emma.

Syl had been an active swimmer in college when he was a member of the YMCA at Carnegie Tech. At some point, he started going to the beaches on Long Island and enjoyed swimming in the ocean. He found a house in Flushing, New York, where it was about a half an hour to Long Beach and Rockaway Beach on the Atlantic and an easy commute into Manhattan to work. He and Emma set up household at 56-40 138th Street and went on frequent swimming excursions with friends.

Syl and Emma's second and last child Raymond Frederick Meurer was born in 1931.

Great Neck

The short definition of "neck" when pertaining to land is a long, thin peninsula. Another more descriptive definition is a narrow piece of land connecting two larger areas across an expanse of water by which they are otherwise separated. Sometimes the word also refers to the shape of the landmass. Throughout history, shore towns or sections of towns, streets (e.g., Middle Neck Road, Second Neck Lane) or even lookout points have been named "neck" (e.g., for a while, Horseneck was the name of a part of Old Greenwich, Connecticut, and modern-day Greenwich Point was earlier named Elizabeth's Neck).

Great Neck, New York, in Nassau County on Long Island is a town consisting of nine villages covering 1.4 square miles. It is located on a peninsula that sits between Manhasset Bay to the east and Little Neck Bay to the west, both of which feed into Long Island Sound.

You may have heard of littleneck clams, a popular appetizer or entrée, and, yes, they originally came from the same Little Neck Bay. Starting in the 1860s, small hard-shelled clams, called quahogs, from Little Neck Bay came to be a favorite food item for diners in the best restaurants in New York City. Eventually, the term "littleneck" came to be the word used as a size category for all hard-shelled clams, regardless of origin. They are tasty served raw (clams on the half shell) or steamed (say, with a butter and garlic sauce).

In 1935, Syl purchased a parcel of land and had a house erected at 40 Valley View Road in Great Neck on Long Island, about 30 minutes outside of New York City and, specifically, from Consolidated Edison so it was an easy commute to work.

Great Neck also was just 30 minutes from Jones Beach on the Atlantic Ocean and 10 minutes from Long Island Sound.

Fred and Fritz lent a hand with the finishing touches to Syl's house whenever they had some spare time.

Life was good, and Syl and Emma and children were a happy family, going about their business. The lifestyle was different from that of today. The men went to work during the week, and the women cooked and cleaned and took care of the children.

The wives were neighborly and enjoyed their coffee klatsches, where they shared everyday happenings and the ups and downs of life. As Ray grew up, he was adored by all the neighbor ladies, and he kept in touch with a few of them into adulthood, particularly Gladys Schofield and her daughter Nancy Hall.

Great Neck was very much a cosmopolitan community. People

from all over Europe settled there. It was a melting pot of disparate rhythms and cultures.

The area also attracted the rich and famous who built majestic homes on the north shore overlooking Long Island Sound and lived a lifestyle most of us only read about. More will be said about this later.

Although the tony section of town was but a few miles up the road, it was a world away from everyday life for many Great Neckers.

Ray grew up in an environment where a number of languages were spoken. And Manhattan was only half an hour away with all its culture and attractions. It was a wonderful place to be raised.

The immigrants were grateful for the opportunity to live in this grand new country with all its promise and freedoms and tried their best to assimilate into the American way of life. Most insisted that the children speak English and not their native tongue.

Emma became fluent in English but, as was not unusual, never did master the proper pronunciation of certain letters or combination of letters. One example was the "w" (she always called the area just north of New York City where Scarsdale was located "Vestchester" County).

The terms "pop" and "grandpop" were used by everyone in the Meurer family until Syl changed that tradition and brought up his two children to say "dad" and "grandpa."

Emma and Alice and Ray journeyed back to Europe most every year to visit family (Syl had limited vacation time and couldn't be gone long enough to take an annual sea voyage). There are photos of Ray as a young towhead entertaining the adults – one on a ship steaming its way across the Pond and another one at a neighbor's house in Great Neck. His fun-loving smile tells all. By nature, he was a happy and positive child and instantly won everyone's heart. He carried those traits throughout life.

Having chosen Great Neck as a place to call home partially because of its close proximity to Jones Beach on the Atlantic, Syl took the family to the shore about every weekend during the summers.

He also took Ray and sometimes Alice on camping trips to destinations throughout the tri-state area. One time, Syl took Ray and cousin Dick on a week's camping trip to High Point State Park in New Jersey. Alice rode along and was dropped off in Stroudsburg, Pennsylvania, where she visited with friends for the week.

Syl took the commuter train into New York City every workday. Most of the time, Ray would meet the homebound train around 5:30 p.m., and the two of them would walk home together (just under a mile). If it was raining or snowing, neighbors would offer a ride, but Syl declined every time. Ray always thought all that walking all those years contributed to Syl's longevity.

Since both Syl and Fritz worked in New York, the brothers periodically had lunch together. One of their favorite restaurants was The Russian Tea Room, located on 57th Street between 6th and 7th Avenues. Carnegie Hall is situated right next door. They also joined forces from time to time and helped each other with home repair projects.

Syl was a modest man. One of the exceptions was when he splurged on an automatic transmission for his new Oldsmobile in the early 1940s. That was a big deal because, generally, Syl was frugal. Having lived through the Great Depression, he did not like to spend money foolishly or frivolously (and did not approve of others doing so either, especially his kids).

Even with Anna's disapproval of Emma, the Meurer clan kept in touch after Syl had a family of his own. One Sunday every month or so during the late '30s and '40s, Syl and Emma and the children would drive from Long Island to New Jersey for a family gathering at Fred and Anna's house. The route took them through Midtown Manhattan to the car ferry that crossed the Hudson River.

In the wintertime, it would get cold on the way home since most cars didn't have an adequate heating system. So Alice and Ray would place their feet on a heated brick to keep their feet warm and tuck a blanket on top. And during the ride, they listened to radio programs like "The Green Hornet," "The Monster Says" and "The Shadow" episodes: "Who Knows What Evil Lurks in the Hearts of Men? Only the Shadow Knows."

Grandpop Fred was quite a character. A day didn't go by that he didn't smoke a couple of packs of Camels or Lucky Strikes and consume his allotment of beer (sometimes by noon or so) and later whiskey. At the house, he kept a supply of the cheapest beer he could find. For many years, it was A&P Tudor beer, purchased from the local A&P grocery store (everyone called it "A&P beer" regardless of the brand). He bought it by the case but was always running low on inventory.

And he drank wine with dinner every night and, from time to time, even tried a hand at making his own hooch. Sometimes the batch was good, and sometimes it tasted like vinegar.

Also, Fred was long remembered for his consumption of raw eggs. He would take his pen knife and tap the skinny end of the egg, breaking a small hole in the tip of the shell. Then he would suck the egg out.

The grandkids found the whole thing disgusting. They dreaded having to kiss their grandpop hello and goodbye (on each cheek, as was the custom) because his full beard was not only scratchy but smelled of stale tobacco, beer, whiskey and raw egg. (Yuck!)

Grandson Dick remembers being dragged to a few bars during visits when he was a mere boy. The story goes like this: Anna would ask Fred to pick up a few items for her for cooking and cleaning. So he would go shopping first thing in the morning and take Dick along.

Afterward, Fred would stop at a bar and get a beer for himself and a soft drink for Dick. Then they'd shop for some other items on the list followed by another stop at a bar for a beer and a soda, respectively. Repeat a third time and add a sandwich. All that, and they'd be home by noon or so. It was fun. Fred had a great sense of humor and was well-liked by all the guys.

Dick's friends thought it was pretty neat that he got to hang out in bars.

Fred had circulatory problems later in life and had to have some of his toes amputated. The doctor said a shot of whiskey every night might make him feel better. So Fred followed the doctor's orders. But he thought: "If one shot is good for me, might not more than one shot be even better?" Thus he started a routine of drinking whiskey in the evening for "medicinal purposes."

Anna made periodic trips by ship back to Alsace to visit family. Her son Fritz told the story of how she ran out of money in Paris on one voyage, and he had to wire funds to her so she could get back to the States.

After a long illness, Anna passed away in 1951 in Hackensack Hospital at the age of 71, eight years prior to Fred's death. After she was gone, his kids kept a close eye on him. He eventually sold the house and lived for a spell with various members of the family, including his sons Erv and Fritz and granddaughter Alice.

In due course, Fred decided to move to Florida. Alice accompanied him to Lakeland and helped get him situated in the Carpenters and Joiners Home for retired members. He acclimated to his new surroundings but didn't like the rule that alcoholic beverages were not allowed on the premises. However, Fred found a way to get beer and whiskey and would sneak into the men's room to make the exchange. Two of his grandchildren, Dick and Anne, visited him there, and Dick told me he can attest to the truth of this story. Fred spent his last years in the Carpenters' home and died in 1959 at the age of 83.

Syl Helping Others

The course was set early on with Syl being taught that helping others was the right thing to do.

As noted earlier, after graduation from Carnegie Tech, Syl paid rent to his parents for three years as a thank you for helping with his college expenses. He also supplemented funding for his next younger brother Fritz' college expenses. And they all assisted each other in building a home.

During World War II, Syl sponsored many Jewish people from

Germany and France who were desperate to escape the Nazis. To be eligible to come to America, one had to have a sponsor who lived here in the United States. To a person, the people Syl stood up for worked hard in their new country and were successful and upstanding citizens. And they were forever grateful.

In return, the Meurers were invited to countless bar (and bat) mitzvahs. Ray's vocabulary was peppered with Yiddish words and idioms that he had heard growing up: chutzpah, futz, gesundheit, glitch, goy, kerfuffle, klutz, kvetch, lox, mensch, nosh, oy vey, schlep, schmaltzy, schmooze, schmuck, shtick, spiel, tchotchkes, tush and "What am I, chopped liver?"

Throughout his life, Syl was partial to those less fortunate and tried to help however he could: via personal effort and through government, church and local programs.

Syl also assisted family members when he could. There is a letter from Erv thanking Syl and Emma for loaning him their car so he could take his bride Teresa on a honeymoon to Washington, D.C.

And there's a letter from Emma's sister Annele Maurer Gervais thanking Syl and Emma for making it possible for her to visit them in America in 1958. Emma had had a serious surgery (a breast removed due to cancer) and couldn't travel to Alsace that year so she and Syl offered to pay Annele's fare to come here.

It was Annele's first trip to the United States and also her first plane ride. She flew in and out of Idlewild Airport (renamed John F. Kennedy International Airport in 1963).

Emma was 15 years old when Annele was born and was designated as Annele's godmother. In 1995, Ray and I visited Annele and her relative Marguerite Gervais in Basel when we were in Switzerland.

In 1978, Ray and I applied for a mortgage so we could purchase our house in Rowayton. Until all the arrangements were finalized, we needed a bridge loan.

Syl agreed to lend us the money – with interest, of course. It was all very proper and formal with a contract that stipulated the details, including installment dates. We were grateful to have Syl's help and paid off the loan ahead of time.

Alice and Ray – the Fourth Generation

Alice and Ray (and respective cousins) were the fourth generation of Meurers that we can track but were the first generation of Meurers born in the United States. As related above, Alice and Ray grew up in Great Neck, New York.

Great Neck High School was renowned for its academic excellence and its social activities. Sororities and fraternities were part of the scene, and the students had meetings and parties regularly.

Many parents belonged to one of the several country clubs nearby, and they encouraged the teenagers to join in the fun and hone their social skills. All in all, there was a party somewhere on most any weekend night.

Alice loved to party, and she was in her element. She was a good-looking girl with dark hair and eyes and olive skin, and the guys considered her a real babe and fun to be with. Her grades suffered because she had more important things to think about during class than the subject at hand and didn't like taking time away from the social scene to do homework.

Her zest for partying caused Syl to pull her out of Great Neck High School for her senior year and enroll her at Mount Aloysius Academy in Cresson, Pennsylvania, a private Catholic school in a quiet town nestled in the Allegheny Mountains 80 miles east of Pittsburgh, population 1,500 (can you imagine?).

Alice tested the nuns' patience every day. But she did manage to find some fun in that desolate environment. Although smart as a whip, she graduated with C's and D's.

Ray attended Great Neck High School, too, rated one of the best schools in the country at the time. A high percentage of the graduates went on to college. With its sororities and fraternities, it was almost like a university environment.

His high school experience was loaded with strenuous academics and packed with endless social affairs. He said the solid educational foundation he had in high school made college seem easy.

From an early age, Ray had an interest in writing and was fascinated with reading books and getting thoughts down on paper. As a pastime during high school, he would sit at his manual typewriter and copy articles word for word from *The New Yorker* magazine to get a feel for how to construct a story.

This exercise became a building block for the career Ray would pursue. He also tried to improve his typing skills (he was a fast typist but made lots of errors) by practicing the phrase that we all know: Now is the time for all good men to come to the aid of their country (or "their party" originally). The typing drill was developed by teacher Charles E. Weller, author of *The Early History of the Typewriter*.

During the summertime, teenaged Ray took a job on a farm in upstate New York one summer and in rural Connecticut the next. He enjoyed the work and talked about those experiences all his life. And he was a lifeguard one summer.

Being just minutes from Manhasset Bay, Ray then landed a job as crew for the owner of a sailboat one season and the owner of a powerboat the next – and thus began his passion for boating.

It was a lifelong love affair.

His cousin Dick was equally fascinated with trains, and his entire life was centered around the railroad world, both at work and at play. Dick graduated from Dartmouth and then the Wharton School of the University of Pennsylvania and spent his career working for the railroad. And every vacation – encompassing dozens of trips all over the world, visiting all seven continents – was centered around train rides.

Ray and Dick spent most every waking moment obsessed with their respective hobby and had fun sharing their adventures when they got together.

Upon graduating from Great Neck High School, Ray matriculated at Wabash College, a small liberal arts men's school in Crawfordsville,

Indiana, 50 miles northwest of Indianapolis. He had read an article written by the school president that inspired him to apply.

Ray had considered skipping college and breaking into the construction business. He knew people up and down the street who were making megabucks as Long Island – and the country in general – was experiencing the biggest building boom in history. And you didn't need a college degree to jump in and make it "big time." There were opportunities everywhere.

Some family friends offered to introduce and recommend Ray to "the right people." In the end, he went on to school because learning was so compelling to him even though the big bucks and excitement were tempting.

So Ray went to Wabash College instead of getting into construction. There were no female students, and most of the male classmates went home every weekend. Ray spent his free time studying and working. For a discount on his room and board, he washed dishes in the frat house (Beta Theta Pi) and, for spending money, he worked in the library; he also sold vacuum cleaners door to door in town. And one summer he accompanied a friend home to Detroit and worked on the Chrysler assembly line. On the lighter side, he was a member of the university choral group and served on the staff of the student newspaper.

The education at Wabash was excellent, but life was a far cry from the active, invigorating days he had experienced at Great Neck High School, along with frequent trips to the museums and theaters and movie houses in Manhattan.

After two years at Wabash, Ray told his parents he'd like to transfer to a college in the New York City metropolitan area, where it wouldn't be so isolated and would be more social.

Syl said, "What you start, you finish."

When Ray persisted, Syl said, "If you don't want to continue at Wabash, you can come home. I'll give you two weeks to find a job and start paying rent."

Ray went back to Wabash.

Upon graduation from college, Ray returned to the East and started his business career with Walden Book Company and a few years later (in 1956) married Jane Schriefer. He went on to work at S&H Green Stamps and the American Petroleum Institute and then took a job at IBM, where he worked for 35 years.

Employees often joked that IBM stood for "I've been moved," referring to the fact that people were transferred frequently. But that was not the case with Ray. He spent nearly all his years with the company in locations in Westchester County and New York City with a short stint in Cleveland, Ohio.

In the meantime, Alice had married John (Jack) Garabedian in 1948, and they lived in an apartment in Great Neck. Jack's father had started a taxi business in town, and his two sons, Jack and Charlie, worked with him. Ray helped out on weekends and summers.

Fairview Taxi did very well. Certain areas of Great Neck attracted the rich and famous due to the village's desirable location on Long Island Sound and its proximity to Manhattan. The cab company had contracts with celebrities to be transported to and from and all around New York City.

These prominent people lived in magnificent waterfront mansions built by nationally acclaimed architects such as Frank Lloyd Wright, Frank J. Forster, Perkins & Will, Emery Roth, Gustav Stickley and Leroy P. Ward. Landscape architects such as Olmsted Brothers created acres of sprawling gardens that were beautifully maintained.

Residents enjoyed the scenic beauty and wildlife of their country estates. Some lived a lifestyle that was extravagant and ostentatious, as depicted by F. Scott Fitzgerald in his novel *The Great Gatsby*. He started writing this book when he was living in his home in Great Neck and describes life in and around New York City during the Roaring '20s, also known as the Jazz Age.

Great Neck is divided into nine incorporated villages. One is called Village of Great Neck Estates. Because the residents live near or on the water, they need to be aware of the tides on Long Island Sound. I have had a standing order for decades from the village office for my tide calendar.

In 1954 at the age of 54, the elder Garabedian died unexpectedly of a ruptured aortic aneurysm, and the taxi business was sold by his wife.

The Garabedian sons formed a trucking company to take advantage of the infrastructure boom going on. Highways and parkways were being built all over Long Island.

Alice and Jack bought a house and moved to Carle Place in 1955. After Ray was married and living on Long Island in a Levittown-like home, he and his wife Jane frequently visited Alice and Jack and their three kids (Bruce, Gregg and Lynn).

Ray and Jane had three children (Diane, Michael and Scott) and moved to Ridgefield, Connecticut, to be close to Ray's work at IBM in White Plains, New York. The two families made it a point to get together often (drive time was under two hours each way).

The trucking company Jack and Charlie had formed didn't work out, and they each pursued another path. Jack joined Snap-on Incorporated in sales and became field manager. Charlie worked as a building engineer and inspector for a municipality.

Both Jack and Charlie learned they had cardiovascular disease, the same ailment that their dad had had. Charlie opted to have surgery. Jack didn't.

In February of 1974, Jack died of a ruptured aortic aneurysm. He was 46 years old. Alice, a widow at the age of 45, moved to West Palm Beach, Florida, four years later. From then on, Alice made periodic trips up north to visit family and friends. And the rest of the family enjoyed vacations in Florida whenever they could sneak away.

Charlie Garabedian, having had a successful surgery years earlier, lived to be in his 70s. He, too, died of a ruptured aortic aneurysm.

Ray and Jane divorced after 20 years of marriage. Then Ray and I met, and we were married in 1978.

Levittown

Ray graduated from Great Neck High School in 1949 during a time when America was being transformed. World War II was over, and 16 million veterans had come streaming home.

This presented two national problems: 1) a job shortage (this was just 10 years after the Great Depression had ended, and people remembered vividly the long years of no work and hardship) and 2) a pre-existing housing shortage made worse as the veterans returned, married and started a family (there were 76 million baby boomers born between 1946 and 1964).

As mentioned earlier, as a senior in high school, Ray was faced with the decision of whether to head off to college and get a degree or go directly to work. If he went to school, he knew it would entail four years of intense studying and concurrently working odd jobs to make ends meet.

On the other hand, he had the chance to jump on board immediately and ride the construction boom that was happening at his front door. There was big money to be made at every turn. He, of course, ended up going to college because he was such a curious person and thrived on learning about everything, but I want to take a few minutes to describe the building frenzy that was occurring.

When President Franklin Delano Roosevelt signed the GI Bill of Rights into law in 1944, the plan was an economic stroke of genius. (GI is a nickname in reference to a soldier's "general issue" uniform.)

The bill prevented the United States from what could have been an unemployment pandemic (no one wanted a repeat of the severe job shortage experienced during the Depression – a lack of jobs meant a scarcity of money to buy even the essentials – which was finally reversed because of the war).

Instead of millions of veterans simultaneously looking for a job, about half (8 million) took advantage of the opportunity to go to college or vocational school. Their graduation dates were staggered over a period of years. With a steady influx of educated and trained workers,

America soon had a workforce that was propelling the country into a level of economic prosperity not seen before.

The other problem – the housing shortage – was being addressed on many fronts, but the single most powerful weapon was a construction firm named Levitt & Sons based on Long Island in New York. That firm was instrumental in taking a cottage industry and turning it into a major manufacturing process by instituting sweeping new methodology in constructing living quarters.

The GI Bill consisted of three components and offered veterans: 1) educational support toward tuition and a monthly stipend, 2) unemployment benefits, and 3) loan guarantees and easy credit.

These enticements were appealing to the masses. Prior to that time, it was generally thought that college was reserved for the elite. Until 1940, around 5% of the population in the United States had graduated from a college or university. Starting with the GI Bill in the 1940s, that percentage grew to around 30% by 2010.

But not everyone was in favor of easy access to higher education. With the onslaught of so many more people enrolling in colleges, some of the prestigious universities said they didn't want institutions of higher learning to become a "device for coping with mass unemployment."

Some went on to say that "colleges and universities will find themselves converted into 'hobo jungles' " (a place where a hobo could rest and repair while on the road; a refuge where a person could eat, sleep, read a newspaper and get cleaned up before heading out again).

Opposition was minor, though, compared with the profound positive ramifications of the bill. The fact that large numbers of citizens chose to get a college degree changed America from an agrarian to an urban/suburban society.

The jobs were in the cities, but the graduates didn't want to live there with all the noise, pollution, overcrowding and disease. They wanted to live in the suburbs in their own home surrounded by a white picket fence.

From an economic standpoint, people who have a higher level of education generally make a bigger salary and, more than likely, have the capability to purchase a home and lots of consumer goods, resulting in a stronger overall economy. That is what happened because of the GI Bill, and it created a large middle class in America.

The program cost the federal government $14.5 billion. But each veteran with a college degree earned from $10,000 to $15,000 more per annum than had they not attended college. In turn, this generated 10 times more tax revenue than the cost of running the program.

In the mid-'40s, the housing shortage in cities across America was already a major problem. Apartments were overcrowded. There weren't enough homes.

So how would the country deal with a heightened housing shortage brought on by the onslaught of vets coming home from war and starting a family?

Being so close to New York City, which was bursting at its seams, Long Island was ripe for growth. The island represented 1,400 square miles of relatively undeveloped land (except in the far west areas closest to the city).

The construction business on Long Island exploded starting in the mid-1940s – especially residential, representing 75% of construction permits issued in the '50s. And wherever people live, they have needs that have to be met, which translates into building the required ancillary commercial businesses such as retail establishments, supermarkets, restaurants, shopping centers, office complexes, industrial parks, hotels, highways, entertainment venues, sports facilities.

Once the highway system was built and the railroad network expanded, transportation and commutation were made easy. For example, by 1950, 80% of male residents living in Levittown, Long Island, commuted into Manhattan, a distance of 35 miles.

The economy was soaring across the board. One statistic shows that land values in the '50s in some prime suburbs spiraled 3,000% over the previous 10-year span, and the population grew 45% during the same period.

To help meet the housing demand, Abraham Levitt and his sons William and Alfred came upon the idea to build not just houses but "census-designated places," commonly known as planned communities. First on Long Island and then in Pennsylvania, New Jersey and elsewhere, the threesome built Levittown communities – a cluster of modest homes that were affordable.

A blueprint was developed that showed not only a grid of the streets to be built but many other elements of the neighborhood. The complex included plans for private meeting areas, swimming pools and recreational facilities. And a formula was developed for providing an adequate number of schools and parks (the cost to be borne by the local municipality or even the state) and churches.

For some, this would be a starter home in the subdivision. Others would stay there for the duration.

Here is the story of how suburbia in America was born.

Abraham Levitt was a real estate lawyer on Long Island who, during the Depression years, handled mortgage foreclosures. After a transaction was completed, he took ownership and would try to sell the property to another party as quickly as possible. His two sons were in the real estate development business, and all three worked together on certain projects.

At one point in the late '30s, a particular tract that Abraham had been holding was not selling. Rather than continue to sit on it, he and his sons decided to take a chance and build a luxury house on the property (America was just coming out of a very long period of hunger and forced frugality, and there was a market for high-quality, high-value products).

It was a successful venture, and by 1941, Levitt & Sons had built 2,600 luxury homes.

When the United States entered World War II, the Levitts turned their attention to the war effort. They won a contract with the federal government to build housing units for military personnel, specifically the Navy.

This was a different kind of market from the upscale homes they'd been building and required utilizing low-cost mass building techniques if a profit were to be made. The Levitts learned the ropes and devised a methodology that would revolutionize the housing industry.

In 1946 after the war had ended, Levitt & Sons returned to a focus on Long Island and put their newly tested knowledge to work. They bought 1,400 acres of potato fields 35 miles east of New York City in Nassau County and, between 1947 and 1951, built 6,000 homes.

They used innovative and unconventional techniques that were cost-effective but not inferior. For example, in lieu of a basement, the house was built on a cement slab with radiant heat; walls were constructed with rockboard rather than drywall; floors were made of plaster rather than expensive hardwood.

The firm also explored options for acquiring materials economically. For example, they purchased timberland on the West Coast, built a mill and produced their own lumber, thus saving 40%.

Non-unionized laborers were hired, which was very unusual at that time but was much more cost-efficient.

The Levitts also streamlined the building process using an assembly line production methodology. They analyzed the entire process and divided it into individual tasks. If there were, say, 36 steps involved in constructing a house, they would hire 36 workers, each to complete one specific task. Since they had so many houses under construction at any given time, each man was kept busy, moving from house to house performing the same task.

With proper planning and execution, a Levitt house could be built in a day.

By limiting the choices to two house models (Cape Cod and ranch), the firm could buy the same raw materials used for both types, thus qualifying for deep volume discounts. That further decreased the total building cost, which was passed along to the homeowner. After all was said and done, Levitt & Sons made a profit of about $1,000 on each house.

The "little Levitt house" was 750 square feet and came with two bedrooms, bathroom, living room with TV, kitchen equipped with modern GE appliances (fridge and range), Venetian blinds, unfinished second floor, parking area (no garage), green lawn and picket fence.

In 1947, a Levitt house cost $7,900. Taking advantage of the GI Bill, the owner was granted a 30-year mortgage with no down payment required.

In 1951 after the Long Island community was completed, Levitt & Sons moved on to the next project in Pennsylvania, a tract of more than 5,000 acres in Buck's County, about 30 miles northeast of Philadelphia. From 1952 till 1958, 17,000 homes were built for 84,000 residents, comprising the second Levittown. The complex, as had the initial development, included various meeting areas, swimming pools and recreational facilities.

People liked living in Levittown. They were thrilled to be out of the grime of the city or the desolation of the farm. They liked the fact that their children played with the kids next door, and the parents could socialize with each other.

Thus the houses were in high demand. In the original Long Island Levittown, 1,400 houses were sold during the first three hours. Keep in mind, these houses were available to vets and not the general public.

Living in one of these planned communities is a study in sociology in and of itself. How was it living with so much sameness: aesthetically, economically, socially? Most of the people were alike: middle class veterans, white professionals. Over time, these communities became somewhat less homogenous but not dramatically so.

You could see row upon row of these cookie-cutter houses sitting neatly side by side (the houses were spaced 60 feet apart), looking much the same. There were plenty of jokes about how, after one too many cocktails, someone might get confused as to which house was home.

Because the target audience was the average John Doe, these homes sometimes were referred to as "the Henry Fords of the housing business." Not often mentioned but obvious as well is the similarity to Henry Ford's production line.

By the end of 1950, building firms across the country were following the Levitt model or a variation of it, and approximately 50 million units were under construction nationwide.

William Levitt assumed control of the firm in 1954. At peak production, 30 houses were completed per day (or 150 per week or one house every 16 minutes), but it was nearly impossible to keep up with demand. William has been called by some the Father of Modern Suburbia in the United States.

After building more than 140,000 housing units, William sold the business to ITT Corporation in 1968 for, according to some sources, $92 million (a value of more than $800 million today).

As part of the Fair Deal, the Housing Act of 1949 was signed into law by President Harry Truman on July 15, 1949. Its goal was to make possible a decent home and suitable living environment for every American family.

The federal government strove to help people achieve the American Dream by making homes affordable.

The Levitt house fit the bill and did just that.

Life Moves Along

Throughout the years that Syl and Emma Meurer lived in Great Neck, Ray and Jane and their three children visited often. Syl was a good, albeit strict, father and grandfather. Grandson Michael describes Syl as "hard but fair."

Michael remembers visiting his grandparents in Great Neck in the mid- and late '60s. Upon arrival, the family would park the car in front of the tidy brick house. Grandma Emma would give Michael a squeeze and a hug and call him her bubula, a Yiddish term used for addressing a small child. And when he was a little older, he recalls her handing out Werther's Original butterscotch candies, named for the German town where confectioner Gustav Nebel created the popular sweets. Grandpa Syl would take Michael to the pond at the bottom of the hill in a nearby park. Syl would pull slices of white bread from his pocket and break off pieces, and he and Michael would feed the ducks. What sweet memories.

Syl retired in 1966 after spending his entire career at Consolidated Edison in Manhattan. He had been a loyal employee and made many contributions to the company. A few years earlier, he had received an award for having "accurately predicted the extent to which the people of the great city of New York will use gas during the winter of 1960-1961."

As so many people do when preparing for retirement, Syl started looking for a place to move that would be quieter and less expensive than the New York metro area. In 1968, he bought a condominium in Leisure Village, a retirement community in Lakewood, New Jersey, that had just been built, one of the first 55+ communities. The complex is situated on 457 acres and encompasses nearly 2,500 units.

There are seven small lakes on the property, and Syl bought an end unit overlooking one of them. The address was 336D Canterbury Court. He would reside there for the next 30 years and enjoy a fulfilling retirement.

It was a good place to live. Syl was active in the association, swam in the pool, planted a garden, played cards and went out to lunch as often as possible. And he frequented the ocean beaches nearby. He and Emma traveled extensively whenever she was physically able.

In 1969, Syl hosted a celebration for Emma's 70th birthday. Ray solicited photos and/or a letter from relatives and friends from around the world. Syl put together a scrapbook that must have taken days and days to assemble. It still is intact.

Emma had health issues throughout her adult life and then suffered a stroke in the early '70s. Syl took care of her through it all. She passed away in June of 1972.

In the years following Emma's death, Syl continued with his interests, especially traveling. In going through his photos – all neatly arranged by date with a notation on the back describing who was in the picture and where it was taken – I was able to construct a travel itinerary.

In the 10 years after Emma's death, Syl traveled to Europe seven times. Each trip lasted anywhere from four to eight weeks and generally included stops in three or four countries. He visited Hawaii three times and took a trip to Japan, Singapore, Bangkok and Bali.

On one of the early trips, Frances Oakley, a widow from River Edge, New Jersey, was in the tour group, and she and Syl found they had much in common. They were married in 1976 and had 20 years together.

Syl was highly respected and well-liked by all who knew him. And he was proactive in an unassuming way in maintaining relationships. For example, in going through his travel notes, I came across on more than one occasion a list of names and addresses of family, friends and neighbors. Syl took this information with him on trips for sending postcards and purchasing little mementos. He traveled light, always carrying just one small suitcase no matter how long he would be gone.

In addition to the overseas excursions, Syl and Frances traveled to destinations around the country. Just to name a few, they went to Philadelphia in the winter to watch the Ice Capades, to Holland, Michigan, in the spring to see the tulips, to the Northeast in the fall to see the foliage, to Rockefeller Center in New York to view the Christmas tree, to the Berkshires in Massachusetts to visit Gladys Schofield, to the Hudson River for a day cruise to help celebrate Erv's farewell, to Washington, D.C., to Charleston, to Boston and Cape Cod. They also rented a condo in Florida a couple of times to escape the winter weather and to be able to visit Alice frequently.

On the afternoon of May 24, 1993 (four years before Syl's passing), Syl and Ray were sitting on a bench overlooking the lake by Syl's condo. Syl started talking about his youth and, for the first time, told Ray the entire story about his having met and married Emma. The fact that his mother Anna never forgave Syl for marrying Marie Dietzi's daughter was very much on his mind.

He was genuinely distraught and broke down and cried for a full five minutes. He kept saying over and over, "My mother never forgave me for marrying Emma. My mother never forgave me, and I do not understand why she couldn't. I so wanted to have her blessing."

It was getting late by the time Syl finished the story.

Syl lived to be 96 years old. His only ailment was poor eyesight (e.g., until he gave up driving, he would count the stoplights to make his way home since he couldn't read the street signs).

On Memorial Day weekend in 1997, on May 25, he had a heart attack and died 20 minutes later (isn't that the way we'd all like to go?).

Sylvain Thomas Meurer was one of the most upstanding, fair and just persons one could ever know. With his German background, he was strong willed and matter of fact, and you could always count on him.

He was a man of his word and never let you down. He believed in doing your best and staying the course and finishing what you start. He was steady, and you always felt as if he could figure out the best and right way to handle any situation or adversity.

Having been "born with the century," I once asked Syl what it was like to have witnessed so many milestones in history during those nearly 100 years. He retorted that most major events occurred one at a time, and the consequence merely slipped into your life without a lot of fanfare. Taken together, however, those happenings were momentous.

As with most families, the Meurer saga encompasses countless stories ranging from happy and sad to colorful and humorous. The chronology above tells part of the story, but there are many others – too many and too lengthy to tell in detail here. Some additional highlights are noted below:

- How Syl, during college, got caught between the sheets with a married lady and escaped through the second-floor window – just in time (like in the movies).

- How Emma was always sneaking homemade cookies to the grandchildren (Gregg especially appreciated that).
- How living through the Great Depression left a permanent impact on people; Syl would painstakingly open gifts with his pen knife so the wrapping paper could be used again and again.
- How Syl, following European custom, drank a glass of wine with dinner each night starting at a young age and ate salad after the main course, passing these traditions on to his children Alice and Ray.
- How Syl always wore a string tie.
- How Syl so often said "One moment."
- How Syl always greeted you with a kiss on each cheek.
- How Syl, at age 87, danced at grandson Gregg's wedding three months after having had a hip replacement.
- How Syl made the best homemade custard and jams.
- How Syl and Frances hosted game nights (cards).
- How Syl read *The New York Times* every day and kept up with current events until the day he died.
- How Syl was an inspiration to us all – his determination and never-give-up attitude.
- How the guys who attended Great Neck High School referred to themselves as "Great Neckers," Ray's classmates were called the "49ers" and the yearbook was named *Arista*.
- How teenaged Ray saved the day by preventing the captain's wife from falling overboard by grabbing the only item at hand – the top of her two-piece bathing suit.
- How Ray dropped 50% of his entire summer's pay overboard, a lesson he never forgot.
- How Ray prematurely picked the last plum on the tree – the plum Syl had been babying for days.
- How Alice and Joyce would sit in the cockpit in some scenic harbor until the wee hours of the morning, chatting and laughing until the moon went down in the west.

Saying Goodbye to Ray

Cancer – that dreaded word. It seems no one knows why we develop cancer, not even the medical professionals. You're healthy one minute, and, bam!, life as you know it is changed forever.

That's what happened with Ray. He was 86 years old but looked to be about age 75. He had always looked and acted 10 years younger than his age (it was an annoyance when he was young but an asset when he was older). He may have been slowing down a bit but not noticeably. Didn't everybody at that age? Ray could run circles around most of his contemporaries.

I was mentally preparing myself for the next stage of life whereby the little ailments become more frequent and signs of "being elderly" start to slip in. I'd seen several people start to show their age in their mid-80s. Ray was healthy, and he looked it. His skin glowed under the summer tan. He had a radiant complexion even in the winter – rosy cheeks, silky smooth skin on his arms and legs. I often told him he had sexy legs (they were shapely compared with most other guys').

Ray took care of himself. He exercised every day. He followed the Canadian Royal Air Force regimen of 20 minutes of calisthenics each morning. He stopped smoking cigarettes in 1978 and ceased drinking alcohol about five years later. His diet was exemplary other than maybe his consumption of too much ice cream.

He did have some dental problems, but he was on top of that – even when we were cruising. On more than one occasion, he took the train or bus home to see the dentist, Dr. Steve Rothenberg, in Darien. As for me, I rarely had a dental issue except for the usual extraction of wisdom teeth when I was young.

Do you know how it came to be that they are called wisdom teeth?

These third molars (there are four of them – one in each corner or quadrant of the mouth) emerge in people starting around age 17 and can arrive as late as ages 21 to 25 or even later. Since these teeth come in during adulthood, people are presumed to be much wiser (have more "wisdom") than when the other teeth, and the first and second molars in particular, come in during the childhood years.

So Ray did his best to stay healthy. He kept trim and took pride in being well-groomed and well-dressed. He had a natural talent for spotting attractive articles of clothing (for him and me). His father Syl had lived to the age of 96, and that was our benchmark for Ray. But it wasn't to be.

Ray had been active in the community for decades and was a "friend to man" (wording from a poem by Sam Walter Foss that hung above Ray's desk in his office).

We both loved our little town. We knew lots of people and, for example, joined in the camaraderie at the annual Memorial Day Parade and would wave to fellow Rowaytonites as they passed by.

The sun shone on our parade, not just in late May every 12 months but every day of the year. The century-old idiom "don't rain on my parade" resonated the wish to keep the dark clouds away and not dampen the many positives in our realm.

We were just so happy together and had a very gratifying life. We encouraged the other person to nurture his/her passions so each was fulfilled. And we leaned on each other – through the tears and the triumphs.

Yes, Ray and I had sailed through the days without too much hardship and with lots and lots of sunshine. Life had been good to us and had demonstrated that "it never rains in Rowayton."

Like everyone, of course, we had had to deal with some major events along the way. Ray had had kidney and prostate cancer and a melanoma on his face and had survived it all. Our parents had passed on. Ray's daughter Diane had persevered through a bone marrow transplant. We had been through a boating accident in Fisher's Island Sound in the '80s, a major nor'easter in '92 and Superstorm Sandy in 2012.

Fast forward to late summer 2018: Dealing with those earlier stumbling blocks had been trying, but it hadn't truly rained on Ray and Joyce's parade until then.

Diagnosis

It was the Tuesday before Labor Day in 2018, and Ray announced that he had made a doctor's appointment because he had a twitch just below the waist. (Ray went to the doctor right away whenever he thought something was wrong.) Our general practitioner, Dr. Philip Negus, said Ray should have either a CT scan or a colonoscopy. Ray said that was a no-brainer – he opted for a CT scan and had it taken on Friday.

The results showed something unusual in the bladder area. A biopsy was performed the following week – the urologist, Dr. Robert Lovegrove, told me on the spot that he suspected cancer.

I wasn't too worried though because Ray had had three cancers before and had survived. And every year brought new medical breakthroughs. I figured that no matter what was wrong, we would overcome it.

A liver biopsy was performed the next week because the x-rays had detected something suspicious there as well. A flurry of doctor appointments, tests and scans took place over the next couple of weeks, and a port was installed in Ray's chest for the many blood draws to come.

On October 2, Dr. Anthony Gulati, an oncologist specializing in blood cancers at Stamford Hospital, met with us and explained that Ray had developed neuroendocrine cancer of the bladder. It is a rare disease that is extremely aggressive and highly invasive. It was treatable but not curable. Because much more research was needed to understand this disease, Ray agreed to be part of some medical studies.

This particular kind of cancer starts in one place (in Ray's case, the bladder), but the cancerous cells float around the body via the bloodstream and attach themselves to any organ they choose. Ray's PET scan showed cancer throughout his torso: in the bladder, lymph nodes adjacent to the bladder, liver, pelvis, vertebrae, ribs and neck. He was to start chemotherapy the following week.

We were advised to get Ray's papers in order: Life expectancy was six months unless the chemo was successful and killed the cancer.

We both were in shock.

Blue Heron Story

It was mid-October, and Ray and I were spending the afternoon on our boat, Blue Heron, knowing it probably would be the last time we'd be on board before hauling out for the winter.

It was a sad and restless time because of Ray's diagnosis of stage IV cancer, and we had had six weeks of countless doctor appointments, scans and biopsies, getting bad news after bad news.

Ray had already started chemo treatments. We were in a state of disbelief and denial, and we were scared of what the future might hold.

We were sitting in the cockpit at the dock, admiring the water view and watching the herons, egrets and gulls flying around the harbor.

All of these birds are frequent visitors to our local waters, and it's not uncommon to see them soaring in the sky and walking on the mudflats. In fact, we named our boat Blue Heron because it goes through the water as gracefully as its namesake flies through the air.

It was getting a little chilly in the cockpit so we went inside the cabin and continued to enjoy the 360-degree view where it was toasty warm.

As we were about ready to leave, a blue heron swooped down from the heavens and made a long pass from the eastern shoreline straight to our boat. The graceful bird flew directly overhead from stern to bow not more than two feet above, then gained altitude and disappeared into the sky to the west.

But this was not the typical blue heron. This was the granddaddy of them all.

Whether around here or in our travels, we had never seen such a gigantic blue heron. This was the big gun.

We were awestruck. Ray let out a gasp and said, "That's a sign that God and all of nature are watching over us. It was a blessing."

The event truly was an epiphany, and we were clinging to every shred of hope that it was a prophesy for good things to come.

As it turned out, that was the last time Ray was on board Blue Heron.

The chemo regimen consisted of three days of infusions every 21 days for six cycles. Ray was a trouper. As expected, he did everything the medics suggested. For instance, he was told to walk after every meal, which he did religiously as long as he could. He concocted an apparatus of flashlights and ropes to wear on his cap and over his coat so when he walked around the block after dark, he would be visible to vehicular traffic.

I usually stayed inside and would watch Ray wend his way down the dark street until the light on his head faded away in the distance, realizing that was a portent of the future when the light he radiated would get dimmer and dimmer until it no longer was. Rain or shine or snow, Ray followed the doctor's orders to a T. He tolerated the chemo fairly well but, as is usually the case, was very tired. He also was shaky and exhibited some of the other normal side effects. But his spirits were good, and his appetite soared.

My world was collapsing. My precious Ray's life was on the line. I was incapable of imagining life without him.

I dropped everything, including work, in order to be with him and cater to his every need. Ray's kids helped with the shopping and cooking, but I found my way to the kitchen about 4 p.m. most afternoons to start dinner so he could eat at 5:00. If he ate later than that, he was so weak he could barely function. The food preparation was new for me since Ray had been doing the shopping and cooking for years to allow me that much more time in my office so I could make the deadlines and keep my clients satisfied.

People from church and the neighborhood brought in all kinds of food – from soups and breads to entire dinners, and both Ray and I were greatly appreciative. Stephanie Close delivered her tasty meatloaf dinner complete with a follow-on cooking lesson. Support came from near and far. Others sent flowers and cards. One couple,

Rich and Chris Bonosky (Scott's in-laws), sent a get well card that included paper cutouts with "Better Day" written on each one and were attached to string. The greeting said, "Wishing you a string of better days." Ray loved it and placed it on the mantle so he would see it every day, saying, "I'll keep it there forever." (It's still there, months after he passed away.)

Our days were full and were fraught with anxiety. We panicked at the slightest concern. Ray had some other medical issues, including a root canal, and our time was spent running from doctor to doctor. We were exhausted. We carried on with that regimen for about three months. Every day seemed like an eternity, and we were on pins and needles every waking moment.

Ray was due for another PET scan in December, and we braced for the worst because we had had nothing but bad news after bad news since this all began in September. But the results showed that about 85% of the cancer had been killed off by the chemo. We were told that since the chemo seemed to be working so well, Ray's life might be extended – maybe by as much as a year or two – due to this unexpected upturn.

We were euphoric!

Thus, life went on with more cycles of chemo being administered every three weeks. Ray was still tired and shaky and all the rest, but we were grateful for this wonderful news. We felt that every day was a gift.

Losing the Battle

In mid-April, Ray started experiencing problems with his memory and his walking. He would shuffle his feet and had trouble climbing stairs. And on Wednesday, April 17, he took a fall on the front lawn while trying to raise the awnings for the second-floor windows.

The next morning, we met with the oncologist, and Ray had a brain scan taken. It showed that the cancer had metastasized to the brain and that there were approximately 30 tumors of varying sizes. We asked how this could have happened when the chemo had supposedly killed off the cancer cells.

We were told that chemo works well on the body but not on the brain. There are countless crevices where cancerous cells have plenty of opportunity to "hide" from the chemo. And all it takes is one cell out a million to start growing and spreading again.

All said and done, the chemo had given Ray four extra months.

We were told the only remaining treatment available was radiation. Full speed ahead, we met with the radiologist the next day, Friday. Ray was prepped on Monday, and the 10 days of full-head radiation treatments started on Tuesday.

That was the beginning of the end.

Ray did not tolerate the radiation treatments well from the very first day, and he was never the same. He said he was in a fog from the moment he woke up in the morning.

The radiation treatments ended on Monday, May 6. On the following Friday afternoon, he quietly and gently told me he knew he would not get well. He said he had accepted it and was prepared to die and enter the next life. And he hoped it would happen sooner rather than later.

We were sitting in a double Adirondack chair at the Boathouse beach across the street. Every time I see that chair, I remember the conversation. I also am reminded of how Ray loved Five Mile River, having been harbor superintendent for 13 years and enjoying the beach across the street and activity on the river for 41 years. I take solace in the fact that being in that place brought him so much joy and peace.

The month of May wore on, and Ray became weaker and weaker. He kept mentioning that his right thigh had no feeling. Since our house had been elevated after Superstorm Sandy, getting outside required maneuvering a flight of stairs. With great effort, Ray was able to get up and down the stairs once a day max during that period, and, on some days, we would take a drive around town in the car.

We made the Loop: We would drive to Wilson Cove Yacht Club and check out the boats being readied for the upcoming season. The next stop would be Rowayton Yacht Club to enjoy the view looking across the harbor toward Tavern Island and several of the other Norwalk Islands. On to Bell Island, we would park at the bend on East Beach Drive and admire the vista looking eastward over the mooring field where we used to keep our boat and toward Sheffield Island where we had anchored for the afternoon a million times. On South Beach Drive, we would park in front of the beach houses where we had met, look out at Green's Ledge Lighthouse and say, "This is where it all began."

Ray continued to lose his physical strength. Even eating was tiring: He would have to stop and rest two or three times during a meal. Ray continued attempting to take his walk after eating, but, by now, he couldn't make the trip up and down the back stairs to go outside. I placed chairs around the house so he could stop and rest about every 10 feet. He lost weight – he was skin and bones even with his ravenous appetite.

Visiting Nurse & Hospice of Fairfield County was brought in, and there were approximately two or three visits a day for the next four weeks with the non-hospice team of nurses, occupational therapists, physical therapists, social workers, and various and sundry medics. Ray and I did walk over to the Boathouse beach across the street a few times to enjoy "Ray's River," as I called it.

On Memorial Day weekend, Ray had a scare, and we called 911 and spent the night in the emergency room at the hospital. At 5 a.m., he was admitted. It was freezing in his room, and it took two hours for someone to find a blanket. He was released by dinnertime, and we went home.

Ray's strength had diminished so much that he couldn't go upstairs anymore. At that point, it was decided to make the dining room into a bedroom for him. There is an incident I have to tell here. Once the hospital bed was installed, we slept apart in the house for the first time in our married life. On one of the first mornings, I was awakened in our bed upstairs by hearing Ray shout at the top of his lungs, "HELP!" "HELP!"

I jumped out of bed and raced downstairs to find Ray at the front window calling to a workman outside. It turned out that the downstairs bathroom light had burned out, and Ray knew I wouldn't be able to change it. So he used what resources were available to him to get the problem fixed. I will never forget hearing him scream for help, imagining all kinds of horrible scenarios.

But it turned out that we didn't have to sleep apart at that time. Ray was still able to move around, and we decided to try sleeping together in the hospital bed. It wasn't by any means the first time we had slept in a twin bed (for example, we shared one for the months we stayed on Bluff Avenue after Superstorm Sandy, not to mention that sleeping in our bunk on the boat for 40+ years was very "cozy").

It was so comforting just holding each other during this frightful time of Ray's uncertain future, and we both got a better night's rest. We did that as long as we could.

By mid-June, Ray's condition had deteriorated dramatically, and we were advised that nothing more could be done. All the medical solutions available had been exhausted.

There was never any doubt about whether Ray would stay home or whether he would go to a facility. I wanted to be with him every minute and cater to his every need, and I could do that only if he was at home. Having witnessed how long it had taken to get a blanket during our recent hospital visit merely solidified that decision.

A little background regarding driving: With my heavy work schedule for most of my career, I put in long hours in my home office and sometimes didn't get out of the house for days at a time. Ray was the one who did the shopping for food and for all those items one needs in order to keep a household running. When we went to social events, Ray drove. Bottom line: I hadn't done much driving for a long time.

When Ray was diagnosed and then went through chemo, he didn't feel like driving. So, all of a sudden, I was thrust behind the wheel every day for all those months, navigating the traffic on I-95 and downtown Stamford.

Ray didn't like the way I drove. He said I needed to go faster and be more aggressive. For a while, Ray sat in the back of the car behind the driver's seat so he couldn't see as much and wouldn't be anticipating and outguessing every move by every vehicle on the road (and tried not to be, literally, a back-seat driver). To anyone noticing, it looked like Ray was a passenger with a chauffeur (me!).

On Friday, June 14, we met with the oncologist at the hospital, who wanted Ray to have one final PET scan for the research being conducted on neuroendocrine cancer of the bladder. Ray's younger son Scott had come along to help get Ray up and down the stairs because he couldn't manage by himself any longer. Scott also offered to drive, and I jumped at that idea – one less trip maneuvering the traffic on the thruway!

The PET scan was scheduled for the next day, Saturday, June 15. It would be the last time Ray rode in the car. Michael, Ray's older son, came this time to help get Ray up and down the back stairs. After such a pleasant experience the day before with Scott at the wheel, I asked Michael if he would like to drive, and he said "Sure." Well, Mike was not familiar with the roads and drove a little hesitantly as he wended his way to the Tully Center in Stamford.

When we were getting ready to head home, Ray looked at me and announced, "Joyce, you're driving."

I laughed – Ray actually preferred my driving to someone else's!

Hospice was brought in on June 19, and Ray announced, "I want to die with dignity." Arrangements were made for aides to be at the house 24 hours a day. The dining room already had been transitioned into a hospital room.

Thanks to Visiting Nurse & Hospice and Lynne Pratt, a friend from church, the house was filled with all kinds of equipment: two wheelchairs, two walkers, canes, a Hoyer lift, a commode, a transfer board, etc. Lynne also brought several changes of sheets and bedding and multiple pillows. Additionally, I ordered a full array of medical supplies, including bed protector pads, wipes and diapers.

As the days wore on, Ray lost all feeling in his right leg from hip to foot and had to be transported by lift. My calendar from that month has this notation: "Ray failing more each day."

One event that helped me get through that scary time was this: Ray was having a hard time breathing one afternoon, and I panicked and telephoned the nurse on call. She said she would arrive in about 30 minutes, and I said, "Hurry!" She said, "Joyce, just stay calm. The purpose here is not to try and save Ray. The goal is to let him die peacefully and without pain."

That put everything in perspective, and I was able to cope better going forward – I was just sad; profoundly sad.

My days were spent trying to make Ray comfortable, and my thoughts centered on ways to do that. My purpose was to do anything and everything possible to make him feel at peace. Having had no background in the medical field, the learning curve was steep, but I tried my best.

So it was a complete surprise when one of the nurses told me that the Hospice team had voted me Best Caregiver of the Week.

Throughout all this, Ray still had a ferocious appetite, believe it or not. The kids helped with the food, and we enjoyed meals together. Ray still insisted on tasteful, properly prepared dishes and was not fooled for a minute with mediocre fare. One morning late in June, I made eggs over easy for breakfast. When I served them, Ray politely said, "Please try not to overdo the eggs next time."

Although making a five-star meal every night was a big deal, I had decided weeks before that we would serve Ray the very best since food gave him such pleasure. Once the aides were on the scene, I was responsible for their meals as well. Ray's daughter Diane was a big help with that. We served lots of Italian dishes from the restaurant where she worked (we were so appreciative that the price of the food was deep discounted to employees).

The aides were available to assist with transporting, feeding, dressing Ray, changing bedding and all kinds of tasks like that. They were not nurses, however, and were not allowed to administer drugs. Ray didn't experience pain until close to the end so I didn't have to give him morphine – which made me uncomfortable – for very long.

One of the aides, let's call him Skylar, was especially skilled, and Ray took an immediate liking to him (even at that point, Ray had an uncanny ability to quickly size up a person).

Just two weeks before Ray passed away, Skylar managed to take Ray to the Boathouse beach across the way. Somehow, the aide got Ray in his wheelchair, out the front door, down the slope to the street and through the sand at the beach. We spent half an hour there chatting with neighbor Tom Lucas's brother Jim, and then Ray got tired. It was his last trip to Five Mile River.

Diane came about every day and made dinner often. Mike and his twin girls Amanda and Rachel visited frequently, making meals. Scott came and prepared dinner. They were all there for their dad and me. Cynthia sent some suggestions on passages to read from the Bible that were particularly comforting.

We all knew the end was near. I stood by helpless and heartbroken.

As it turned out, the kids were in and out of the house but didn't visit for long during those last three days. They were exhausted and strung out. So I had quiet time with Ray alone, and I'm grateful for that. I had started writing a farewell letter to him, reflecting our powerful love and wonderful life together. I never read the letter aloud to him, but I felt he knew what I was saying because we were so attuned to each other. It was like osmosis or telepathy: Thoughts in my mind were unconsciously assimilated into Ray's mind without saying anything.

He slipped away on a Saturday night at 7:30. He died in my arms – his breathing just got shallower and shallower until it stopped. I couldn't speak much during those last few moments so I just whispered over and over, "Everything's going to be *just* fine" as he had said to me so many times in his life.

As sad as it was, it was beautiful.

A Toast for the Ages

It had been only 10½ months from the time Ray was diagnosed until he passed away on July 6 – not very long, and, yet, it seemed like a lifetime.

After he passed away, I stayed by Ray's side most of the evening. The nurse from hospice came. The person from the crematorium was here. Pastor John came by.

Then they came to take Ray's body away, and Diane, Michael and Scott took me over to the Boathouse beach. We talked about Ray and told stories and watched the moonlight on Five Mile River for a long time.

The kids stayed here at the house that night. After they retired, I opened the liquor cabinet and pulled out the bottle of Johnnie Walker Blue, one of the most rare, expensive and exquisite brands of scotch on the market. The bottle had been a treasured gift, and I reserved it for special times, the last being over Christmas six months before. I had saved the final portion for the memorable occasion that I knew would be coming: Ray's passing.

I filled the shot glass with the remaining liquid of the finest of scotches – and made a toast to the finest of men.

As we had celebrated at every meal during our years together, I whispered "Cheers! To our love. I love you!" one last time while his spirit was still in the house.

While the others slept, I sat alone and gave tribute to Ray and his perfect life and the culmination of our lives together:

His – from immigrant family to sea captain to gentleman and scholar.

Mine – from Grass Creek to this moment and all the growth and fulfillment with him and through him.

His – from the moment of arriving to the moment of leaving this life on earth.

Salud!

The Aftermath and Healing Process

The next day the spouses and grandkids came, and we went to Wilson Cove Yacht Club and had lunch on the deck. We went aboard Blue Heron for a while and then, for dinner, barbequed hamburgers on one of the grills at Rowayton Yacht Club. Diane stayed with me until Wednesday. On Friday, we drove to Long Island for a family wedding and then picked up my good friend Loisann Crimmins at LaGuardia Airport on Saturday.

I don't know how I would have managed to get through those days without Loisann. We dismantled the "hospital room" and made it into a dining room again. We sorted through Ray's clothes. We straightened up the house and packed away clutter. We went shopping and bought my dress for Ray's memorial service. We laughed, and we cried. And we prayed.

We had fun, too. There were boat rides, lunch at a friend's house on one of the Norwalk Islands, church in Pinkney Park on Sunday mornings, dinners out, and walks on the beach and around town.

When Ray was first diagnosed, I found my life support was the phone, texts and emails. All through those months, I gained strength from communicating with people. People from far and near called.

Cynthia, Loisann and friend Mary Pat McGuire were in touch almost daily.

Generally, Ray would go to bed at 8 p.m. I would wait till then to do the dishes because I didn't want to take time away from being with him when he was awake. So after the kitchen was cleared around 9:30 or 10:00 at night, I would sit in the rocking chair in the living room and communicate the day's events and provide an update on Ray's condition to my steadfast friends.

Most every message ended with "It is so sad." I could always count on hearing back immediately from Mary Pat as she is a night owl, too. After Ray died, I continued sending messages to people although not on a daily basis. But that helped get me through the summer.

One thing that happened almost immediately after Ray passed

away was that I heard music. First, there would be a loud crashing sound of cymbals. Then came the joyous sound of a choir a hundred voices strong – much like the Mormon Tabernacle Choir.

I couldn't always understand the words, but the chords ringing in my ears made me marvel. I would experience this music and singing on and off throughout the day.

This phenomenon would happen as well when I was having difficulty. One time when I was stressed about something, I heard the refrain again and again, louder and louder, as if someone were shaking my shoulders with both hands. I have no doubt that Ray was trying to tell me he was right there and would try to help.

This went on for a couple of months. It was soothing to me to think Ray was right up there hovering just above the October glory maple tree by the driveway and looking down from the sky almost close enough to touch.

Then there were lyrics that I could recognize. One song that came to me often was the refrain in "How Great Thou Art." Another was the last line of "Silent Night": "Sleep in heavenly peace." Then there was the singing of the beautiful "Hallelujah."

For Ray's memorial service, I requested these songs be part of the music, and Marsha Hall worked them into her prelude.

There was another time last summer when I was at my computer, working on the program for Ray's service. I happened to glance out the window. The sky was clear blue except for one puffy white cloud skirting by on the wind. I just knew that was Ray floating by and saying hello.

I felt Ray's presence everywhere. He was here in the house, he was at the Boathouse beach overlooking Five Mile River, he was at our beach down the street overlooking Long Island Sound, he was up and down the streets of Rowayton, he was in "our" pew at church and, of course, he was aboard Blue Heron.

The songs have receded, and now I don't hear them as often. I think Ray stayed in close proximity until he saw that I could go on without him. One afternoon last fall, I looked out at the eastern sky off the beach facing the expanse of Long Island Sound, where sky meets water, and realized how big the universe is. You could see forever.

It seemed as if Ray wasn't as close by anymore. I sensed that he had been called to leave Rowayton and go to another place that's much bigger than here to learn the ropes and to start a new life with different responsibilities. I hoped he was having fun and rejoicing in being reunited with his parents and sister and all those who had gone before him. I hoped he was enjoying the food, too. He had once had a dream whereby a friend who had passed away shouted down that the strawberries and ice cream in heaven were the best. In fact, Ray had a recurring dream that he was flying through the air up in the sky on his own accord. Afterward, he always woke up rejuvenated.

Somehow, I felt as if Ray had finished his job on earth and now was embracing a whole new world. He was that way in life here on this planet, and I just knew he would carry on the same way in heaven. I felt as if God had called him away. That singing did come back for a while when I was handling the sale of the boat, Blue Heron, on the first anniversary of his passing, and I felt as if Ray was back overseeing all the details and lending me a helping hand.

I also believed that Ray expected me to pull myself together and forge ahead and embrace life without him, as he was doing in his new circumstance. That gave me some backbone because I would never want to disappoint Ray.

The private pain was raw. I couldn't imagine life without Ray. He filled my very soul. He had died at 7:30 on a Saturday night. Every Saturday night for weeks thereafter, I relived his last hour in my arms. But I was torturing myself and decided to cut it to 15 minutes and then to five, and, eventually, it became a short toast to our love and wonderful life together. It wasn't as if I didn't want to remember his last minutes on earth – I just didn't think it was healthy to get so emotional every week. Believe it or not, I got through a few Saturday nights and didn't even remember to check my watch at 7:30. Later that night, I would be surprised to realize that I had actually forgotten. I guess time does heal some things – at least a little bit.

One day when Michael came to see me, he told me about a dream he had had. I felt so much better after he described it to me, and it has given me solace in knowing that Ray is doing all right.

Here's the dream: Michael said he saw an apparition that was floating toward him. The nearer it came, he realized it was someone in a long, flowing white gown. It was getting closer and closer. He could see beautiful long sandy-colored hair billowing in the wind. He looked again, and it was his dad coming straight toward him. Ray positioned himself facing Mike, put a hand on each shoulder, looked him right in the eye and said, "Mike, I'm okay." And then Ray was gone.

I told Mike I wished I had had that dream, but I was comforted in knowing that Ray was okay. I'm glad Michael shared the experience with me.

That is a true story.

I did start a prayer regime that I try to make time for each morning. It takes about half an hour. It is an important part of my day. I start out with asking God to bless this day here in pretty little Rowayton. Before I move on to give thanks for all the good things in my life and for God to be with those who need special help today, I ask him to watch over and guide Ray and other dear ones as they go about their days in heaven. I hope they are spending their time doing the things up there that they had most enjoyed doing down here on earth.

I cried every day for six months after Ray died. I've always been a crier and would embarrass myself and those around me by tearing up for the slightest reason – even watching a movie or reading beautifully written words in a book.

Ray used to tell the story about one morning when the car service came to pick him up to go to the airport for a short business trip. I gave him a hug and kissed him goodbye, tears in my eyes. He got in the car, lowered the window and smiled, saying, "I'll only be gone two days." Then he gave me a thumbs up, and the car rolled away. I stood on the street and watched until the limo faded in the distance and was out of sight. Finally, the tears stopped, and I started counting the minutes till he would return. It was comforting to know he would always be coming home.

So when Ray was given six months to live on that fateful October day in 2018, I cried every time I thought about Ray being terminally ill and going away permanently, and I shed a million silent tears. I didn't wail or keen – I just quietly slipped into a teary state on and off all day long, day after day, at the mere mention of his name. As much as possible, I tried not to cry in front of Ray.

At this writing, I'll have to say I never did have a good, hard cry (they say it's healthy to do so, but you can't force it). I just felt sad from that day on.

Death is so permanent.

I tried to keep busy in the weeks that followed Ray's passing and am grateful to all those who invited me for a boat ride, to lunch, to cocktail hour, to dinner, to any activity. I felt better when I was around people, and I worked hard at filling the calendar. And I wasn't cooking anymore – I was spent when it came to that. I just picked up prepared food at Palmer's or Stew Leonard's or one of the other local markets. Or I ordered takeout from some restaurant or, occasionally, would throw a steak on the grill.

The boating community helped me get through the summer. It was just so natural to be out on the water, something Ray and I had done about every day in season (we averaged 100 days either under way or aboard at the dock). Longtime friend Alex Mackintosh took me out on his boat Loch Moy every week or so, and he and I had frequent phone conversations discussing politics and the state of the world.

David Snyder, Ray's successor as harbor superintendent, and his wife Carolyn graciously invited me for a ride on their boat and called often to see how I was doing. We started going to lunch regularly.

There were more parties and Friday night happy hours, and it was good to spend time with boating friends. In particular, Carola and Stefan Precht and Karen and Buck Miller made sure every get-together was a fun event. And then there were more boat rides and dinners with the Prechts and the Millers, and I especially appreciate Carola's generosity in including me in so many activities. We became good friends.

Tom and Mimi Towell, longtime boating friends from New York City, had been so good about checking on Ray throughout his illness, and we continue to get together for lunch and dinner.

Wilson Cove Yacht Club was to host its 60th Anniversary gala in mid-September, and I played a big part in the planning process all summer long. Having been an active member for about two-thirds of the club's longevity, I knew a lot of the history and wrote some remarks for the big event.

I expended a huge amount of time planning Ray's memorial service set for September 7. Making arrangements for it was akin to planning a wedding, and I wanted every detail to be perfect. It gave me purpose and filled the hours. I wanted it to be a joyous occasion, celebrating Ray's life and reflecting who he was and what he stood for.

A major project was putting together the program for the service. I wanted it to be of the highest quality to reflect Ray's keen eye and quest for excellence when it came to publications (for instance, he was a stickler about the quality of the photos selected for the Darien Men's Association newsletter).

My colleague and friend from JPMorgan Chase, Gerben Hooykaas, offered to design the program, and it was a handsome tribute to Ray. David Snyder, among other niceties, created photomontages depicting Ray's steady-at-the-helm demeanor (see Dedication page and page 129 herein).

And Des McLaughlin was a big help. He had said over lunch during the summer to let him know whatever I needed, and he would make it happen. And he did.

The service turned out to be exactly what I had wanted, and I know Ray would have been pleased in every way. It was a nautical theme, of course – from the scripture and songs to the floral arrangement, which was orchestrated by June Strubinger.

I requested that the men wear a nautical tie and the women nautical jewelry. Those who came to say their goodbye that day had fun showing off their yachty attire. I wore an anchor pin because Ray had been my anchor for four decades.

Lyle McGuire, Janice Strauss, David Snyder, Michael Meurer and Ann DiLeone each spoke about Ray. And my dear friend Loisann Crimmins read my farewell letter to Ray, which can be found at the end of this book.

After the closing words, I asked Pastor John to set the stage for a final goodbye. While Judi Livingston rang bells in the background, John requested that everyone present close their eyes and think about Ray – think really hard about him for a few minutes: some conversation they might have had or some committee they worked on together, remembering his soothing voice, his smile, his twinkly eyes … his kindness.

It was very touching.

The reception afterward was held in Fellowship Hall adjacent to the church. Marcia Smith and Joanne Brown organized the food, and several people from church brought refreshments. And Michael arranged for an array of confections from a local bakery that he had discovered at the Rowayton Farmers' Market.

That evening, I hosted a dinner for the family at the RBA Boathouse. Steve Mason, who considered Ray a second father, made the introductory remarks. Cynthia cited a nautical Biblical passage, and eight-year-old granddaughter Charlotte recited the poem "Sea Fever" by John Masefield. The sunset was spectacular, and we said our final goodbye to Ray overlooking the river that had been so much a part of his life.

The next day, the Hizer entourage met for church and then the whole gang of out-of-towners congregated at the house. The caterer from the night before had stuffed all the leftovers in the fridge so there was plenty to eat.

Life went on. I had note cards printed and wrote more than a hundred thank you notes to those who had shown their concern and provided support through it all or helped in some way. That kept me busy into the fall, and it was therapeutic to write about Ray in so many ways.

In late October, Buck Miller and Frank DiCeglie took the canvas biminis off the boat for the winter, and a few days later, Norm Edwards, John Tou and I ran the boat to Norwalk Cove Marina for winter storage. Blue Heron was on the market, and the broker was located on the premises. He thought it would be easier to show the boat there rather than make potential buyers trek over to Wilson Cove Marina.

Just before Thanksgiving, Skylar, the aide Ray had liked so much, came to the house to pick up Ray's summer clothes, which I had offered. Skylar is from Haiti and was going back for a visit for the first time in several years. Ray would have been happy to know he had helped Skylar's family and friends by donating a wardrode full of shorts and shirts and socks.

There are five stages of grief: denial, anger, bargaining, depression, acceptance. I've experienced most of these emotions to some extent. Because of the age difference, Ray figured he would go first (in fact, he said he hoped he would so he wouldn't have to live without me).

As I said earlier, I could never bring myself to think about Ray passing away and imagine what life would be like without him. So when he was diagnosed and given a few months to live, I wasn't angry. I was enormously sad – my mind and body were consumed with sadness.

It had been a long six months since Ray's passing, but I started feeling stronger right after the holidays. Cynthia had been here in December, and her visit helped me get through the normally festive time. We put the tree up and affixed Ray's Merry Christmas cap at the very top with a dozen angels hovering just below. It was lovely and comforting.

Being an Episcopal priest, Cynthia urged me to accompany her as she made her rounds to a number of holy services. At my own church, Pastor John, who has a beautiful tenor voice, sang a solo, "Joseph's Song," especially for Ray during one of the holiday services.

On Christmas Day, I was alone. Each of the kids had invited me to join them, but we had spent Christmas Eve together so I opted to pass. In the end, I had a wonderful day. At noon, I called a friend from church who I knew was home and alone. At age 101, Martha Cook had told me she would not be going out that day. We had a pleasant chat and wished each other a good year in 2020.

At 2 p.m., I drove to the home of a gentleman with whom Ray and I had spent time over the years, John Geoghegan. He is younger than Martha, a mere 95 years old on that Christmas Day, and we had a delightful visit. I was comforted knowing that maybe I had made someone else's day a little happier.

The next stop was at the Lamendola's, a young couple who had a four-year-old and, at the time, a baby on the way. Veronica's mother was visiting from Ecuador for the holiday, and we all had a pleasurable conversation. Rob and Veronica had prepared and delivered a dinner to Ray and me on that fateful day the year before when we had been told of Ray's diagnosis and prognosis.

Rounding out the day, I stopped at Mary Ellen and Jeff Walsh's, yacht club friends who have a home in the heart of Rowayton. They have a gingerbread house that has been remodeled and updated over the course of their many years in town, and it was the ideal setting on Christmas night with all the holiday decorations and a fire burning brightly in the fireplace. The house was full of people and laughter and yacht talk.

I had gone to each home that day bearing gifts. The one I was most proud to present was the fresh-off-the-press 2020 Long Island Sound Tide Calendar, the 34th edition.

I was back home by 9 p.m. It had been a full day covering the spectrum of people from "one to 92," as the holiday song goes.

Even with the passage of time, I miss Ray every day. He was so easy to be with. He was kind and caring in every way. And I miss the hugs and the cuddles.

Throughout the stories told here about Ray, a constant theme is revealed: He lived his passion.

And isn't that the goal for each one of us?

Moving On

By the new year, I felt as if life would go on, and I could get along without Ray. I believed it was critical to keep foremost in my thoughts my gratitude for the happiness Ray had brought me for more than 40 years. Not everybody gets that lucky, and I became a better person because of him.

Then COVID-19 changed life as we all knew it. I guess this pandemic has speeded my grieving because we now are focusing on ourselves and are trying to fulfill our own basic needs, such as getting groceries. But I keep thinking it would be so much easier to cope with all these restrictions and isolation if Ray and I were going through this world crisis together. We sometimes don't realize what a support system and sounding board our loved ones provide until they are not around.

Writing this memoir has helped in the healing process. Ray was the one who talked about writing a book one day, not I (I offered to edit his book). His advice was: "Write about something you know." Well, that certainly was a prophecy in this case. Writing about Ray and our lives has been easy – the words just flew from my fingertips. We were good together and so in sync.

There are many more stories I could tell, but I've said enough.

I want to say, too, that this is not a normal book where characters are introduced and developed. It is a collection of vignettes and some historical facts during a given period of time. I have tried to capture as much detail as possible in order to describe "the way we were."

Another benefit of writing this book has made me understand how the pieces of my life follow a theme and fit together. For example, I originally had selected a bright and "happy" solid blue for the front cover because it was nautical looking and reminded me of all the good times I've had throughout my life surrounding the water – from Lake Maxinkuckee to Five Mile River to Long Island Sound and beyond.

The color I selected, for no reason other than I liked this shade best, is Pantone Matching System (PMS) 287. Later I realized that this PMS number is very close to the color Ray and I chose for Blue Heron's hull 20 years ago. It also is the color I've used in printing my tide calendar all these years. Apparently, it's my favorite blue.

As you will have noticed, the front cover of this book is not solid blue. Instead, it features a photograph taken from Roton Point in Rowayton looking toward the Rowayton Beach Association beach and entrance to Five Mile River. The Adirondack chairs shown here can be found at beaches and sitting areas around town. They are quite popular. And they dot the shoreline at both our RBA beach and the Boathouse.

Mark Smith, former neighbor and RBA resident, became involved in this project near the end and helped in the design and production of the book. It was he who encouraged me to consider using a photo of Rowayton on the cover, and he presented six choices of scenes he had taken of Long Island Sound, the RBA beach and Five Mile River. I surveyed about 30 people and asked which cover they liked best, including the solid blue choice, and, to the person, the favorite was the Adirondack chair photo. Thanks, Mark, for your guidance and input.

There are a couple of things to do yet. Ray and I have a joint plot at the Grass Creek Cemetery, and I will have a marker installed that has our names, dates of birth and death, and the words: Reunited in Heaven. A rendering of a ship's wheel will be etched above Ray's name (because he was the captain of the ship and the captain of my soul) and an anchor above my name (because Ray was my anchor).

I do believe I will be reunited with Ray in heaven. I think about it often. Heaven – it's a place where, in my mind, there are endless blue skies and puffy white clouds; a place where there is no tension or stress; a place where everyone is kind to each other, and there is no backstabbing; a place where it never rains and the sun shines every day, and heaven's residents are eternally peaceful and happy.

Next summer, I will spread the remainder of Ray's ashes in Long Island Sound out past Cable and Anchor Reef on an outgoing tide on a line between Green's Ledge Lighthouse and Eaton's Neck (per Ray's instructions), and he will be one with the sea. Before we do that, we will visit the local waterholes that he loved so much – Sheffield Island, Five Mile River, Ziegler's Cove, Goose Island – and pay tribute to the wonderful human being that he was.

Immediately after Ray passed away, I placed a photo of him here and there around the house so I could glance at his image from any room. That helped. Again, I felt he was here with me. I can tell I'm healing because I'm not conscious of looking at those photos a hundred times a day anymore.

I joined a bereavement group at the hospice center, and that has been very beneficial. Each one of us has lost our spouse, and we share our thoughts and fears. And we celebrate when we have small triumphs or take baby steps toward healing.

When Ray was diagnosed, I joined the Bible Study group at our church, and I have continued with that and find it meaningful.

Our Sunday worship service is held in Pinkney Park overlooking Five Mile River during the summer. In the fall, we resume with services in the sanctuary. Ray and I always sat in the front left pew – that was our spot. After he died, I sat anywhere else but there. But I started sitting in "our" pew again this past fall and could feel Ray's presence. That was a big step. I could almost feel his body next to me with my shoulder tucked into his and hear his beautiful rich voice singing hymns or repeating "The Lord's Prayer." Nancy Dauk has mentioned on several occasions her memory of sitting behind us and sensing the closeness we obviously felt for each other.

My work has been a godsend and keeps me centered. I derive great satisfaction from reviewing copy and making sure it is correct in every way. It keeps my mind active and occupied. I actually lose track of time when I'm editing and now writing – for a client, for pro bono purposes, or for myself in the form of a special project or interest (such as this book, the family history, the yacht club). I hope to continue with these endeavors for a long time.

Learning to live alone is a huge adjustment. I lived by myself when I was single, but that was different. I was young and enthusiastic about my future. I had a demanding job, night school and a busy social life, and I had a lifetime ahead of me.

Living alone today is not the same because I'm in the opposite phase of life. Many of my relatives, friends and colleagues are not healthy or have passed on. It makes me realize again how lucky I am in so many ways, and that spurs me on to make sure I remember to appreciate every day – carpe diem.

Pastor John Livingston makes a good point when he suggests you think about this scenario: Let's say you and several others are sitting around a table. Each of you is asked to put your troubles in a bucket, place it on the table and describe what's in it. After everyone has had a turn, you are asked to select one bucket from the batch. In all likelihood, John predicts, you would choose your own bucket over the others.

So Ray is gone, and I'm trying hard to carry on in a manner that would make him proud. Of Syl's direct descendants and their spouses, I'm the family matriarch now (that's mind-boggling in and of itself).

On top of all that, we are in a pandemic. We cannot be around other people. We have to remain isolated. Dealing with grief along with the restrictions surrounding COVID-19 has been doubly hard.

Although I have had the privilege of having the support of a lot of people, it's not possible to be with another person all the time. So I have to accept that. And I have to learn to be comfortable and content with being alone.

I'm working on that.

I'm seeking happiness and joy. I know I'll get there one of these days. And I look forward to writing a next chapter of my memoir.

In the meantime, I still find Rowayton captivating after 50 years and enjoy living here. I spend time at the Boathouse beach across the street and never tire of watching the boats coming in and going out of Five Mile River. From the beaches on Long Island Sound, I see Green's Ledge Lighthouse – part of the DNA here in our pretty little town – and hear the soothing sound of the foghorn on misty days.

I walk the docks around town and admire the beautiful boats.

Then there's the Loop: From Wilson Cove Yacht Club to Rowayton Yacht Club to the top of the hill on East Beach Drive on Bell Island to South Beach Drive where my life with Ray began, I applaud the spectacular water views.

I take in the salt air. I watch the gulls soaring through the sky. I marvel at the cloud formations above the water and the breathtaking sunsets.

And I never turn down a chance to take a boat ride to any one of the many coves and harbors that we are blessed to have in our local waters.

Rowayton is a special place, and I've had the good fortune to call it home for most of my adult life and to have found a soulmate to have loved with all my heart.

Life is good, and I am thankful every day for all the gifts that have been bestowed upon me.

Farewell Letter

Below is my farewell letter to Ray. My dear friend Loisann Hartzler Crimmins read the letter at Ray's memorial service. It is a testament of the deep love and wonderful life we had together, thus the title of this book *It Never Rains in Rowayton*. When my time comes, I truly believe I will be reunited with my beloved Ray in heaven.

Good afternoon. My name is Loisann Crimmins. I live in Indiana where Joyce became an Indiana University graduate, and Ray graduated from Wabash College.

Joyce and I have been friends since our freshman year in high school – 58 years.

Because of my friendship with Joyce, I have had the pleasure of knowing and loving her beloved husband Ray.

Forty-one years ago, I was in this very church when Joyce and Ray pledged their love for each other and became husband and wife. Their marriage has always been an example of devotion and respect for each other.

My husband and I loved Ray and will miss him and the many good times the four of us had together.

It is a great honor that I now share with you the beautiful letter that Joyce wrote to Ray two days before he passed away.

My Dearest Ray –
It's the 4th of July, and I sit by your side watching you writhing in pain from the cancer. My heart aches for you, my love, and I feel your pain.

I know you will be leaving me soon. Your year-long struggle has been daunting, and you have been brave and courageous. Through it all, you did not express self-pity or ask "Why me?"

Last fall, I joined the Bible Study group at church. One day, Pastor John asked us to think about a gift we had to give someone. My answer that day was that my gift was to be able to care for you in your illness.

My gift to you today, Ray, is that I am giving you my blessing to leave me. I don't like it, and I'll never be ready to let you go, but I want you to be spared from any more misery and suffering.

So I'm taking this time to reflect on the wonderful years we've had together.

Ours was a great love right from the beginning. We loved, we laughed, we cried and now I mourn. Even in sadness, I am grateful for the 40 years we've had and all that we've shared.

You possessed a combination of traits that drew people to you and who immediately respected and admired you. You always looked for the good in others and helped them recognize their own strengths.

You certainly empowered me to be the best I could be.

You supported and encouraged me to follow my star, and, together as a team and as a partner, you embraced my dreams. My own success is attributed to you, too. So, again, thank you. You even did the shopping and cooking so I had more time in the office. However, that wasn't such a blessing this past year when I had to learn to cook again and prepare meals that met your expectations. I would do it all over again, though, if it meant having you with us even for another few days or weeks.

You taught me a lot about life. I stood by your side and learned those lessons and became a better person. You were my anchor, and you always centered me. With such a solid foundation, there wasn't anything I couldn't accomplish.

Your uncanny ability to size someone up in about two minutes was amazing. And you were right on every time. It was just like taking that first bite: Within five seconds, you knew whether the food was excellent, mediocre or unsatisfactory.

You used your abilities to enable others to feel good about themselves, always complimenting or thanking a person for the smallest deed. And you had such an incredible vision and could see through the details and get to the heart of any issue.

You were a peacemaker. You diffused conflict, and everyone walked away from the table with a better outlook and perspective. And you always comforted people. You were famous for saying, in that soothing voice of yours, "Everything's going to be *just* fine."

You also jumped in and got involved in the community – from church activities to the Swanky's group to the Darien Men's Association. Your contributions are endless and will live on.

Our shared passion for the water and boating enriched our lives, and we had so much fun. One of your favorite sayings was, "A bad day on the water is better than a good day at the office." And our motto was that the day was not complete without a boat ride.

I came across a file folder the other day that contains dozens of cards and mementos from our birthdays and anniversaries and all kinds of special occasions. In every instance, the message was a pledge of love and a declaration of our wonderful and happy life together. The word cherish appears in many of the passages.

You often called me Miss Hallmark because of the meaningful notes I wrote to people on various occasions. So here's one last thought for you as you leave on your journey: The love we share is as timeless as the tides and as deep as the sea.

And now, my sweetheart, it's time to say goodbye. Life on earth will never be the same without you. But I'll be joining you one of these days, and we'll be together for eternity in a happy, healthy, peaceful place called heaven.

Godspeed, my love.

Joyce

Ray and Joyce – 41 years of bliss.

-30-

About the Author

Joyce Hizer Meurer was born and raised in Indiana. She earned B.S. and M.S. degrees from Indiana University and an M.B.A. from the University of Connecticut. After moving to Fairfield County, Connecticut, in 1970, she taught at Greenwich High School and, later, was named academic dean at the Berkeley School in White Plains, New York.

She started her own corporate communications business in the late 1980s and has served clients ranging from small and midsize businesses to Fortune 500 companies. She reviews all types of communications projects from brochures to corporate reports to whitepapers to websites and specializes in annual reports and proxy statements.

During their 41 years of marriage, Joyce and her husband Ray lived in Rowayton, Connecticut, and were avid boaters, traversing the waters of Long Island Sound and the entire East Coast, including the Intracoastal Waterway to and from Florida. Joyce recently served as commodore of one of the local yacht clubs.

After 50 years, Joyce still finds Rowayton captivating and continues to reside in the seashore village, where you can smell the salt air and hear the soothing sound of the foghorn from the lighthouse one mile offshore. She appreciates and takes full advantage of the amenities offered in this picturesque coastal community featuring boating and beaches.

Made in the USA
Middletown, DE
14 June 2025